THE COMPLETE IDIOT'S GUIDE® TO

W9-BLP-413

Marathon Training

by David A. Levine and Paula Petrella

ALPHA

A member of Penguin Group (USA) Inc.

From David:
To all those runners with whom I have ever or will ever run. You are all an inspiration.

From Paula:
To my husband, Peri Pastor.

ALPHA BOOKS

Published by the Penguin Group

Penguin Group (USA) Inc., 375 Hudson Street, New York, New York 10014, USA

Penguin Group (Canada), 90 Eglinton Avenue East, Suite 700, Toronto, Ontario M4P 2Y3, Canada (a division of Pearson Penguin Canada Inc.)

Penguin Books Ltd., 80 Strand, London WC2R 0RL, England

Penguin Ireland, 25 St. Stephen's Green, Dublin 2, Ireland (a division of Penguin Books Ltd.)

Penguin Group (Australia), 250 Camberwell Road, Camberwell, Victoria 3124, Australia (a division of Pearson Australia Group Pty. Ltd.)

Penguin Books India Pvt. Ltd., 11 Community Centre, Panchsheel Park, New Delhi—110 017, India

Penguin Group (NZ), 67 Apollo Drive, Rosedale, North Shore, Auckland 1311, New Zealand (a division of Pearson New Zealand Ltd.)

Penguin Books (South Africa) (Pty.) Ltd., 24 Sturdee Avenue, Rosebank, Johannesburg 2196, South Africa

Penguin Books Ltd., Registered Offices: 80 Strand, London WC2R 0RL, England

International Standard Book Number: 978-1-61564-058-4
Library of Congress Catalog Card Number: 2010915378

13 12 11   8 7 6 5 4 3 2 1

Interpretation of the printing code: The rightmost number of the first series of numbers is the year of the book's printing; the rightmost number of the second series of numbers is the number of the book's printing. For example, a printing code of 11-1 shows that the first printing occurred in 2011.

Printed in the United States of America

Note: This publication contains the opinions and ideas of its authors. It is intended to provide helpful and informative material on the subject matter covered. It is sold with the understanding that the authors and publisher are not engaged in rendering professional services in the book. If the reader requires personal assistance or advice, a competent professional should be consulted.

The authors and publisher specifically disclaim any responsibility for any liability, loss, or risk, personal or otherwise, which is incurred as a consequence, directly or indirectly, of the use and application of any of the contents of this book.

Most Alpha books are available at special quantity discounts for bulk purchases for sales promotions, premiums, fund-raising, or educational use. Special books, or book excerpts, can also be created to fit specific needs.

For details, write: Special Markets, Alpha Books, 375 Hudson Street, New York, NY 10014.

Publisher: *Marie Butler-Knight*

Associate Publisher: *Mike Sanders*

Executive Managing Editor: *Billy Fields*

Senior Acquisitions Editor: *Paul Dinas*

Development Editor: *Lynn Northrup*

Production Editor: *Kayla Dugger*

Copy Editor: *Cate Schwenk*

Cover Designer: *Kurt Owens*

Book Designers: *William Thomas, Rebecca Batchelor*

Indexer: *Brad Herriman*

Layout: *Brian Massey*

Proofreader: *Laura Caddell*

Contents

Appendixes

Introduction

"Training has to be a relatively enjoyable experience to get peak results. Otherwise, you won't be willing to put up with the discomforts that come with hard effort."

—Jack Daniels, Ph.D., author of *Daniels' Running Formula*

If you ask most nonrunners what they think of running a marathon, most of them will tell you it looks like a painful, difficult, next-to-impossible feat best left to super-humans. But if that were true, how could thousands of Americans run marathons each year? In this book, we show you the reality behind the myths, and how training for and running a marathon can—and should—actually be fun.

Running or walking 26.2 miles—the official length of a marathon—is certainly a grand goal that takes a lot of work, dedication, and strategy. But it doesn't have to include terrible pain or injury. Medical and scientific advancements have helped us to understand the human body so well that marathon training has become a science in itself. Modern training techniques break down the process of training so that it's both understandable and effective for the average person. Advancements in the nutrition and sporting goods industries have also helped to make marathon training more comfortable, healthier, and easier.

The first rule of endurance athletics supersedes everything else you do in training or racing—everything! That rule is critical to your success as an athlete.

Rule Number One: You need to have fun!

Rule Number Two: If you aren't living up to rule number one, something is wrong, and you need to fix it.

We now know that if you start your training and find yourself asking, "When is this run going to be over?" you are pushing yourself too hard or overtraining, or you may not have a strong-enough endurance base to do what you are doing. If it feels as if you are beating yourself up, you probably need more aerobic (low-intensity) work before you can do the fast, high heart rate work involved in running a marathon. Once you have that base of low heart rate work, pushing yourself to new limits can be exciting, not painful.

Similarly, many athletes feel that being tired all the time is a natural element of training. Nothing could be further from the truth. This is a sign that the runner's hormones have been depleted by overtraining. There seems to be an epidemic of overtraining within the nonprofessional marathon community. If you are tired the next day after a workout, you are overtraining. A little overtraining is good. But overtraining for long periods of time leads to less energy for the rest of that training season. This makes you slower and more prone to injury. Simply stated, you need rest. Rest and recovery are necessary for muscular and system adaptation, or growth. Exercise + Rest = Optimal Energy Output (greatest ability). Training is tailored to use your body's natural tendencies to your best advantage. We show you exactly how to do that and why it's so important. We also show you how to avoid injury and how to tell if you are pushing yourself too hard. We have had more success holding people back than in pushing them for more.

Undertraining can also cause many problems. If you lose your endurance base from missing too many workouts, jumping into the longer runs can be a nightmare and can easily lead to injury. We give you tips and advice on how to stay consistent in your training and how to fit it into your very busy life.

Training for a marathon shouldn't tear you down; it should build you up. When done properly, preparing for a marathon will leave you healthier than you were when you started. Of course, your endurance will increase, your cardiovascular system will improve, and you will build and strengthen muscle. Many people also report feeling mentally sharper and more at peace after an endurance run. In short, the idea that training for a marathon is torture is based on misinformation and faulty logic.

Americans are consistently hard workers who aim for the finish line not only in our jobs but in our daily lives as well. In your training as well as in life, we encourage you to enjoy the road it takes to get to the finish line. Enjoy feeling alive, with air filling your lungs. Enjoy running outside in nature, or run inside and appreciate the comfort that it provides. Have fun in life, love, and running. Creating balance and harmony in your life is an important part of maintaining balance in your training, and this book shows you how to achieve both.

How to Use This Book

This book has 17 chapters organized in 3 parts, which we recommend you initially read from beginning to end. They are arranged to help you organize your thinking and then your training as you approach the idea of running a marathon. We also give you the tools and guidance you will need as you embark on a training program. We describe how a marathon is organized and what you should expect on your first marathon run. Then, as you advance through your training plan, you can refer to individual chapters that align with your journey through training up to the finish line.

Part 1, Me, Run a Marathon?, gives you the history of the marathon, as well as factors you should consider when deciding to train for a marathon. We also help you prepare for training and offer tips and advice on health issues and modern running gear.

Part 2, Training Regimen, introduces you to the way your body runs and how to improve your athletic efficiency. Here you will find tips on nutrition and setting up a training routine, as well as guidance in choosing the best training plan for you. We describe the theories behind different training programs and the best methods for preventing and recuperating from injuries.

Part 3, The Main Event, takes you through the last few weeks before race day. We show you how to taper your training, tailor your diet, and get the rest you need. Then we walk you through the marathon course from starting line to finish line and beyond. And once you've crossed the finish line, we show you how and when to do it all again!

We also include five helpful appendixes for your reference: a glossary to help you navigate the terms and phrases used in marathon training; a list of recommended resources to complement your training; a look at the most popular U.S. and international marathons and shorter races; sample training programs for both the marathon and half marathon; and suggested stretches, strength training exercises, and drills to improve coordination and flexibility.

Extras

To enhance your understanding of the text, look for the following types of sidebars sprinkled throughout the book:

DEFINITION

These sidebars define key words and concepts to aid in understanding the challenges of marathon training.

YELLOW LIGHT

These warnings illuminate things you should avoid and prevent while training for and running a marathon.

COACH SAYS ...

These tips and advice from a certified and experienced coach provide perspective and reliable information on training concepts and athletic practices.

MILE MARKER

These sidebars expand on the text with little-known facts and trivia on training and running, as well as miscellaneous information you should know.

Acknowledgments

From David:

I wish to thank LA Roadrunner Coach and Pro Athlete Rod Dixon for his important contributions; Matthew Mahowald, nutritionist at NPN for the menus; Robert Forster of Phase IV training lab for lactate tests; Kamal Oudrhiri and Katherine Gluck of USA Marathon Training; LA Running Club Execs; The Coach, Pat Connelly; my loving parents in Toledo, Sid and Rita; all those friends who peel me off the floor; and Phoenix, Devora B., Julie W., Bill S., and Kevin K., who I learned the most from.

And last but not least, to my amazing writing partner, Paula Petrella. No winning marathoner has ever had the drive and determination to win more than you have with writing. You were amazing to work with, and I could not have done this without you.

From Paula:

This book has had a long genesis, and my gratitude must follow. In approximate chronological order:

I would like to acknowledge my late parents, Eleanor and Frank Petrella, for their brilliant and incomparable encouragement and support in all of my endeavors. I grew up watching them work together on my father's writing projects and am eternally grateful for their creative and intellectual influence. My dear brother Peter has been a kind and supportive friend for as long as I can remember. My aunt, Rose Davi, among her countless graces, also encouraged my early writing with, "No one ever showed the first poet how to write poetry." My precious friend and fellow writer Danielle Collins has made me a better person and a better writer—and also manages to keep me laughing all the while. And I couldn't have written this book without the support of my husband and best friend, Peri Pastor. His patience, humor, strength, and compassion are my oxygen and sunshine.

Allison Troxell, my dear friend and fellow runner, introduced me to the Santa Monica Trail Runners Club, which was founded by Stan Swartz. Stan's wise and compassionate advice still rings in my ears whenever I run or even just think about running. He, in turn, introduced me to my agent, Marilyn Allen, whose generous support and sage advice are legendary. At Alpha Books, I was extremely fortunate to work with Paul Dinas, a powerhouse of intelligence and wit. I am forever grateful to

Marilyn and Paul for their guidance and kindness. Warm thanks to Lynn Northrup, our development editor, for her guidance and tireless efforts, as well as to Kayla Dugger and Cate Schwenk, our omniscient production and copy editors, respectively.

I must also extend my gratitude and respect to my co-writer and colleague, David A. Levine. David was a pace leader in the marathon training program I joined in 2009. I realized, after watching him patiently answer countless training questions from runner after runner, that he would be the perfect person with whom to partner for this book. His love of running and his genuine desire to help people succeed in reaching their running goals is inspirational. Tremendous thanks go to Rod Dixon, for his gracious generosity and brilliance in sharing his advice and love of running with us. And, finally, a fond thank you to Monica Howe and Robert Phillips for their patience and creativity as our models.

Trademarks

All terms mentioned in this book that are known to be or are suspected of being trademarks or service marks have been appropriately capitalized. Alpha Books and Penguin Group (USA) Inc. cannot attest to the accuracy of this information. Use of a term in this book should not be regarded as affecting the validity of any trademark or service mark.

Me, Run a Marathon?

In this part, we show you how to wrap your mind around the idea of running a marathon. Countless runners throughout history have completed marathons without any of the advanced training techniques or modern nutritional sciences we all enjoy today.

We give you the history of the marathon, statistics on the popularity of the race, details on how a marathon is organized, and how to prepare for training. You'll see that running a marathon is entirely achievable for "regular" people. We help you define your goals in running a marathon and also dispel stubborn marathon myths. We underscore the myriad benefits of distance running, and we show you how to fit training into your busy lifestyle.

Lastly, we discuss common medical issues and how they can affect distance runners. We also describe modern types of running gear, and nutrition and hydration options that are available.

The World of Marathons

In This Chapter

- How "going the distance" started with the ancient Greeks
- The many reasons people run marathons
- What's involved in running a marathon?
- What you need to know to get started

Marathons are growing in popularity every year, but to the uninitiated, they can still seem overwhelming and discouraging. All those happy, healthy people running together in apparently joyous harmony can seem intimidating from a distance. But when you get a little closer, the bigger picture starts to come into focus.

Step over the line from spectator to participant, and an entirely new world opens up to you. It's a welcoming world where you are free to challenge yourself among supportive peers and knowledgeable instructors. You will find training plans tailored to your needs and ability, and coaches and trainers ready and willing to help you reach your goals. There are also foods, clothing, and equipment specifically tailored to help you in your journey. Suddenly you will find yourself running a little farther every day, doing better than you had dreamed. And before you know it, you will be one of those joyous runners with your eyes on the horizon and a very achievable goal in your heart.

The Greek Roots of the Marathon

Before we get into what makes marathons so popular, let's take a brief look back. You may know that a *marathon* is defined by its length: 26.2 miles. Any longer or shorter, and it's no longer a marathon. While that may seem a random distance, it's actually rooted in ancient Greek history as well as in more recent British tradition.

> **DEFINITION**
>
> A **marathon** is typically defined as a foot race of 26.2 miles, or 26 miles and 385 yards. It is also the name of a town in ancient Greece, but the term has come to signify any long and enduring event.

There are many versions of the legendary story of Pheidippides, the ostensible "founder" of the marathon. He was a Greek messenger who was dispatched by his Athenian general in 490 B.C.E. to request aid from Sparta in fighting the invading Persian army. Professional runners were used as messengers in those days as they could cover difficult ground and use shortcuts unavailable to mounted cavalry. According to most historical accounts, the Persian army had landed at Marathon with the intention of invading nearby Athens. As ordered, Pheidippides ran the 150 miles to Sparta in two days, but despite his efforts the Spartans couldn't arrive in time to help. Miraculously, the Athenian forces defeated the much larger and better-equipped Persian army on their own.

At this point, Pheidippides was again sent out with a message, this time from Marathon to Athens, which was only about 25 miles away—considered a short hop for a runner of his caliber. He is believed to have arrived safely in Athens with the word *Nike!* (victory) on his lips only to drop dead a moment later. Now this may seem like a bit of a discouraging story to start off with, but bear in mind, the guy probably fought all night, then ran the distance on no sleep, dehydrated, starving, and in sandals. He also didn't have this book to advise him, nor did he have modern training, sports medicine doctors, anti-inflammatories, or … well, you get the picture.

In 1896, the approximately 25-mile marathon run was included in the first modern Olympic Games in Athens. It covered the route from Marathon to Athens and was won in under three hours by a Greek citizen with a seven-minute lead. Thereafter, the distance remained at about 24 or 25 miles until the 1908 Olympics, which were hosted by the city of London. In order to accommodate the location of the British Queen's viewing box, the length of the race was extended to its current 26.2 miles. This inspired the popular practice of shouting "God Save the Queen!" around mile 24. There are other things that marathoners also call out at mile 24, knowing that they have to go 2 more miles because of the queen, but we will be polite and not repeat them.

Who Runs Marathons and Why?

From the beginning, marathon running has been the exclusive province of exceptionally dedicated runners. Starting in ancient Greece and lasting until the 1980s, it was also exclusively a man's game. Women weren't allowed to participate in long-distance competition based on its alleged dangers for the so-called "weaker sex." Public and Olympic committee disapproval, however, couldn't dampen the spirit of early female distance runners.

Not only did two women "unofficially" run the course in the 1896 Olympics, one of them finished in four-and-a-half hours (04:30). In 1926, a British woman clocked in at approximately 03:40. By the 1960s, two women runners were tackled on the Boston Marathon course and one was forcibly removed. Katherine Switzer broke the barrier in Boston, in 1967, by being the first woman to finish the Boston Marathon. She signed up as K. V. Switzer, and got her number without a problem. But as she ran the course, co-race director Jock Semple tried to grab her. Her 235-pound boyfriend knocked Semple to the ground, allowing Switzer to continue running. Her finish time for that race was approximately 04:20, though not officially recorded. She went on to win the 1974 New York Marathon. By the early 1970s, women had broken the three-hour mark, and by the end of the decade had broken 02:30. After much struggle and protest, the women's marathon competition was finally included in the 1984 Olympics. Today, women runners make up over 40 percent of all U.S. marathon finishers. Carrying the torch for her forebears, British marathoner Paula Radcliffe set a world record at the 2003 London Marathon, finishing in 02:15.

So what is it about running a marathon that inspires such perseverance and fearless dedication? While every runner gives you a different reason, the bottom line is apparent: marathon running is rewarding. Countless people face the challenge of running 26.2 miles in one shot for the simple reason that it repays them much more than it costs them.

There isn't any one type of person who runs marathons. Organized marathons take place on all seven continents of the world (yes, even on Antarctica). There are few age restrictions, as 10-year-old children run alongside octogenarians. The unifying characteristics of people who run marathons are generally an interest in challenging oneself, a love of adventure, and a good deal of focus and determination. And, of course, their doctors give them the thumbs up before they start training.

More People Are Running

Marathon running has exploded in popularity in the last decade—annually, over 400,000 people have finished almost 400 marathons in recent years. Men still out-number women, but their majority is declining. In 2000, men made up 62.5 percent of finishers, and women made up 37.5 percent. In 2009, the split was 59.6 percent men, 40.4 percent women. Finishers' average age has hovered around 38 since 2002, although men in the 40 to 44 age range generally rack up the fastest average time.

Similarly, the average finish time across all age groups has been decreasing, to about 04:35 in 2009. Hence, runners in general are getting faster. The world record currently stands at about 02:05—which works out to an average pace of approximately 13 miles per hour.

The major marathons are generally hosted by America's largest cities such as New York, Boston, and Chicago. In 2009 the New York City Marathon set a record with over 43,000 finishers. Although they are run year-round, most marathons are held in fall and spring due to the more manageable weather.

The Top Reasons People Run Marathons

So what is it that inspires so many people to run marathons? The most popular answers center on health benefits, the challenge, the adventure, and the incomparable feeling of accomplishment. Many people are motivated to run a marathon in order to raise money for a cause or a charity. But most of all, people run marathons in order to find the best in themselves.

MILE MARKER

When running marathons, men generally find inspiration in the goal of lowering their finish time. Women tend to focus on the process more, citing reasons like feeling better about themselves and enjoying the challenge.

Quite often, completing a marathon changes people's lives. In training and during the marathon itself, you will explore your inner resources in ways you never knew existed. You will take on challenges you never would have thought possible. And once you cross that finish line, your perspective on life will be forever changed. You will gain confidence and your fitness will improve. You will understand how a marathon is a metaphor for life, and how strategy, perseverance, and patience really do matter. You will learn that you can accomplish great things by taking small steps.

Upon crossing the finish line, many realize that other challenges in their lives may not be so insurmountable as well. Marathoners often go on to change their diets and lose weight, quit smoking, get a better job, etc. The bottom line is, you don't need a big, poetic reason to run. Running a marathon is its own reward.

What a Marathon Entails

Unfortunately, the mystique surrounding marathons tends to deter less experienced runners. With its storied past, intricate training plans, and grand tales of glory, the marathon may seem like an insurmountable goal to most people. It shouldn't. Perhaps the most important thing you need to complete a marathon is good planning. It's often said that the athlete is in the mind, not the body. And as an endurance sport, running a marathon is very much an exercise for the mind. While you train your body to run longer and longer distances, your mind will undergo beneficial changes as well.

We could list any number of attributes that a marathon runner needs to get to the finish line, such as discipline, perseverance, focus, determination, a sense of adventure, patience, and goal-oriented behavior—but that isn't the whole story. Fitting yourself into the right training plan will carry you along when any of those character traits falter. The human body improves in training in predictable ways, and a good training plan is firmly based on this pattern. Therefore, it will be challenging but it will be structured to succeed. Sticking with your carefully thought-out training plan will likely be your biggest challenge, but if you plot your time and weekly mileage appropriately, you will find it much easier to stay on track. (We describe various training plans and methods for choosing the right one for you in Part 2.)

Before you embark on a training regimen that will last several months, you need to learn what you're capable of at the present time. This will position you to find an appropriate training plan, and this plan in turn will dictate your time frame. Then, you will have to educate yourself regarding equipment, nutrition, hydration, marathon rules, and how to deal with injuries. As far as cost, running a marathon is not an expensive undertaking. Other than running gear and some special foods, you can expect to pay from $100 to $200 in registration fees, depending on how early you sign up.

Three to Six Months of Training

Before you can choose a training plan, you need to know two things:

- What is your level of endurance now?
- What is your goal in running the marathon?

If you don't have any running experience under your belt, you will need to choose a longer plan that allows extra time to build up more mileage. If you want to compete and finish with your best time possible, you will likely need a more aggressive plan. If your goal is simply to finish, you might want to choose a run/walk or strictly walking plan. Most runners will do well with a three- to six-month training plan, which entails running several times each week. (See Chapter 10, which introduces training ideas, and Appendix D, which describes sample training plans.)

> **COACH SAYS ...**
>
> Pick a training plan and a running intensity level that starts out comfortably.
> You don't want to overtrain. As your efficiency progresses, you will speed up.
> And if your training is scheduled correctly, your marathon finish time won't look
> anything like your early training times.

Travel May Be Required

Not everyone is lucky enough to have a marathon scheduled in their hometown, so you may need to factor travel time and expense into your training plan. If you will have to travel to your race, it's best to start making travel plans as soon as you register for the race, because flights and hotels will undoubtedly be booked as you get closer to the date. You should also plan to arrive at least two days ahead of time, or even longer if you will need to acclimate to a higher altitude or different climate. You will need to allow sufficient time to recover from jet lag or a long car ride. Of course, being organized and thorough when packing up your gear is critical so you don't forget anything important. To minimize unnecessary stress, a marathon close to home is best.

Marathon Structure and Rules

Most marathons are set up on a similar blueprint, as they are generally large civic events. Many people will be converging on one place at one time, and this takes tremendous structure and organization. Not surprisingly, the host city's police and fire departments will take part in planning the marathon, and emergency medical support will be available. The 26.2-mile course will be marked and closed off to traffic for the duration of the race. Keep in mind, closed streets are a serious obstacle to arriving on time on race day. Plan to arrive early at the start line. Online registration is the norm, during which you will have to sign a waiver and pay the entrance fee. Only registered participants will be allowed on the course, and there may be age or finishing time restrictions. Generally, pets, vehicles, and electronics like cameras or personal music devices are prohibited for runners, who must stay on the official course. Each marathon race has its own rules of conduct which are generally similar to common rules of civil propriety. You are expected to be courteous and cooperative just like at any crowded civic event.

Many marathon organizers arrange special travel deals for marathon participants, such as with airlines or hotels. Hotels close to the starting line sell out early, so it's best to plan ahead. Many hotels offer shuttles to and from the starting line and/or finish line. An expo will be set up two days prior to the marathon at which registered runners will pick up their registration bibs, timing chips (more about these at the end of this chapter), and usually a T-shirt and a bag of goodies from corporate sponsors. At the marathon, spectators can line up along the route, but aren't allowed on the route itself. Quite often a traditional pasta dinner is held the night before, though its timing and nutritional value are questionable. The camaraderie at such events is generally worth the price of the food, but take care to eat wisely. (We talk more about this ritual in Chapter 13.)

How a Marathon Is Organized

Marathons are usually organized by civic groups or athletic associations. It takes a lot of staff a great deal of time to put a 26.2-mile race together, and they are usually assisted by a large contingent of volunteers. The marathon route must be measured and certified by USA Track & Field in order to be considered an official marathon course. Once the race route is accepted by the host city, arrangements must include the highway department as well as the police and fire departments. The race usually begins early in the morning and ends at a specified time. Runners or walkers who can't complete the course before the end time will generally be bused to the finish line. You will find medical tents at certain intervals along the course, but anyone in need can be picked up from any of the water stops, which are generally spaced about one mile apart. Bathrooms—usually of the portable toilet type—are also available at various locations along the route. Those bathrooms available near the start of the course are usually the busiest.

Participants line up at the starting line according to their estimated finish times, with the slower runners in the back followed by walkers. Some races use corrals, while some use staggered start times, or "waves." Wheelchair and disabled participants usually start the race before the rest of the runners. Your time will likely be measured at each mile along the course, and at the finish line, your photo will be taken and you will receive a finisher's medal. Your finish time will be displayed on a clock as you cross the finish line. Medical personnel, snacks, and refreshments will usually be available at the end of the race and you may even be wrapped in a complimentary plastic blanket by a friendly volunteer. At this point, provisions made by the organizing committee usually end, and you will be responsible for getting back to your hotel or home. Some marathons provide shuttles back to the starting line or to prearranged parking lots.

Do You Need to Qualify?

There are very few marathons in the United States that require a *qualifying time* prior to registration. One such race is the Boston Marathon. Official qualifying times currently stand at 03:10 for men and 03:40 for women ages 18 to 34. The accepted times and races change from year to year, but the fact remains the same: Boston is one of the most difficult races to enter. Even with such stringent rules, Boston sells out far ahead of time. You can still register for the Boston Marathon after it sells out if you join an affiliated run-for-charity program. In that case, you must agree to raise a certain amount of money, and you will be entered in a sponsored training program. On the other hand, all you need to qualify for most marathon races is the entrance fee and some way to get from the start to the finish line on the official course under your own power. Read your chosen marathon's information pages and application carefully so that you don't apply for a race for which you don't qualify.

DEFINITION

A **qualifying time** is a certified finish time for an approved marathon race. The runner's time must be officially recorded within the 18 months prior to the Boston Marathon. The list of approved marathons may change every year, and they must be USA Track & Field–sanctioned courses.

There are a few races for which competition to get in is so fierce, they require a lottery in which registrants are chosen at random. The New York City Marathon, the St. George Marathon in Utah, and a few other popular races use a lottery system for admission. New York City does offer guaranteed entry to runners with certain finishing times, but most runners are subject to the lottery. New York currently charges an $11 fee to enter its lottery, though the cost varies from year to year. With that one marathon, you forfeit your lottery fee whether your name is chosen or not. Most marathons don't make as much money in total as the New York Marathon makes from lottery money alone.

How to Enter

Once you have chosen your race (more details on the best way to do that in Chapter 2), entering is quite simple. The race organizers likely manage a website that allows online registration. With credit card in hand, you can pay the registration fee, which will generally be lower if you register early in the season. For the larger marathons such as New York and Los Angeles, the cost generally runs from around $100 to $200 depending on when you register; it gets more expensive the longer you wait. Smaller marathons generally cost less (and offer fewer services). You may find an online waiver to sign electronically, indemnifying the race organizers if you are injured or unable to complete the race. At that point, you will likely be placed on the event mailing list and will begin to receive updates and advice. You may also be offered an "official" marathon finish photo, which must be purchased in advance. These photo companies are generally very reliable and use your bib number to identify you. They take photos of everyone who crosses the finish line, but only those who pay for their service in advance will receive an official photo. It makes a nice memento, especially for your first race, so remember to smile as you cross the finish line!

Several of the larger marathons are supported by their own training programs, or at the very least, their websites will offer training tips and advice. You can learn a lot by following the recommended links that are listed on the marathon's website.

Nonrunners Are Allowed, Too

Most marathons allow walkers as well as disabled and wheelchair-bound participants. Be sure to fill out your application appropriately, because your placement behind the starting line will depend on your estimated finish time, and certain groups such as wheelchair participants generally start the race before the rest of the pack. As a walker, you will be expected to stay toward the edge of the course so that others can pass you easily. Special arrangements can often be accommodated for disabled runners, such as an escort along the course. Finish times are calculated separately for each category of participant, and awards may be given to the top finishers in each category. You should be aware that all marathon routes will eventually be re-opened to traffic after a certain time, and stragglers may be bused to the finish line. This occurs when the open streets become too dangerous to allow slower athletes to finish. Aid and water stations will also be dismantled at this time. If you are planning to run or walk slower than 15 minutes per mile, check for any early cut-off times for your chosen marathon.

MILE MARKER

Walkers make up a large percentage of marathon finishers. In some of the largest races, walkers can make up between 20 and 40 percent of total finishers.

Competing for Your Age Group

Although you don't have to run with anyone in your age group, your finish time will be reported in relation to others in your particular age group. Starting line corrals are organized by estimated finish time, not age. Most age groups cover about four years, such as 35 to 39 or 40 to 44 years of age. This is a convenient way to compare yourself to your contemporaries. In marathons with qualifying times, the required finishing times are staggered according to age group, with older participants allowed to finish later. For example, Boston currently requires men age 35 to 39 to finish before 03:15 and men age 70 to 74 to finish before 04:30. Generally, awards are given out for the top finishers in each age group.

How Finish Time Is Calculated

Chip timing is a relatively new invention, and its widespread implementation has helped improve timing accuracy a great deal across the sport. The chips also keep people from cheating, as the timing company can track you at intervals, and knows where you are on the course. When you register for a marathon, an electronic timing chip will be assigned to you and linked to your identification number. It will either be attached to your bib, or will be designed to tie onto your shoelaces. At the starting line and finish line, your chip will register the exact time you crossed each line and your "net" finish time will be the elapsed time between those two measurements. Official time, or "gun time," is based on the time of the start of the race, not the time you individually crossed the starting line. This can be very different from your particular finish time, because it can take several minutes to actually cross the starting line in large races. Hence, the time you see on the clock as you cross the finish line may be very different from your net finish time.

Sophisticated chip timing systems calculate your net finish time automatically. It's always a good idea to wear a watch with a stopwatch and turn it on as you cross the starting line, because the race's electronic timing system can fail. This is a rare occurrence, but it has happened.

The Least You Need to Know

- The marathon's roots begin in ancient Greece in 490 B.C.E., when a military messenger ran approximately 25 miles from Marathon to Athens.
- Almost anyone can participate in a marathon—men, women, runners, walkers, and disabled competitors. There is generally no upper age limit, and many races allow children above a certain age.
- Time and effort will be your biggest expenditures in training for a marathon. There are no great monetary costs involved, but you should count on three to six months of dedicated training.
- Choose your race wisely and enter early. Many races fill up quickly, and travel amenities will also sell out as you get closer to race day.

Making the Decision to Run

In This Chapter

- How much time you will need to invest in training
- Cost considerations
- Three important criteria in choosing your first marathon
- Defining your goals in running a marathon
- Common marathon misconceptions
- The many benefits of long-distance running

Many runners remember their first marathons with great affection. The experience is often compared to a favorite first kiss, in that you're very nervous at first, but then after it's over you're quite relieved and you never forget it for the rest of your life. And quite often, it changes your life in a multitude of ways.

The decision to run your first marathon is a unique and pivotal moment in your life that will likely have long-ranging effects. A variety of factors will influence your decision, and you should take the time to consider each one carefully. Certainly, time and effort will be your greatest investments, but there are some minor financial considerations as well. Proper training and planning will make the difference between a challenging but memorable marathon experience and one fraught with injury or difficulty. Finding the race that is the best fit for you is of primary importance at this stage. (See "Choosing Your Race" later in the chapter.)

Making a Weekly Time Commitment

Whichever training plan you choose to pursue, a weekly commitment of time will be integral to your regimen. For the next three to six months, you will need to run several times each week according to your plan. Consistency is key in your training, as your progress is directly tied to your weekly mileage as well as to your strength and speed training. All of this takes time and can't be rushed. Like steps on a ladder, each week builds on the previous week and brings you closer to your goal of running 26.2 miles. There is a little leeway built into most training plans, but not a lot. If you miss too many training runs, you will fall behind, and your endurance base will suffer. It's extremely difficult if not impossible to make up the missed mileage and still stay on schedule. The upside is, you are investing a good deal of time in yourself and in healthy living, which is rewarding in itself. You will find sample training plans for reference in Appendix D, and training concepts in Chapter 10.

In general, most training plans will require you to run shorter distances two to three times a week with a longer run on the weekend. Interspersed with these runs will be hill challenges and track work to improve your strength and speed. Hence, several hours of each week will be dedicated solely to running. It may actually be misleading to say that you will need to dedicate a few days a week to running. The fact is, your days off will also have to be in service to your training. You will need to eat nutritious foods, drink enough water, and rest so that you are recovered and strong enough for your next run. (See Chapter 6 for more on nutrition and diet.)

COACH SAYS ...

Remember to allow appropriate time in your schedule to plan meals and recovery time in support of your new running habit. These requirements will demand more time as your mileage base increases. You may also need to allow time for travel to and from your training locations.

Running Is Not Expensive

In comparison to other sports that require more elaborate equipment, running is relatively inexpensive. A popular notion is that all you need is a good pair of running shoes and the open road. We recommend much more thorough preparation than that, of course. The costs associated with marathon training can vary greatly, depending on several factors. You can train on your own for free, invest in a managed training program, or hire a trainer. Nutritional supplies and gear come in a wide range of costs, from bagels to sophisticated carbohydrate and electrolyte gels, and from low-end fitness apparel to high-tech clothing that is fitted and engineered to stay dry. Some cost considerations include the following:

- Professionally managed training programs can cost $120 to $250, although you can always follow a published training plan on your own or with friends.

- Hiring a coach or trainer can run you as much as $30 to $60 per hour for a one-on-one session, or a bit more depending on the coach. General coaching fees range from $150 to $250 per month. One way to cut costs here is to go in with some friends and request a group rate.

- Equipment is available in a wide variety of prices, with clothing generally costing about $20 to $75 for shirts and $30 to $80 for shorts or leggings.

- Quality running shoes will usually cost over $100, and you may require professionally fit orthotics to correct your stride and running form. Most athletes don't need orthotics, however, given the vast array of shoes available for different types of feet.

- It's also a good idea to invest in a hydration system such as a water belt with pockets to hold personal or nutritional items. Smaller belts that hold one or two bottles cost about $20 to $40, while larger backpack-style systems can be as much as $40 to $100 and more.

- Registration costs for most large marathons hover around the $100 mark. If you sign up early, you can often get in on a reduced price, but prices usually go up from there, based on how late you register. Smaller races will generally charge less.

- Don't forget to factor in travel and accommodation expenses if your marathon will be out of town.

Injuries can cost you time and money as well—and we'll show you how to avoid them in Chapter 12.

Choosing Your Race

Strategically choosing your race is one of the most important things you can do to ensure a rewarding experience. Some races are notoriously more difficult than others, so it's best to do the research and choose a less challenging course for your first marathon. Races are held throughout the year although race organizers typically aim for the most temperate seasons in their particular locations. Here are some questions you should ask yourself when contemplating which marathon to target.

- How much time do you need to complete your training program?

- Do you prefer to run in a warm climate or in cool conditions?

- Are you prepared to travel a long distance to the marathon?

- Do you plan to run or walk the race, or some combination of both?

To help you organize your thinking, you can group these concerns into three important categories: time frame, location and date considerations, and difficulty. It's the intersection of these three crucial considerations that should direct your decision. You will have to balance each criterion against the others in order to find the race that best matches your priorities. Keep in mind, many larger races sell out quickly—even as much as six months in advance. Check availability before making your final decision.

Time Frame

If you are relatively new to running and need a full six-month training program, set your sights on a race that is half a year away. Likewise, if you feel you can do well with a shorter training program, start researching marathons that take place at the end of that time frame. This is a crucial consideration, as you don't want to finish training too far in advance of your target race date—you may lose conditioning or end up overtraining to fill in the extra time. And obviously, if you don't allow enough time to complete the training program that's best for you, you risk being ill-prepared for the race, or even worse, injured. Be realistic and allow yourself an adequate amount of time to train and prepare.

Location and Date Considerations

As you follow this path in your decision-making process, you will see that the time of year tends to dictate race location and vice versa. If you expect to complete your training during the summer, your pickings may be a bit slim because much of the country is too hot to run a marathon at that time of year. Northern latitudes might be your best bet at that point. Conversely, in fall and spring you will have the most races to choose from thanks to the more moderate weather throughout most of the country. As you might expect, many southern marathons take place during winter. If you have the time to wait, and you have a strong preference for running in a particular type of climate, you can pick a location or a specific race and then choose your training start date by backtracking to figure out the amount of time you will need to train for that race.

Don't forget to consider altitude when choosing your race, as altitudes of approximately 8,202 feet (2,500 meters) and above will likely require special training and preparation. The lower concentration of oxygen in the air may make your race extremely difficult even if you allow time to acclimate to the higher altitude in the days before the race. Some of our understanding of the effects of altitude on athletic performance comes from the 1968 Olympic Games, held in Mexico City at an approximate elevation of 7,545 feet (2,300 meters). Marathoners there found their abilities impaired by 5 to 7 percent. Interestingly, races shorter than one half mile (800 meters), held during that same Olympics, found athletic improvement at that same altitude. The theory behind this is that shorter, faster races utilize less oxygen in the muscles used for running than longer, slower races. Therefore, the athletes in the shorter, faster races were impacted less by the lower oxygen levels than were those athletes in the longer, slower races.

YELLOW LIGHT

At 5,000 feet, or 1,524 meters (the approximate altitude of Denver), the air only contains 84 percent of the oxygen it would contain at sea level. Among other adjustments your body will make, your respiration rate will increase to help compensate for the scarce oxygen. This means you will exhale more water vapor at higher altitudes, increasing your chance of dehydration.

Many first-time marathoners are attracted to the idea of running a marathon in a foreign country. While this is a fantastic way to see the world, it may add unnecessary stress to your first race. The long trip may affect your performance if you don't allow enough time for rest and recovery from jet lag and any associated time zone change. A good rule of thumb is to allow one day for every hour of time change. But even if you can schedule enough time, the challenge of traveling in a foreign country can be overwhelming when combined with the pressure of preparing for your first race. Different foods, unpredictable water quality, unfamiliar locations, and a new language can all add up to disaster on race day. It may be easier on you to choose a race that doesn't require extensive travel on your first time out. Choose your battles for your first race, and keep it simple.

Difficulty: "Fast" or "Slow" Course?

As you do your research, you may see course descriptions like "fast" or "slow." Ironically, as a beginner it will benefit you to aim for a faster course. What this means is that the marathon route isn't very hilly, or features more downhill mileage, and is therefore less challenging, resulting in generally faster finish times. Conversely, a slow course will take more time to complete thanks to its hills, altitude, or tricky terrain. In a nutshell, the flatter the course, the faster it is.

You should be aware that trail marathons, which are run off-road, are typically more challenging—or slower—than road races. For example, Chicago is considered a fast marathon because it is relatively flat. Boston, conversely, is considered difficult because it's hilly and even boasts Heartbreak Hill, which looms near mile 20 when runners are already close to exhaustion. If you plan to walk most or all of the race, the difficulty of the course will probably not affect you as much.

Define Your Goals

Now that you're getting a feel for the when and where of your race, it's time to think about the how and why. How are you going to run this race? Why are you running, or what is your ultimate goal? Your answers to these questions will dictate the type of training plan you require as well as the length of time you will need to train. Is improved fitness your primary goal? Are you striving for the absolute best you can do, a personal record? Or are you planning to simply finish, with no set time frame in mind? There is no "right" answer, of course, and most beginners tend to fall in between the two extremes of competing and simply finishing.

Your goal in running a marathon should also play into your choice of races. If you aim to test yourself and run the fastest race possible, then a faster course might serve you well. Or, if you plan to run at a slow pace or walk, then a more scenic route might be preferable, and its "fastness" or "slowness" will be less important. Also, if you are sensitive to climate or humidity and you want to ensure a fast and efficient race, then you should aim for a marathon in a location that is most likely to provide the conditions you prefer. Perhaps you don't like crowds and would like to run in a smaller race near home. Then the course details may have to take a backseat to these preferences, and your finish time will become less of a controlling factor. Having a clear set of priorities will help you narrow down your choices. As you will see, this type of organized thinking will help you throughout your marathon training. Choosing the best race for you is good practice in learning to plan and strategize.

MILE MARKER

Warm weather generally causes slower finish times. According to a study conducted by the U.S. Army Research Institute of Environmental Medicine, as the ambient temperature increases from 41°F to 77°F, marathon finish times get progressively slower, and the slowest runners are the most negatively affected. Cooler temperatures are more conducive to long-distance running.

Racing vs. Noncompetitive Running

The difference between training for a competitive race versus a noncompetitive run is a question of intensity. Running competitively—that is, competing with yourself as well as with the other runners—demands a more intense training schedule. Depending on your running experience, this approach will put more strain on your body than would a less aggressive training schedule. No matter at which pace you intend to complete the marathon, you will need to train to increase your endurance. That is a given whether you plan to run or walk. But if you plan to run competitively, you will have to focus heavily on your speed and strength work as well. Depending on the training plan you choose, this may mean additional sessions of speed and hill work, or a faster accumulation of mileage, or both. In the broader view, this also means you will need to adjust your nutrition and rest to compensate for the greater demands you will be placing on your body. This calls for even more focused time off so that you can reach your nutrition and recovery goals.

Conversely, running or walking noncompetitively calls for a training plan in which you accumulate mileage and work on speed just like a competitive runner does, but at a lower intensity. Your marathon experience will also last longer than that of most runners, so you will need to plan your nutrition and hydration accordingly. Many run/walk training plans are available, and some even claim that you will finish before some strong runners who do not run/walk. This can happen, thanks to the fact that your slower pace will allow you to progress at a more consistent rate than runners who go out fast and have to slow down later from exhaustion or injury. This type of plan is also more forgiving on your body.

Fitting Running into Your Lifestyle

As you can see, long-distance running takes some planning. It also takes considerable time, energy, and dedication. But because your training must be accomplished a little at a time, in weekly increments, it shouldn't be too difficult to fit into your current lifestyle. Some of your shorter, mid-week runs can be accomplished in less than an hour. Many people are able to run during their lunch hours, or before or after work. With some minor tweaks in your nutrition and rest schedule, you can become a long-distance runner with very little disruption to the rest of your life.

You already eat and sleep, of course. No huge changes there. What training asks you to do is eat and rest with more structure, more awareness. Pay attention to how food makes you feel and how much energy it provides. Experiment with different foods and eating at different times to find your optimum nutrition plan. Try to notice how much rest you need to feel your best. Taking on new habits is a challenge, but after a few weeks of the same routine, it will start to become second nature. Then, once your training starts to make a difference and you start to experience the rewards of long-distance running, the positive feedback loop will help to keep you motivated.

You also need to be realistic, and understand that while your friends go on with their usual routines, they might not understand your new routine. It's best to inform your friends and family of your plans so they can support you and give you the time you need. Including family and friends in your training can also help to keep you on track.

Going Solo vs. Group Training

If you are new to long-distance running, you may feel that you're moving away from your usual life and routine and everything that is familiar to you. That can feel lonely and a little intimidating at times. One way to combat these feelings and find support and camaraderie is to join a group training plan. You can train with runners just like yourself and learn from professional trainers and coaches. You will also forge new bonds with people who are experiencing exactly the same things you are, and you can compare notes and laugh about your challenges. The collective experience and expertise you encounter in group training, both from veteran runners as well as trainers, can be a great boon to your morale. Training in a group setting is also a good way to stay motivated and focused.

On the other hand, many runners find solo training to be a better fit. This gives you more flexibility in scheduling your training runs, and allows you the space you need to progress at your own pace. Or you might choose to run with a friend or family member, which can give you the benefits of camaraderie as well as some of the flexibility of solo training. Many new runners train on their own for the first few miles and then join a group program after they have a small mileage base under their belts. In any case, you will have to find the plan that works best for you. After all, you need to create positive reinforcement in your training experience so that you stick with it.

Common Misconceptions

Perhaps the biggest obstacles for runners who are contemplating their first marathon are the many myths and misconceptions that surround marathons as well as marathon training. To make matters worse, the legacy and history of the marathon itself can be quite daunting. Because such a small segment of the population actually runs marathons, there is very little accurate word-of-mouth information out there. And because marathon runners are relatively rare, they carry a certain mystique. But just like Lao-tzu's proverbial "Every journey of 1,000 miles begins with a single step," every marathon runner was at one time a beginner with no running experience.

The only thing that can turn a beginning runner into a marathoner is a healthy training program. There are no secret societies or magic tricks to help you run a marathon. What is needed, instead, is a tried-and-true method of preparation. The marathon is completed one step at a time, and marathon training is no different. And, the process of training for a marathon can be broken down into manageable and predictable parts. The only secret that marathon runners have is that they implement a structured training program, strategic rest and nutrition, and a good amount of common sense and dedication. Taken together, these very achievable measures add up to a successful marathon experience. These are the only secrets you need to know.

Marathons Are for Elite Runners

The most pervasive marathon misconception is that only elite runners are capable of completing a marathon. Elite runners have existed throughout history, even before the legendary "first" marathon was run in ancient Greece. And it's true that many elite runners have set world marathon records over the centuries. Elite finish times have improved dramatically over the last 100 years. For example, in 1908 John Hayes finished in 02:55:18; and in 2008 Haile Gebrselassie set a record with 02:03:59. A big part of the faster finish times during this long period is simply due to more efficient training principles and better running shoes. But elite runners don't make up the majority of the field of runners. In fact, given the thousands of people who will run a marathon in any given year, they are a distinct minority.

Every year, more and more "regular" people run or walk marathons. And, as our understanding of biology, athletic endurance, and medicine advances, finish times are improving across the board. Average finish times for all runners are decreasing year over year: in 2002, average finish time was 04:38:21, and in 2009 it was 04:35:42. As recent statistics show, the largest number of finishers—approximately 40 percent— come in at between four and five hours. That is an average pace of 5.25 to 6.55 miles per hour. (The average person walks at about 3 to 3.5 miles per hour.) As you can see, the majority of marathon finishers are middle-of-the-pack, nonelite runners and walkers. This shows that no matter what your experience or speed, you can improve with training and finish your first marathon.

Do Marathons Promote Weight Loss?

One of the most often cited reasons for running a marathon is to lose weight. Aerobic exercise is an important tool in any weight-loss plan, but training for a marathon is a bit more complicated. Many people don't realize that running the marathon itself actually uses up less than a pound of fat. And, since most runners will eat and drink while running the race, some of that fat will automatically be replaced. The real opportunity to lose weight is during marathon training due to the total amount of running you will do. But, as discovered in a recent study published in a journal of the Public Library of Science, exercise makes you hungry and can lead you to "compensation" eating. That is, exerting yourself can increase your appetite, or make you feel you deserve a reward, or both. This leads to compensatory eating during which you may consume more calories than you would have if you hadn't exercised. And in practice, it's close to impossible to tell how much is too much compensation. Of course, you need some additional calories to perform the exercise, but if you supply those calories and more by eating more, you will not only *not* lose weight, but possibly gain it.

You may also add a small amount of weight as muscle while training. You will tone up your leg muscles and may even build them up a bit with your hill work and cross-training. Hence, weight loss is a slippery slope while training for a marathon. It takes good control of the diet as well as an understanding of exactly how many calories you are using during your workouts. A good rule of thumb is that an average-sized person uses approximately 100 calories per mile, whether walking or running. Walking takes longer, and running requires more effort. Certainly, keeping your caloric intake below the number of calories you expend will make you lose weight. In marathon training, you have to keep a close eye on both in order to make a difference.

Benefits of Distance Running

Also widely misunderstood are the many benefits of running marathons. Not only does long-distance running work the leg muscles and cardiac system, it also challenges the pulmonary, neurological, and skeletal systems. There are also numerous mental and emotional benefits, which are often overlooked.

Physical Benefits

Your heart muscle, like your leg muscles, will become stronger and therefore better able to pump your blood, meaning it doesn't have to work as hard to get the job done. In most cases, your left ventricle in your heart will grow, improving your ability to pump blood to your extremities. Among other benefits, this additional blood flow will enhance your ability to regulate your body temperature, which is especially important in long-distance running. In addition, your blood pressure and cholesterol levels will likely go down. Your lungs will become stronger and you will be able to take in more oxygen with each breath. Similarly, your trained muscles will learn to use more oxygen, making them more efficient. Red blood cell count increases, giving your body the ability to get more oxygen to the muscles.

Running has also been shown to improve bone health, as it's a weight-bearing, "pounding" exercise. Placing this kind of stress on your bones actually causes them to become stronger, which carries long-term benefits and will help you to avoid osteoporosis as you get older. (See Chapter 3 for more about running and bone health.) Neurologically speaking, marathon training is also likely to enhance your coordination, as you will become more efficient in your stride and your *proprioception* will improve. You will also induce your body to engage different types of muscle fibers when you run, increasing your muscle power. And the stronger you are, the faster you can run.

DEFINITION

Proprioception is your perception of your body and its actions. It's your instinctive understanding of how your body moves and how it's oriented in space.

Many older runners are faced with the question, "How are your knees?" It's almost expected that running too much or for too many years will ruin one's knees. Two recent studies, however, have shown that long-distance running may actually provide protective benefits to knee health. In a surprising turn, a 10-year study by the Radiology Department of the Danube Hospital in Vienna in 2008 showed that marathon running doesn't cause any permanent damage to the knees where there was no damage before. And in a 2009 study conducted by the Stanford University School of Medicine, 45 long-distance runners age 50 to 72 years exhibited less arthritic damage to their knees than a control group of 53 men. It's contemplated that the knee cartilage "learns" to accommodate the motions of running and becomes stronger by reinforcing itself. In short, these studies show that if you have healthy knees, there is no reason to believe that running a marathon will change that.

Mental and Emotional Benefits

Marathon running carries nonphysical benefits as well. The "runner's high" is a well-known effect of running. It comes from your body's natural tendency to flood the brain with endorphins during intense physical activity. Endorphins are the body's own pain-relieving and stress-reducing hormones. After stressing your body in a challenging run, you may feel slightly euphoric, and your sensitivity to pain may go down. You may also feel more energetic than you felt before the run. This is due to the effects of adrenaline, which increases when you exert yourself, and the opiatelike effects of endorphins.

In addition to enjoying the benefits of the runner's high, many people run to relieve stress or to clear their heads. The sense of accomplishment that results from long-distance running also leads to confidence and a more positive outlook. Many marathon runners report feeling mentally sharper and more optimistic in general. Setting goals and reaching them is a sure-fire way to feel better about oneself. The camaraderie of running in a group or with friends brings lasting benefits as well. It's not unusual for runners who are training for a marathon to look forward to their weekly runs as a way to make friends or network.

The Least You Need to Know

- You will need to run at least three times per week to prepare for the marathon.
- Training for a marathon doesn't generally cost a great deal of money. Your greatest expense will likely be your marathon registration, which can run between $100 and $200.
- When choosing a marathon, consider difficulty, location/date, and time frame.
- Before starting your training, define your goals and decide whether you will run competitively or not.
- Marathons aren't just for elite runners; no matter what your experience or speed, you can finish your first marathon.
- Long-distance running can benefit every system in your body and can enhance mood and self-confidence as well.

How's Your Health?

In This Chapter

- How to prepare for your marathon training
- When to give yourself a break from running
- Tips for running with chronic conditions
- Running and physical disabilities
- Smoking and other health concerns
- Handling women's considerations while in training

The first question on every beginning marathoner's lips should be: am I healthy enough to run a marathon? Although you are likely to reap many benefits from marathon training and from running the marathon itself, you need to ensure that you start out on the right foot, so to speak. Running is generally beneficial, and under a doctor's supervision it can even be useful in treating certain health issues like high blood pressure or high cholesterol. However, it can also aggravate certain conditions, which should be monitored carefully or altogether avoided in marathon running.

Watch any marathon race for a few minutes, and you will probably see quite a few health challenges represented. In addition, most large races have wheelchair divisions, and it's becoming more and more common for amputees to compete as well.

First, Talk to Your Doctor

Your first step before beginning any new exercise regimen is to speak to your doctor and get a complete physical. Tell him your plans and be sure to obtain his approval before you start training. After the results of your physical are in, you should then address any outstanding problems that may have been revealed by your test results. With a little care and conscientious health management, many long-distance runners are able to forge ahead despite certain health issues. The key is to know what your issues are and then take the necessary steps to solve whatever problems you can before embarking on a training regimen.

You should also use common sense as you prepare for your training. After you obtain your doctor's okay, you can start increasing your aerobic activity by walking for a half hour each day or running slowly for a few minutes at a time. Start paying attention to what you eat and when, and try to get regular rest. If you smoke, try to cut down or quit altogether. In addition to all the health benefits you will enjoy by quitting, your lung capacity is of utmost importance now. Alcohol use can affect your running in various ways. Even at low levels, alcohol in your system can change your blood sugar levels and can lead to dehydration. These effects can last into the next day after use or longer.

Just as racecars or thoroughbred horses are pampered, you, too, will need to care for yourself with increased awareness and dedication as you begin your marathon training. The time and effort you invest now will come back to you in spades during your training regimen and during the marathon race itself.

Running with a Cold or Flu

We all get sidelined with a cold or flu now and then. The idea that you can "sweat out" your cold or fever by running doesn't appear to have any foundation in truth. In fact, it could make things a lot worse, as you simply shouldn't run with certain conditions, like sinus or chest infections. Immediately following exercise your immune system is slightly depleted. The tougher the workout, the greater the immune system depletion. This is a temporary condition, but it can make your illness worse, or make you more susceptible to illness.

Many common illnesses such as cold or flu will also dehydrate you, especially if you have a fever. Dehydration limits energy output and impairs many normal bodily functions. This is why everyone always tells you to keep drinking water when you're sick. Don't worry about your training. Heal first, before you stress your body and make your illness last a lot longer. Sometimes it's better to allow yourself to be sick for a few days rather than forcing yourself to run and increasing the risk of making it worse.

COACH SAYS ...

It's best to give yourself a break if you're not feeling well. If you really want to get out there, though, consider the "neck rule" if you're thinking about running while sick. Illnesses with symptoms above the neck, such as runny nose or headache, are less risky for running. However, issues below the neck, including chest cold, bronchial infection, and aches from the flu, can be more hazardous in running.

Following illness, most feel as if they have lost their entire endurance base, and that all the work they have done is gone. This is a very common concern. But fear not, after a few days or a week you haven't lost a tremendous amount of conditioning. You are probably dehydrated and you also need to get your airways opening wide again. With some stretching (see Appendix E) and possibly some strength training (see Chapter 8), you will be back to your higher levels of ability in no time.

It's also important to keep warm after exerting yourself, especially when outdoors in cool weather. Immediately following exercise, your body may feel warmer than normal. However, as your heart rate drops, breathing lowers, and other metabolic functions go back to normal, you will begin to feel cooler or even cold. If you are still wet with sweat, the cooling effect will be even more intense. You may be more susceptible to illness at this point. This is why most marathon organizers give out sheetlike plastic blankets to participants at the end of the race. There is a higher risk of bronchial infections among healthy marathon runners right after they finish. That's a good reason to grab a jacket and stay warm right after any longer or more intense runs.

Running with Chronic Conditions

Many *chronic conditions* can be managed so well that they don't present a major problem for long-distance runners. Either with medication or dietary changes or equipment, these issues can peacefully co-exist with endurance running. Being informed and prepared is the best preventive medicine in most cases. If you need to take medication while running, make sure you plan ahead and bring enough with you. If you will need to run with an assistive device, ask your doctor or coach how it will affect your stride and your running in general. You may need to make adjustments in your training schedule or running form to accommodate such requirements. The point is to avoid worsening any preexisting conditions and to prevent any new ones.

DEFINITION

A **chronic condition** is one that can be managed but not cured. It generally lasts longer than three months but doesn't necessarily progress.

As you advance through your training, you may develop new chronic conditions that may or may not be related to your running. It's a good idea to develop relationships with sports medicine doctors, trainers, and coaches so you can stay informed and address any issues as they arise. Try to develop a support system to help maintain your health. Being proactive will diminish your likelihood of encountering any serious health issues and will help keep you on your feet. The less time lost to illness and recovery, the better.

Should you experience a flare-up in any chronic condition during your training or during the marathon, stop running immediately and consult with a medical professional.

Allergies

Allergies such as hay fever can present a major hurdle in long-distance running. Congestion, itchiness, watery eyes, and runny nose can make it all but impossible to breathe well and stay focused on your running. Persistent sneezing can also mess up your breathing rhythm. Not to mention, many antihistamines cause drowsiness or nervousness and can dry out your sinus membranes. If you can't schedule your training for a location or time of year that doesn't harbor your offending allergens, the best thing to do is to experiment with different allergy medications to find a brand and a dosage that works best for you. You may need to ask your doctor for a prescription medication if over-the-counter drugs don't do the trick. It might be necessary to trade off a little medication strength for more manageable side effects.

In addition to airborne allergens, you should be aware that running equipment and supplies can carry some dangers for those who are sensitive. Many types of apparel are reinforced with rubber, for example, as are some wristwatches, water belts, and fanny packs. Quite a few energy bars contain soy or nuts, which can trigger severe allergic reactions. Protein drinks may use milk or egg proteins. Many sports drinks are sweetened with aspartame, which can cause trouble in sensitive consumers. If you are a victim of allergies, make sure to read labels and ask questions before you try anything new or untested.

Arthritis

The term arthritis actually describes over 100 diseases of the joints. The most common type, osteoarthritis, is a degenerative disease that consists of a breakdown of the cartilage between bones. This causes the bones within the joints to rub each other, resulting in pain, swelling, stiffness, and loss of movement in the affected joints. At its worst, osteoarthritis can be debilitating. Long-distance running hasn't been shown to cause arthritis, and according to a report by the Surgeon General of the United States, regular moderate physical activity can actually control joint pain and swelling. If you have arthritis in your lower extremities, talk to your doctor about whether running is a good idea. If your arthritis is minor, you just might benefit from the protective effects of running.

Asthma

Asthma is a serious condition that can make breathing difficult or impossible. During an asthma attack, the airways swell up and secrete excess mucus, causing congestion, coughing, and in some cases severely reduced airflow. Without treatment, serious asthma attacks can result in death. Asthma can have many triggers, such as allergies or even exercise itself, and it's generally managed with inhalers and/or oral medication. Once you have your asthma under control, running a marathon shouldn't cause you any particular difficulty. Always make sure you have your medication with you, and advise your running buddies of your condition.

Some asthma sufferers prefer warm, moist climates while others can breathe better in cool, dry environments. Make sure you understand your asthma triggers before you sign up for a marathon in an extreme climate or at a high altitude.

Most asthma patients require a greater amount of time to warm up before a workout. This slower approach can help keep the bronchial tubes from narrowing. A little walking, followed by a slow jog of about 5 or 10 minutes, followed by short amounts of running, can usually do it. Under normal conditions, this can better prepare the asthmatic athlete for the workout ahead.

MILE MARKER

If Olympic track and field athlete Jackie Joyner-Kersee could win three gold medals with asthma, and seven-time marathon winner Paula Radcliffe could set a world record with asthma, there is tremendous potential for anyone with well-controlled asthma.

Diabetes

Diabetics must take insulin shots or pills to help control their blood glucose levels. Keeping blood sugar at optimum levels can be a challenge for any long-distance runner, as running demands a lot of energy which is ultimately supplied by glucose in the blood. Therefore, running a marathon is a special challenge for those with diabetes. The body must cycle through a lot of glucose for energy, and the diabetic runner's body has little or no natural control of those glucose levels. Extreme variations in blood glucose levels can cause a wide range of problems, including impaired circulation and neurological function, unusual behavior, and even unconsciousness. Unchecked blood sugar swings can result in coma and death. Hence, diabetics must choose their foods carefully before and during their runs, and must monitor their blood glucose levels often during training and during the marathon. On the other hand, distance running does make the diabetic more efficient at metabolizing blood glucose. That's one benefit of distance running for everyone. However, please consult a doctor before altering any prescribed medication, including insulin.

Eating small amounts often will help to prevent large swings in blood glucose. Complex carbohydrates like whole grains, which take longer to digest, can also help by delivering their carbohydrates more slowly. Keeping sugar tablets on hand is a good idea as well. It's also important to watch for depleted glucose levels *after* long runs, as the muscles may use extra glucose in order to repair themselves. The anxiety and excitement of the marathon race itself can also result in higher adrenaline levels, which may cause the body to use more glucose. Endurance running is a delicate balancing act for those with diabetes, but it can be done with careful planning and monitoring—and under the guidance of a physician.

Heart Disease

No doubt, running a marathon places a big strain on even the healthiest heart. The months you spend in training are meant in large part to strengthen your cardiovascular system little by little. It's no small feat to go from breathlessness after running one block to sustained deep breathing during 26.2 miles. This points to your body's ability to adapt to the demands you place upon it in structured training. Even so, if you have heart disease, running a marathon can stress your heart enough to cause real trouble. While running can help some problems associated with cardiovascular disease by reducing cholesterol and blood pressure, your heart muscle must be healthy enough to sustain high-intensity, long-duration running workouts.

Recent studies in Australia have found inconclusive evidence that running a marathon can result in a biochemical marker, creatine kinase, in the blood, which indicates heart muscle damage, even in veteran marathoners. However, this is the same enzyme that occurs during neuromuscular disease, or any muscle damage. More studies must be conducted to clarify these results. Still in question is whether the enzyme is released by all muscle cells as a normal part of the exertion-repair cycle, or whether diminished kidney function (possibly caused by dehydration) could have resulted in a build-up of the enzyme due to less efficient kidney filtration of the blood. If you have any cardiac disease, it is best to review your condition in detail with your physician before starting any exercise program.

Endurance running increases the size of your heart's left ventricle. This is a good thing, and a sign of increased power and efficiency. Yet this symptom is the same found in cardiac patients with enlarged hearts due to clogged arteries or high blood pressure. Years ago, doctors wrongly theorized that the increased ventricle size in endurance athletes could be symptomatic of a heart condition. Long-distance running doesn't appear to cause any cardiac damage in healthy individuals. More information is sure to surface in the near future. In the meantime, this is an obvious reason to speak to your doctor before starting your marathon training.

The bottom line is that long-distance running stresses your heart. In healthy individuals, this generally makes the heart muscle stronger and more efficient, just as repeated exercise makes any muscle stronger. In those with compromised cardiac function, however, this type of exercise can be too much of a strain and should not be attempted without a doctor's permission.

Hypertension

Hypertension, or high blood pressure, is a dangerous condition that should be monitored closely. Most people with high blood pressure take medication to manage the condition. Left unchecked, hypertension can cause heart and circulatory system damage, neurological damage, and even organ damage. The high-pressure flow of blood can disrupt the lining of the blood vessels, making them vulnerable to a build-up of plaque. The resulting narrowed arteries can starve muscle tissue and cause cardiac distress, which can enlarge the heart muscle. Hence, it's crucial to have your blood pressure checked regularly and take steps to reduce it if it's elevated. Maintaining a healthy weight and reducing sodium intake are two effective ways to manage your blood pressure.

If your hypertension is well-controlled, you may benefit from long-distance running, as it has been shown to reduce blood pressure. If, however, your blood pressure is very high, it can be dangerous to exert yourself for long periods. Endurance exercise can cause your blood pressure to rise temporarily, but if your pressure is already high, this small change can have big effects. Some blood pressure medications have diuretic effects, meaning that they cause your body to flush out water and sodium. This can affect the fluid balance in your body, making endurance exercise difficult or impossible. If you are on medication, talk to your doctor about its effects and take it slow until you know how you feel during exercise.

YELLOW LIGHT

Exercise-induced hypertension affects a small segment of the population. If the blood pressure rises significantly during exercise but is normal otherwise, frequent exercise could lead to some of the damaging effects of long-term high blood pressure. A simple treadmill test can rule out this condition.

Running with Physical Disabilities

Luckily, modern technology is doing its best to keep up with the indomitable human spirit. Nowadays, marathon finishers include wheelchair-bound participants and amputees as well as those who are blind and/or deaf. Most larger marathons have wheelchair and hand-crank divisions, and there is hot competition within those divisions. Hand-crank wheelchairs are operated differently from push-rim wheelchairs. The rider sits upright and grips two crank handles that resemble bicycle pedals. This type of positioning is better for certain types of disabilities. Wheelchair participants use their arms as their primary method of locomotion, and must train to improve their strength and endurance just like runners in any other division. The wheelchairs are designed for aerodynamic racing and can cost thousands of dollars. The rider sits low to the ground, the rear wheels are angled outward at the bottom for stability, and one steerable wheel in front generally acts as a stabilizer. Lower-limb amputees often use a prosthetic leg with a flexible, curved foot module made of carbon fiber that absorbs shock and provides spring just like an anatomic foot would.

Eugene Roberts, a 62-year-old double amputee and Vietnam veteran, recently completed a 3,100-mile run across the country on specially designed artificial legs, traversing 11 states. In 1970, he was also the first person to finish the Boston Marathon in a wheelchair (though he wasn't officially registered).

Running a marathon with disabilities such as blindness or deafness is becoming more common all the time. If certain safety precautions are observed in training and throughout the marathon, there is no reason for blind or deaf running enthusiasts to stay on the bench. For example, for the blind an escort can provide guidance and companionship. In 2008, a British gentleman named David Heeley, who lost his sight as a young man, became the first blind person to complete seven marathons on seven continents in seven days. Nowadays it seems that disabilities provide little deterrence to dedicated runners.

Other Health Concerns

Several other health issues can impact your training and running. Certain medical situations will take more planning and preparation than others. It's best to be proactive and address possible complications before you start training, rather than face difficulty and/or injury after you have already begun. If you smoke or are overweight, for example, you will need to adjust your training plan to accommodate certain challenges presented by these conditions. You may need to resolve any nagging aches and pains before starting training, or you may risk making them worse. Female runners face certain challenges that don't affect men, and may need to make certain adjustments to avoid discomfort and stay as healthy as possible (more on this later in the chapter). With proper preparation and appropriate lifestyle changes, endurance running can be a healthy pursuit for just about anyone with their doctor's approval.

Smokers' Issues

The dangers of smoking are well known, but they take on special significance for long-distance runners. Just one cigarette a day can lessen lung capacity and cause dangerous changes in the cardiac system. Nicotine causes the blood vessels to constrict, which raises blood pressure and can also increase the risk of stroke. Narrowed blood vessels can be especially troublesome for distance runners, as adequate blood flow and oxygen delivery are crucial for hard-working muscles. Restricted blood flow also delays healing of injured or stressed muscles. A small rise in blood pressure may be risky for endurance runners, as blood pressure may become slightly elevated during exercise, so an additional increase could become damaging.

The nicotine in one cigarette also causes a rise in heart rate. Again, this is of utmost importance to endurance runners as much marathon training is centered on low heart rate exercise. It's also crucial to conserve energy and control exercise intensity by controlling heart rate. Starting a long run with too fast of a heartbeat could lead to early fatigue and could stress the heart.

COACH SAYS ...

Try to cut down or quit smoking cigarettes before starting a marathon training program. You will benefit from the increased lung capacity and healthier cardiovascular system.

The lungs are the oxygen powerhouses of endurance athletics, and they take the brunt of damage caused by cigarette smoke. Bronchitis, or inflammation of the bronchial tubes, and emphysema, a debilitating disease of the air sacs in the lungs, are commonly caused by smoking. And, thanks to a protective system called the muco-ciliary escalator in your lungs, you also tend to swallow whatever you inhale. Tiny hairs called cilia constantly beat in rhythm to remove impurities from your bronchial tubes and lungs. These impurities then work their way into your throat to be swallowed and eventually expelled through your digestive system. Hence you also digest the impurities you are inhaling. This could be a cause of stomach cancer in many long-term smokers. Smoking tends to interfere with this system, which in turn makes the smoker more prone to infection and inflammation of the lungs and bronchi. As a long-distance runner, all of your biggest assets are damaged by smoking: your lungs, your cardiovascular system, and your digestive system.

Age and Weight Considerations

Most marathons have a lower-limit cutoff at 16 or 18 years of age. Some marathons do allow minors to run, and in 2010, a 10-year-old boy finished the Los Angeles Marathon in 03:03:40. But because there are no conclusive medical studies regarding children running marathons, most marathon organizers prefer to restrict the entry pool to adults. At the other end of the spectrum, there are generally no upper age limit restrictions. Finishers in their 80s aren't as rare as you might think. At that stage, most octogenarian runners have already been at it for many years, and have cultivated and maintained a healthy running lifestyle. It all comes down to general health and the approval of your doctor.

Weight carries a more direct bearing on one's running ability than age apparently does. Most endurance runners are lean and light, which makes for less work as they propel themselves down the course. Larger runners, however, make up the majority of marathon participants. Finish time is generally proportional to weight, as larger runners must simply work harder to run. Carrying excess weight can affect running biomechanics as well as joints and bones. This additional stress on the joints can cause the cartilage in the hips and knees to break down, which could start the cascade of events that leads to arthritis. In general, it is recommended that larger runners walk or run at a slower pace in order to protect their bones and joints.

MILE MARKER

It's estimated that every extra pound of weight you carry places 4 additional pounds of stress on your knees.

Recent studies have shown that it's healthier to be overweight and active, or "in shape," than it is to be of average weight and inactive, or "out of shape." Running groups for "Clydesdales," or larger men, and "Fillies" or "Athenas," or larger women, do exist. They tend to focus, however, on shorter races such as half marathons. There is no set weight for each division, as it varies from race to race. In races that offer such divisions, it's up to you whether to register in that division or not. Weight is certainly not a requirement.

Everyday Aches and Pains

Everyone has some aches and pains now and then, but how do you know if they should preclude running? It depends on where they are, how bad they are, and when they started. If it's an old injury, it's best to allow it to heal before starting any new activities. If a joint or muscle is achy, you could start with some gentle stretches to see if it's just stiff. Inactivity can cause stiffness and achiness, and your body may protest a bit when you do become active. This is normal and is an expected part of the exertion and recovery cycle. Your back may be stiff from sitting at a desk all day, or your legs may feel achy from too much standing. In any case, a gentle approach to exercise will tell you if activity will lessen your pain or increase it. If your pain increases, stop exercising and try to isolate the cause of the problem. Talk to your doctor about any nagging pains that worsen or don't go away. Generally speaking, if you feel achiness or pain for two workouts in a row, consider yourself injured and see a doctor.

Bone Health

Running is generally considered good for your bones because it's a "pounding," weight-bearing exercise. This type of activity stresses the weight-bearing bones just enough to cause them to reinforce themselves, making them stronger and denser. However, conditions such as arthritis, osteoporosis, and *osteopenia* may put you at increased risk for injury. If you have osteoporosis, your bones aren't as dense as they should be, meaning you are more susceptible to breaks or other bone injuries. Running may help reverse osteopenia, but if you have this condition you and your doctor should devise a treatment plan that encompasses exercise and diet. Calcium and vitamin D are crucial for healthy bones and can be obtained in dairy products and leafy green vegetables. Daily exposure to sunlight can help your body to manufacture vitamin D. There is much debate lately regarding how much vitamin D is required every day, and doctors are increasingly prescribing vitamin D supplements.

Like osteopenia, mild arthritis may be helped with running. The pounding action can stimulate new cartilage formation in the knees and other joints, offering protection against the development of osteoarthritis. Check with your doctor regarding any arthritis or osteoporosis medications you may be taking, to make sure they are compatible with long-distance running. Some of these medications involve hormone replacement, which can negatively affect many other systems in the body.

Special Considerations for Women

For most women, menstruation hardly interrupts their lives. Thanks to modern feminine hygiene products and pain relievers, monthly menstruation can be just a minor inconvenience. For the most part, menstruation hasn't been shown to hamper running performance in any way. But for those with monthly cramps, bloating, and moodiness, menstruation is a burden and is difficult to manage whether they are running or not. If you get your period on race day, you can take several steps to minimize your discomfort so that you can focus on your running. Even if you aren't due for your period on race day, don't be surprised if it arrives early. The adrenaline and anxiety you experience just prior to race day may alter your usual cycle. Cramps and bloating can be managed with pain relievers, though diuretics aren't a good idea because of your need to stay well hydrated. Tampons may be a better choice than pads to reduce friction.

It may be a good idea to schedule a long training run on a day that you have your period, so that you can practice your management techniques. It's at this time of the month that running's mood-enhancing effects can be very desirable. At a time when physical discomfort and hormonal swings may be affecting you, the endorphins or "feel good" hormones generated by long-distance running can offer some welcome relief.

One risk faced by female athletes is amenorrhea, or the cessation of menstruation. This can occur if the body is overly stressed by too much exercise, too much dieting, or both. It can be dangerous, as it's a symptom of hormonal imbalances which could lead to osteoporosis and other health issues.

Many women are also anemic and don't realize it. The monthly loss of blood can lead to depleted iron in the blood, which causes reduced oxygen delivery to the tissues. Symptoms can be very mild and include fatigue, dizziness, shortness of breath, irregular heartbeat, and cold hands and feet. You should check with your doctor if you have any of these symptoms. An iron supplement can usually reverse the condition.

Running in pregnancy is a controversial subject. Since every woman and every pregnancy is unique, you should consult with your doctor as soon as you know you're pregnant. A woman who has been running for quite some time should generally be able to continue running into her second trimester. At any stage of pregnancy, it is critical to stay hydrated, not overheat, and not allow your heart rate to rise above approximately 150 beats per minute. These are all guidelines that would benefit long-distance runners as well. Wear a heart monitor when you run and carry a fast-read thermometer (preferably a rectal thermometer) to make sure your core temperature stays near normal, as overheating is a major danger for the fetus. Because of hormonal changes, your joints will loosen up, which can make you more prone to injury. You may therefore want to use knee and/or ankle braces—or better, strength train—especially if you have been injured in the past. Be sure to listen to your body, and if it says stop, then stop.

COACH SAYS …

Doing some running in water during this time can be a healthy bonus for mother and fetus, as it doesn't involve any pounding or impact. A special floatation device called an aqua-jogger can help you maintain proper form in deep water. The rubber vest snaps around you, keeping you floating upright. Though you cannot increase your endurance ability, you can maintain the hard work you did by running in water. It's also useful for those recovering from injury.

Lastly, it's best to avoid running in the last trimester, as the changes your body experiences are liable to become unmanageable when running. Your center of gravity will change as your belly grows, throwing you off balance and placing you in greater danger of falling. The added weight in your belly will probably cause a great deal of jarring and bouncing. As it becomes too cumbersome to run, you can always walk comfortably, with the approval of your doctor. The good news is, the rigors and discipline you put yourself through in endurance athletics can only help you in your pregnancy and throughout motherhood. And your improved pulmonary and cardio-vascular systems will serve both you and your baby during your pregnancy. Not to mention, you can return to running shortly after you recover from delivery.

The Least You Need to Know

- Always speak with your doctor before starting any new exercise plan.
- Try to take a break from running when you have a cold or flu, or you may risk a longer and/or more severe infection.
- Many major health conditions such as hypertension and arthritis can be improved with running.
- Physical disabilities don't have to prevent you from running a marathon.
- Smoking and alcohol consumption place additional stress on your body that can make running difficult and potentially unsafe.
- With proper care and precautions, women's considerations such as menstruation and pregnancy can be compatible with long-distance running.

Gearing Up

In This Chapter

- Running apparel and footwear for every situation
- Gear for any kind of weather
- Using orthotics and braces
- Staying hydrated and keeping your energy up
- Secret weapons to combat common problems
- A few technological tools

As is true with most sports, there is an entire industry passionately dedicated to running gear. This is a good thing, as your choice of clothing and equipment can make or break your entire running experience, not to mention your spirit. (Try taking a long run in the cold rain wearing a cotton T-shirt. You might never run again.) Fortunately, most manufacturers of running apparel have embraced recent advancements in fiber technology and running ergonomics. Likewise, the science of nutrition has taken giant steps forward in recent years, leading food manufacturers to flood the market with innumerable products that are tailored for endurance athletics.

If you do your homework, you can find the most appropriate equipment and nutritional supplements for your situation and preferences. After all, the best gear is the stuff that you *don't* notice, because it's doing its job.

Clothing and Footwear

One of the biggest challenges in long-distance running is staying dry—not only for comfort but also to allow your body's thermostat to work correctly. Sweat is your body's way of cooling you off because the evaporation of water pulls heat away from your skin. But staying wet for a long time will force your body to use up much of your valuable and limited energy just to keep warm. Therefore, fabrics and shoes that wick moisture from your skin and dry quickly are the only ones to use.

YELLOW LIGHT

Never wear cotton! While it may feel soft and cushiony when dry, it can hold more than its weight in water and can stay wet for hours. And running with a cold weight around your neck is never recommended.

Running shoe manufacturers offer almost limitless choices in style and design. Much has been made in recent years of different tread patterns, materials, cushioning, and structure. There is also a movement promoting barefoot or near-barefoot running. While barefoot distance running has its fervent supporters, we believe that the protection and support offered by modern footwear far outweighs any purported drawbacks. Given the wide variety of running shoes available today, you are likely to find the style that best supports your feet and keeps you running safely and pain free.

It's best to buy your running shoes from a specialty store with qualified personnel who can analyze your gait and recommend the best type of shoe for your individual needs. We'll discuss buying running shoes in more detail a little later in the chapter.

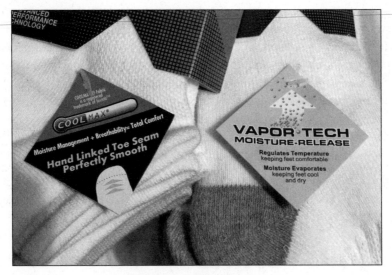

Moisture-wicking fabrics.

Shirts and Tanks

Running shirts come in all styles, from long-sleeve turtlenecks to wispy tank tops or *singlets*. Of course, the weather will play a big role in your choice of style, but you will also develop your own preferences as your training progresses. Some people like a lot of room in their garments so they can move more freely. Some prefer closer-fitting clothing to cut down on chafing and wind drag. A little experimentation will go a long way in finding the styles that work best for you. Look for man-made fabrics that are labeled as "wicking," "fast-drying," "comfort," and the like. A few popular brands are Dri-FIT, COOLMAX, and Vapor Tech, all of which are woven polyester.

DEFINITION

A **singlet** is a loose-fitting tank top worn by many types of athletes.

Shorts and Leggings

Just like shirts, running shorts and leggings come in all styles: loose or tight; long, medium, or short lengths; high-waisted or low-waisted. You will need to try different styles in different types of weather to find your favorite fit. Look for sturdy fibers touted for their wicking and quick-drying abilities. Many manufacturers offer matching outfits complete with tops, bottoms, and jackets. Women can even buy "skorts" for running, which are shorts with a panel in front to resemble a skirt. What will they think of next?

Socks

Ah, your poor feet. As a marathoner, you had better be as good to them as possible or they will surely take their revenge on you when you need them most. Therefore, keeping them comfortable, dry, and blister free must be a top priority. Socks that are made from modern fibers (no cotton) and designed to conform to the shape of your foot are best. Blisters result from moisture and rubbing, so excess sock material poses a danger. Some manufacturers also offer double-layer socks, which help reduce friction.

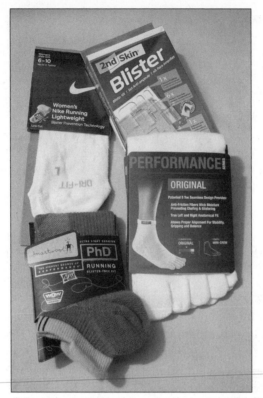

A few of the choices available to keep feet dry and prevent blisters.

Shoes

When it comes to running shoes, you not only have to consider fabrics and breathability, but fit, cushioning, support, tread, and weight. The idea is to balance the amount of structure your feet require with the need to keep things light. For example, running shoes for a road marathon will require less tread, and therefore less weight, than an off-road or trail marathon. A more structured shoe may weigh more than a more cushioned shoe. Just a few extra ounces in your running shoes can mean that during the thousands of steps you will take in a marathon, your legs will have to lift a total of many extra pounds. This cumulative effect can tire you out and slow you down.

Before buying your first running shoes, it's best to have your gait analyzed at a qualified athletic equipment store or by a sports doctor or orthopedist. In this way, you will learn about your arches, your particular *pronation*, and whether more cushioning or structure is right for you. It's always a plus to go to a specialty shoe store, where salespeople know running shoes and can help guide you to the right shoe. You will need to try on the shoes and see how they feel. Stand in them, walk in them, and then finally run in them. Specialty running shops will always let you take new shoes for a run outside their shop, for a block and back, or they may have a treadmill for you to run on. Pay close attention to how the shoe feels. How comfortable is the shoe? Do you feel any aches in your feet or joints? Often a more cushioned shoe may not be the best, most supportive shoe. If you overpronate, you may need more of a "control" shoe.

DEFINITION

Pronation is the rotation that your foot makes as it strikes the ground.

Understanding whether you over- or underpronate is important in resolving any joint and muscle problems that can develop as a result. If your foot strikes the ground at the wrong angle, you can get injured and throw off your body's alignment, which could result in a lot of pain. The proper running shoes can do a great deal to keep your feet level as they strike the ground, and this will literally have a great impact on how well your ankles, knees, and hips align. Good shoes equal no pain. You can find annual shoe reviews in some popular running magazines (see Appendix B for running resources).

Depending on your weight, running style, and weekly mileage, plan to replace your running shoes approximately every six months or 300 to 500 miles. The shoes' internal cushioning will wear out before any changes become visible, which can result in fatigue and pain in your feet and legs. Likewise, be cautious when buying from discount shoe merchants. Their stock may be older, and that can mean dried-out and ineffective cushioning in your otherwise-new shoes. Well-designed, name-brand running shoes will generally cost between $80 and $120.

Hats and Hoods

It may seem counter-intuitive, but many runners find it helpful to wear hats in all kinds of weather. The nature of marathon running and training means you will likely be outdoors for long stretches of time. Long-term sun exposure can dehydrate you, cause sunburn, and can sap your energy. Conversely, staying dry in rain or snow is key in maintaining a comfortable body temperature. Baseball caps are available with sunshields that convert them into hoodlike hats to protect your neck and ears. Hoods can be useful in blocking wind and rain, but they can also restrict movement and visibility. Visors can help improve visibility in bright sunlight.

Underwear

Most of us wear it, but is it necessary in running? Some runners prefer not to use underwear in order to reduce bulk and the possibility of chafing or wayward elastic bands. For this reason, many types of shorts and leggings are equipped with ventilated crotch and support panels. The rule of thumb is the same here as it is with all running apparel: fast-drying, wicking fabrics are essential. Avoid cotton wherever possible. Bras are available in most sizes and all levels of support. Firm support is best in high-impact sports such as running.

Reflective Gear

Your training schedule may cause you to run outdoors at night or at dusk or dawn. Be sure to choose clothing and shoes that are equipped with reflective material. You can also buy reflective armbands, strips, vests, and lights to wear with any gear. Staying visible is the best way to stay safe in low-light conditions.

Hair Accessories

For those with long hair, it's best to pull it back and keep it off your neck while running. Long hair acts as insulation and will hold in body heat and moisture, both of which are enemies of long-distance runners. It can also fly into your eyes and compromise your visual field. Soft elastic bands and scrunchies are the most comfortable alternatives. Short hair can be restrained with headbands, visors, or light barrettes.

Weather-Specific Gear

As intrepid runners, weather doesn't deter us, right? Many endurance runners will tell you that some of their best running experiences took place during dramatic weather events. There is something about challenging yourself on several levels at once that adds to the exhilaration and sense of accomplishment. And, to help keep you intrepid there are plenty of choices in weather-specific gear and apparel. From hot and dry to wet and icy, long-distance runners successfully inhabit every climate … with a little help.

No matter what kind of weather you're running in, your body temperature will rise after you warm up. Therefore, dressing in layers is a good idea in cool and cold weather. Light jackets and long-sleeve overshirts can be removed and tied around the waist if necessary.

YELLOW LIGHT

Not even the best gear can protect you from the most intense weather events. Use common sense and avoid dangerous or unpredictable situations such as flooded areas, icy conditions, lightning, and the hottest part of the day in summer.

Sunglasses and Sunscreen

Sunglasses may be an obvious choice on a bright day, but they are also useful in protecting your eyes from the drying effects of wind. Sun and wind can make your eyes feel tired, which can affect your focus and energy. Bright winter sun can be as fatiguing as summer sun. Choose a light, close-fitting style that won't bounce or fog up. You can find elastic bands that gently secure the glasses to your face, if needed.

The use of sunscreen is also a good idea due to the amount of time you will be spending outdoors. Of course, exposed skin is most at risk, but keep in mind that most clothing provides less than 30 *SPF*, so even unexposed skin can burn. Therefore, protecting your skin against sunburn requires additional precautions. Choose a light, nonoily sunscreen formula that will allow your skin to breathe, and apply it to both exposed and unexposed areas. Look for brands that block both UVA and UVB, the two types of ultraviolet sunlight that cause sunburn and skin damage. A water-resistant formulation is best if you expect to sweat, but in any case you should reapply it every two hours for maximum protection. Choose your SPF based on skin type and expected length of exposure. Generally, the minimum recommended rating is 15 to 30 SPF. You can also use sunblock on your nose, lips, or other exposed areas, but because it is a thick, opaque cream containing zinc oxide, it may stain clothing or come off easily when rubbed.

DEFINITION

SPF stands for Sun Protection Factor, a measure of the strength of sunscreen expressed in terms of time. An SPF of 10 will allow you to stay in the sun 10 times longer than it would take you to burn. If the sun is strong enough to burn you within 15 minutes, a lotion with a 10 SPF rating would only give you 150 minutes, or two and a half hours before you burn.

Water Resistant vs. Waterproof

When it comes to protective clothing, outerwear such as jackets or windbreakers can be waterproof or water resistant but they should also be well-ventilated. While you need to stay dry and shielded from rain and snow, you must still allow sweat to evaporate from your skin. Hence, shoes and clothing can't be truly waterproof or they would seal in your perspiration while sealing out the elements. Fortunately, many fabrics are available today with tiny holes that allow water vapor to escape but aren't big enough to allow water droplets to enter.

Outerwear and Gloves

Whether you're running in a temperate climate or an extreme environment, there is a jacket to meet your needs. Popular fabrics are lightweight and combine breathability with warmth. Ergonomic design is also important to ensure ease of movement. For example, longer jackets should feature a double zipper so that you can unzip the hem to allow your legs their full range of motion. Because your body temperature will change based on your level of exertion, you will need to experiment with different fabric weights to find your comfort zone.

Many runners find that their hands get cold while running, even though they are working up a sweat. This is due to the centrifugal force generated by swinging their arms for long periods of time. Blood can pool in the hands, slowing down circulation and causing some swelling. Gloves are available in several types of breathable fabrics to help insulate your hands and maintain adequate ventilation. A glove that is too tight can limit circulation of blood and actually cause your fingers to get cold, so be sure whatever gloves you choose fit comfortably. Some styles incorporate small pockets for keys, or have reflective strips for safety at night.

Orthotics and Braces

For some runners, even professionally fit running shoes don't alleviate foot and ankle pain. Moderate to severe overpronation and underpronation can cause a host of problems in the legs, hips, and back that must be addressed with medically prescribed orthotics. Allow some time to adjust to orthotics, as you must "break them in" just like new shoes and allow your feet to become accustomed to them.

COACH SAYS …

Orthotics that are prescribed specifically for running are generally more durable and resilient than those that are used only for walking. A podiatrist who specializes in sports medicine can give you the best advice.

The use of knee braces is very common in long-distance running. Several styles are available to provide stability to the knee joint while allowing adequate freedom of movement. Quite often, simply stabilizing the kneecap can relieve chronic pain. An elastic sleeve with an opening for the kneecap is best. You don't want to lock down the kneecap, only stabilize it. Ankle braces are also available to help treat and prevent foot, tendon, and ankle pain. Again, an orthopedist or sports medicine doctor can direct you to the proper brace for your particular situation.

Nutrition and Hydration

Even more important than what you wear on the outside of your body is what you put into it. Long-distance running demands strategic nutrition and hydration, and modern technology has stepped up to meet the challenge. In the early days of running, the science of sports nutrition didn't even exist. Long-distance runners had to invent novel ways to meet their unique energy demands, such as carrying easily digestible baby food in plastic bags on their belts, believe it or not. Thankfully, nowadays there is a multi-billion dollar industry just waiting to serve your every nutrition and hydration need. See Chapter 6 for more detailed information on nutrition and hydration.

Sports and Energy Drinks

Lest ye dare to think that plain water is enough to quench your exercise-induced thirst, take a walk into any convenience store in America today. There you will find a veritable rainbow of sports drinks containing an array of vitamins, *electrolytes*, flavorings, and even herbal additives. Of course, water itself is the most critical component of adequate hydration. But for endurance athletics, it's also important to replenish electrolytes. Quality sports drinks can accomplish both quite efficiently. Some runners experience nausea when drinking sports drinks straight, so you might want to experiment by diluting them with a little water.

DEFINITION

Electrolytes are minerals such as sodium and potassium that allow electrical impulses to flow inside the body. They are essential for the proper functioning of the cardiac and nervous systems, and they also play a critical role in regulating fluids throughout the body.

Don't confuse energy drinks with sports drinks. Most energy drinks contain high concentrations of caffeine. Although many athletes use caffeine in moderate amounts to help boost energy, it does have the side effect of increasing your heart rate, and in large amounts it's is believed to have a diuretic effect, which means it can pull water from your tissues. This isn't ideal for endurance athletes, as maintaining adequate hydration is often a challenge in itself. Therefore, caffeine can be useful for an occasional energy boost, but the higher doses in energy drinks could affect your fluid balance. Not everyone is affected in the same way, though, so you should experiment a bit. See Chapter 13 for more details on caffeine.

Carbohydrate Gels, Blocks, and Beans

A good way to keep your energy up in long-distance running is to eat while you run. Luckily you have a plethora of choices when it comes to convenient and energy-packed snacks. While some people prefer natural foods like granola or fruits to keep them going, you can also find good sources of energy in the latest carbohydrate gels, blocks, and jelly beans. These foods are manufactured to be easily digestible. They give up their energy rather quickly and are also packaged so that they are easy to carry. An effective strategy is to alternate these fast-digesting gels with foods that take longer to break down, such as pretzels, bagels, or more traditional energy bars. This ensures a more even delivery of energy. Quite a few of these carbohydrate gels also provide small quantities of electrolytes to help keep your fluids in balance.

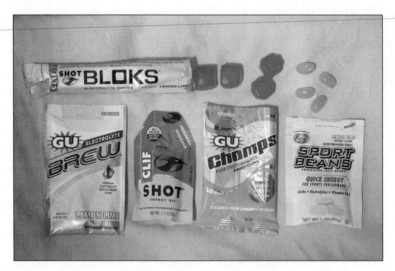

You have a wide variety of choices when it comes to energy bars, blocks, gels, and beans, some of which also offer electrolyte replacement.

Another helpful item is sour gum to keep your mouth from drying out. While it's advertised as a thirst quencher, it only helps to keep your mouth moist by stimulating your salivary glands. It doesn't actually aid in your hydration in any way. Use chewing gum with caution, however. Keeping anything in your mouth during a run, when you are breathing hard, is not advisable because you can choke on it when inhaling.

Many natural foods offer carbohydrates in a variety of flavors and textures.

Water Bottles and Hydration Systems

Plastic is still the most common type of bottle in long-distance running. Although metal is quickly growing in popularity, plastic is lighter and safer to use while running. Most runners learn to eat and drink while running, so a metal bottle could cause some damage if you inadvertently hit yourself in the teeth with it or fall on it. Belts are available to hold all sizes of bottles, and some are made to carry several small bottles instead of one big one. This helps to spread the weight around your waist and reduce bouncing. It also gives you the option of filling some of the bottles with sports drinks if you prefer. For your longest runs, backpacks are available that can hold up to 100 ounces of water, and they are equipped with a small hose and mouthpiece.

Belts are available to carry bottles of up to 1 quart.

Fanny Packs and Totes

"Keep it light" is a mantra of long-distance runners. For those few items that you just can't part with, you'll find an infinite variety of fanny packs and totes. Some fanny packs are simple and consist of a single zippered pocket. But there are also totes that are designed for practically every use. You can tie one kind of tote to your shoelaces and carry just one key in it. You can clip another kind to your belt to carry your carbohydrate gel pack. You can wear one around your wrist for small items such as keys and folded bills. In short, if you need it, someone has already designed it and put it on the market for you. Most fanny packs and totes are constructed from rugged water-resistant fabric, and they come in a wide choice of colors.

Secret Weapons

Either through trial and error, or through the benevolent advice of seasoned runners, most athletes develop their own arsenals of secret weapons. Endurance running requires diligent preparation and sometimes ingenious solutions. We're not talking lucky charms here, though of course they have their place in running, too. We're talking about effective ways of managing chronic problems and preventing disaster. After all, did you ever really think you would have to protect your nipples in a marathon? Aren't you glad that someone thought of it for you?

Blister Prevention

Blisters can incapacitate even the strongest runners. As we've already discussed, socks play a very big role in preventing blisters. Close-fitting, noncotton, double-layer socks work best for many athletes. Some runners wrap their feet with athletic tape to prevent blisters. It's also very important that your running shoes fit properly and that you break them in before using them on long runs. Keeping your feet dry with a light dusting of talcum powder can also help. Wet skin is soft skin, which is far more susceptible to chafing and blisters. Beyond these precautions, many runners use lubricants such as petroleum jelly to reduce friction. There are also several specialized preparations on the market that accomplish the same thing. They can be used as a preventive measure on almost any part of the body that is prone to irritation from friction.

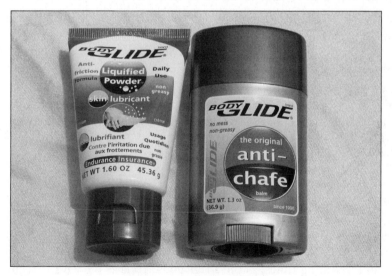

Options for reducing friction.

Nipple Guards

While we're on the subject of friction, we must include nipples in the discussion. This is quite often a bigger problem for men than for women, as most women wear sports bras that protect their nipples. Hours of running can cause chafing in many body parts, and the nipples are at particular risk because they are elevated above the surface of the skin. Body lubricants can help reduce friction, but nipple guards provide more enduring protection. Nipple guards are small bandages that adhere to the skin surrounding the nipple and protect them from rubbing on your clothing. Regular small bandages placed over the nipples could also work, if needed.

Athletic Tape and Wraps

Athletic tape or wrap can be used in injury prevention and as a way to aid healing. The tape itself is available with or without elastic and in a variety of weights. Ankles and knees can be wrapped to help provide stability. A new form of adhesive tape has become popular that is designed to support specific muscles or muscle groups without limiting their movements. It's best to consult with a sports medicine professional before using tapes or wraps to ensure you use them correctly.

Music Devices

Music may soothe the savage beast, but it also can help inspire your running. A good music mix can make the difference between a long, difficult run and a fun and challenging run. You can create your own soundtrack of running-compatible tunes to help carry you through even the longest workouts. The best music players are small and light with no moving parts. They are generally available with clips or armbands to help keep your hands free.

YELLOW LIGHT

Use caution whenever you use earphones, as you need to stay alert to your surroundings while running. Keep the volume down to a level at which you can still hear what's going on around you.

Technology and Tools

We live in interesting times, as the adage goes. Today's pioneering technology is used in many ways to assist endurance athletes. The very nature of long-distance running will push you beyond your self-imposed limitations, both internally and externally. You will push your body's performance into new territory, and you will literally cover new ground in your long training runs. Lucky for you, there are monitors to help you track your progress in both realms. For runners/walkers, some monitors and sports wristwatches have programmable alarms that can mark the start of each run and walk period.

Heart Rate Monitors

Keeping track of your heart rate is important in marathon training, as it's an indicator of low and high levels of exertion. You will train at both levels for specific benefits that are explained in Chapter 5. Heart rate monitors work by picking up your heart's electrical signals and transmitting them to a wristwatch-type of receiver that calculates your heart rate, or beats per minute. Generally, you wear the transmitter around your torso, under your clothes like a belt. More advanced receivers can keep track of your maximum heart rate, calories burned, and length of workout. Keeping track of your heart rate is also helpful in learning how you feel at different levels of exertion so that you can manage your energy output and not run out of steam.

GPS

As your training progresses, you will take on longer and longer runs as well as hill work. A *GPS* monitor can be very useful in keeping you from getting lost during these challenging runs. Not only do GPS monitors give you a live map of your location and altitude, they can track your average pace. Countless models are available and can be worn on the wrist or on a keychain. They aren't fail-safe, however. If you are running between tall buildings, mountains, or trees, they may not be able to find open sky to communicate with their satellites. Another type of GPS monitor is designed as a wristwatch specifically for runners. Among other features, it's also sensitive enough to track not only the distance you have run, but your pace as well.

DEFINITION

GPS stands for Global Positioning System, which tracks your location based on satellite information. These monitors can generally pinpoint your location and altitude to within a few feet. They are also sensitive enough to calculate your pace, or distance in terms of time.

This GPS wristwatch model shows time, pace, and distance at a glance.

The Least You Need to Know

- Moisture-wicking, breathable clothing and footwear are important in maintaining proper body temperature.
- Running shoes and orthotics should be professionally fit.
- Carbohydrates are the best source of quick energy.
- There is a wide variety of products available for staying hydrated and energized while running.
- Try to carry as little as possible while running, but never skimp on carrying food or water.
- GPS monitors are useful to track location as well as altitude and pace.

Training Regimen

In Part 2 we show you how to wrap your body around the idea of running a marathon. We explain how your body runs on the inside, so you can manipulate its strengths in your training.

Then we describe how cross-training, stretching, diet, and rest can support your running. Strength training is recommended to help improve balance and coordination, and to help power you over hill and dale.

Finally, we help you start slowly and show you how to improve your speed. You learn about various training tools, and how they can make you a better runner. We discuss the pros and cons of different types of training programs. You'll also see how tapering during your training will actually make you faster and stronger. Then we'll show you how to stay motivated and avoid injury. If you do get injured, we describe how and when you can start running again.

How Your Body Runs

In This Chapter

- How your muscles work
- The roles of dietary fat and carbohydrates in exercise
- The benefits of variable-intensity training
- How training affects your hormones
- The role of lactic acid and hydrogen
- Fine-tune your training plan with fitness tests

Running a marathon carries a certain mystique, much of which is based on misunderstandings that revolve around the science behind endurance training. For example, many marathon runners train at one speed of running, figuring that their marathon race will be run at one speed as well.

In this chapter, we show you the simple science behind why this isn't an efficient method of training, and why the best methods work so well. Training takes place at specific levels of intensity that are powered by two main sources of energy (fuel). These various intensities of training will turn your body into an efficient, energy producing engine that will propel you through your first, or best, 26.2-mile run.

How Muscles Work

Muscles are like rubber bands. To generate force, they contract. A rubber band can never expand with force; its strength is exhibited only when it contracts. Take for instance the muscles in the front of your thigh, which are called quadriceps. When they contract, your lower leg straightens out. Then, when the hamstring muscles in the back of your thigh contract, the knee bends. These two sets of muscles are a prime example of muscles that work in opposition to each other. One muscular contraction causes the opposing muscle to relax. That relaxed muscle is now ready to contract again, and on it goes. Your lower leg goes up, down, up, down, etc. Now combine this action with the efforts of scores of other muscles, and you can actually take one step.

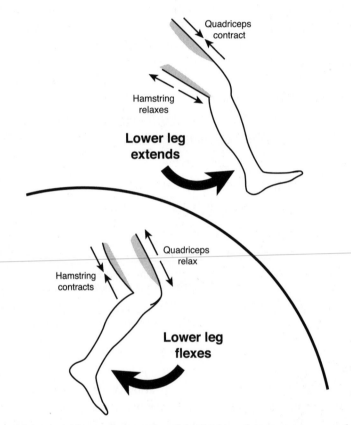

The quadriceps and hamstring muscles of the thigh work in opposition to each other.

Of course that step, or any muscular contraction, requires fuel. It's the same principle behind a car's piston. To move the piston, the engine's combustion chamber requires gas. Just as that force generates movement with your car, muscular contractions generate movement with your body. Similarly, your muscles require fuel in order to do any work. You will be using the largest muscles in your body to propel yourself down the road for several hours straight. That demands a lot of fuel. It's crucial to understand how to make your muscles efficient, avoid fatigue, and not run out of fuel.

Muscles Run on ATP

So where do your muscles get this fuel? Despite what you may like to think, your cells can't actually burn a cheeseburger and beer for energy. The foods you eat are first broken down into their most basic molecular components, and then reassembled into compounds that your cells can use.

The final fuel used to fire, or contract, your muscles is generated in every one of your cells by tiny factories called mitochondria. These specialized, microscopic structures reside in each cell of your body and provide the energy needed to power all of the biological processes that keep you alive. They take simple fuels (by-products of digestion), and reassemble them into ATP (adenosine triphosphate), which your muscles then use as their primary energy source. ATP is a molecule that stores energy and is continually being produced and broken down by your body. The more mitochondria you have, the more ATP you have, and the more quickly it's generated. Without ATP, your muscles would stop working, making any movement—and life itself—impossible.

Your body uses different fuels or resources to generate ATP. Here is the key for long-distance running: your body naturally switches between two primary fuels to meet the demands of low- and high-*intensity* exercise. At a low heart rate (low intensity), you use more fat to generate ATP. During higher heart rates (high intensity), a molecule called glycogen plays a bigger role as a fuel. Glycogen is produced primarily from carbohydrates in your diet, such as grains, bread, pasta, and sugars. It's an altered form of glucose, a sugar, that is stored in your liver and muscles. Fat is an essential, energy-storing nutrient that is available in many foods we eat, including nuts, animal products, and oils. It's also produced by the body when excess calories are consumed.

DEFINITION

In terms of exercise, **intensity** means the level of energy output or heart rate. Terms such as "fast" or "slow" running aren't relevant. You may run slowly up a hill, but at a high intensity. Likewise, you may run down a hill at a fast pace but at a low intensity.

Glycogen can be broken down more quickly than fat, and is readily available right in the muscles, as opposed to fat, which is predominantly stored outside of muscle cells. In other words, glycogen is already inside the engine, ready to be used, while fat must be broken down and burned more slowly. Unlike fat, however, your body only stores a small supply of glycogen. It can be depleted in a rather short period of time, or extended by lowering your level of exercise intensity. You are always using both fat and glycogen to generate ATP. But as your heart rate goes up, your body transitions from using more fat to using more glycogen in order to fuel its increasing demand for ATP.

A third major fuel used by the body for explosive energy, CP (creatine phosphate), can only last about 10 seconds at a time (2 seconds of ATP and 5 seconds of CP). Think of a sprinter when the gun goes off, or football players at the "hike." Studies indicate that orally consumed creatine may benefit body builders and short-distance sprinters. It's not useful to marathon runners. This highest level of intensity is considered level five, or 90 to 100 percent of your maximum. See "Training at Different Intensities" later in this chapter.

Low-Intensity Fuel: Fat

Our bodies carry an abundance of fat. For our purposes, fat can be defined as a stored source of energy or fuel. It's created by eating more calories than you use. The average person, it's believed, carries about a month's supply of fat-based fuel in his or her body. Fat is primarily used at lower-intensity levels of exercise, and can be used for longer periods of exertion, such as in marathons. Therefore, we aim to use more fat in our early marathon training, which will begin at a low intensity. By training consistently at this lower level of intensity, your body will become more efficient at metabolizing fat. You will become a "better butter burner," as one authority calls it.

 MILE MARKER

There are 3,500 calories in 1 pound of fat. Running a marathon, however, uses on average, 2,600 calories (approximately 100 calories/mile). Therefore, you will usually burn off less than a pound of fat during the marathon.

For example, if you were to walk or jog a marathon at a low heart rate, you would have more than enough fat to get you to the finish line. Ultra-marathon runners (any distance longer than a marathon) race at a lower level of intensity (generally slower) than marathoners, and therefore use a preponderance of fat to get them through. As you can see, a lower heart rate and the use of fat as fuel are critical for those running a marathon or beyond.

High-Intensity Fuel: Glycogen

A reserve of glucose is generally always available in the blood as blood sugar. After this limited reserve of readily available energy is depleted, the body must turn to glycogen, the stored form of glucose, to continue its activity. Your body does use some glycogen and fat at all times. But as you approach higher levels of exercise intensity, you will tip the balance toward more glycogen use and less fat.

After your early training at the lower-level, fat-burning intensity we mentioned, you will push yourself into medium and high levels of intensity later in the season. Your body's reservoir of glycogen can last you a day at low levels of activity, but you begin using it in greater amounts as you approach medium and high levels of intensity. In this case, your glycogen reserve can last about 80 to 90 minutes. Any longer, and you will need to consume carbohydrates to replace the lost glycogen. If you pace yourself at a lower level of intensity, your reserve of glycogen will last longer.

For example, because 5K and 10K competitors (approximately 3 and 6 miles, respectively) run at a higher average intensity than marathoners, and for a shorter time, they use greater amounts of glycogen for the entire race than they would in a marathon. In contrast, marathoners who start out slower, at a lower intensity, initially use more fat as fuel. They tap into glycogen more as the race progresses and their heart rates go up. Ideally, this should occur mostly toward the end of the race, as dehydration and fatigue set in, because these conditions put stress on your body and cause your heart rate to increase.

 MILE MARKER

Studies show that about 10 grams of glycogen are used per hour at rest. Thirty to 60 grams of carbohydrates per hour are used during enhanced running performance. This higher consumption rate can deplete blood glucose concentrations (hypoglycemia), leading to limited performance, or "hitting the wall."

When all sources of glycogen are used up, the athlete "hits the wall," or "bonks." Those are the most popular euphemisms to describe the awful feeling of running out of energy. The athlete's muscles are simply out of fuel, and she can't go on. In the middle of a marathon, she will find herself walking slowly if at all, which isn't a fun way to complete any race. It can take time to recover from bonking, so you will need to plan carefully to prevent it. However, with good hydration, strategic consumption of carbohydrates, and a disciplined control of your energy output or intensity, bonking can be completely avoided.

Aerobic and Anaerobic Training

Your marathon training will be split generally into three types: low intensity or aerobic, high intensity or anaerobic, and somewhere in between at marathon race pace, which is the intensity at which you will run the marathon. *Aerobic* means "with oxygen," and *anaerobic* means "without oxygen." At low or aerobic levels of exercise intensity, your body burns fat, which requires oxygen. At higher levels of intensity, the body begins to burn glycogen for energy, which does not require oxygen. This variable-intensity training will teach your body to become more efficient in running long distances and will also make you stronger and faster.

Aerobic Training Benefits

Oxygen is necessary to turn fat into ATP, so in general, low-intensity exercise is predominantly an aerobic process. When you push your body into long periods of low-intensity exercise, your cells' extra demand for oxygen causes your body to generate more capillary veins and arteries. These tiny blood vessels bring additional oxygenated blood and nutrients to your hardworking cells and also help to remove waste products more quickly. This is similar to having more hoses to drain a body of water. Imagine the efficiency of one hose draining or filling a swimming pool. Then imagine two hoses for the same job. Water is now flowing twice as fast. Add a few more hoses and your efficiency level jumps dramatically. More capillaries work the same way. This is the way in which your body becomes more efficient at supplying additional oxygen and other resources to its cells and removing waste products that can cause discomfort and fatigue.

YELLOW LIGHT

You may have noticed a small chart on or near your treadmill at the gym. These charts give you rough estimates of how heart rate relates to levels of intensity (high, medium, low), or calories burned. Note: these charts are designed for the average person, and aren't accurate for everyone.

This long-term, increased demand for energy also causes your body to expand the size and number of mitochondria to meet that demand. Indeed, throughout your body, there are more mitochondria in very active cells than there are in less active cells. These new capillaries and expanded mitochondria are generated by periods of aerobic exercise only, but develop during periods of rest. Therefore aerobic work and rest are both critical parts of this process.

Aerobic Training: Basework and More

In short, prolonged aerobic activity increases your efficiency, and prepares you to sustain a low level of exercise intensity for a longer duration. It will also train you to do more for longer periods of time before switching over to glycogen as your main fuel. This is called developing a "base." Your base describes the range of activity intensity over which your body transitions from primarily fat to primarily glycogen use. Most beginners have no base, and high glycogen consumption begins almost immediately, as does high waste production. As proof, when a beginner starts a run, breathing increases almost immediately. This is evidence that their glycogen consumption has jumped quickly and therefore they aren't using much fat as fuel. In contrast, when a runner with a good aerobic base starts running, a very different set of events takes place. The experienced runner has a longer aerobic base, during which the use of glycogen won't jump, but will increase more slowly. His breathing will increase less dramatically. His more efficient body will keep him comfortable at a higher level of intensity for a longer time. These are the key reasons for low heart rate work early in the season. It's critical. As the famous New Zealand coach Arthur Lydiard used to say, "It's more money in the bank."

There are several concepts that are counter-intuitive to what makes sense regarding endurance athletics. The heavy breathing as one goes anaerobic is one of those things. Your body switches to heavy breathing because your cells have depleted their oxygen reserves and are switching to anaerobic processes to continue to create energy. You breathe harder to exhale waste product gasses, even though you are using less oxygen in the muscles you use to run with (mostly arms and legs). Keep in mind, some oxygen is always used in the body, as in the brain, for example.

MILE MARKER

Runners can benefit from living at high altitudes, as the lower concentration of oxygen causes the body to make more oxygen available in the blood.

Anaerobic Training

As your heart rate goes up, you eventually reach your anaerobic threshold (AT). At this point you no longer use fat or oxygen in the muscles that you use for running. Your body transitions to glycogen as its main fuel, which as we mentioned is much more limited in supply than fat. Therefore, delaying this transition point is a major goal in your training.

Aerobic training won't raise your AT, but it will increase your aerobic range. Only training above your AT (high heart rate) will push your body to raise your anaerobic threshold. In other words, your body will learn to use more fat as fuel at a higher level of intensity. This will enable you to run at a higher intensity for a longer period of time. That generally means faster. Before you become faster, however, it's critical that you develop a strong base of aerobic efficiency first. This is accomplished by weeks of low heart rate activity such as easy-intensity running or walking.

Training at Different Intensities

During your early aerobic training, you will take your running intensity down a notch or two for several months and will find yourself running more slowly than you might think is necessary. By keeping intensity low, your body can more easily grow accustomed to longer distances. You will also give your body the chance to evolve and improve its efficiency, as we described earlier (more capillaries and mitochondria). Then, as you become more efficient, you will switch to a higher level of training. This higher-intensity training period will add some shorter anaerobic training runs to your repertoire. For the most part, this portion of your training regimen will take place at a level below anaerobic, similar to your "race pace," or the intensity at which you will run the actual marathon. Your race pace would generally be run at lactate threshold, an intensity level that is below anaerobic, allowing you to use both fat and glycogen. This keeps your intensity high while still permitting you to use fat as a fuel. By incorporating both low and high heart rate training at proper times, you will better prepare your body for all of the rigors of endurance running.

There are five levels of training intensity, although your marathon training will only encompass the first four. During the marathon itself, you should only use the first three. The five levels are:

- **Level one: at rest.** The body has been resting for over an hour, using mostly fat, at a low consumption rate to create ATP.

- **Level two: aerobic threshold, 60 to 70 percent.** This stage includes walking or jogging, using more fat than glycogen to create ATP. You are generating more capillary blood vessels and mitochondria at this level than any other. High amounts of oxygen are utilized.

- **Level three: lactate threshold, 70 to 80 percent.** This is roughly marathon race pace, between a jog, where talking is easy, and faster running (about 20 percent slower than a 5K race), where your heart rate is high and you can't talk easily. You are utilizing both fat and glycogen, with less oxygen.

- **Level four: anaerobic threshold, 80 to 90 percent.** This is at 5K or 10K pace, possibly sprinting. You are at a high heart rate and breathing hard, using mostly glycogen and no fat or oxygen. This is a higher level of intensity than is used in marathons, as it cannot be maintained for long enough periods of time.

- **Level five: explosive level, 90 to 100 percent.** You are just below your maximum heart rate (HR Max) at your peak level of energy output, usually sprinting. Creatine phosphate is used for seven seconds at this level. Marathoners would have no reason to run at level five, as sprinting plays no part in running marathons. Slower, lower-intensity running is the key to success in any marathon.

Start Easy—Talk Comfortably

How do you know you are at a low enough heart rate (or aerobic intensity level) to use more fat than glycogen? Remember that your body utilizes some fat and glycogen at the same time. To utilize more fat, exercise at a level where you can talk fluidly and breathing isn't as labored (level two: aerobic threshold). In contrast, at high levels of intensity, such as at the end of a 5K where you are really pushing it and can barely talk, you aren't using any fat.

 COACH SAYS ...

After completing a period of aerobic training (possibly 12 weeks) with all low heart rate runs, you will notice a difference in your running. You will feel you can access more energy more easily, almost as if you're idling at a higher level. Your training will become easier and you will feel less drained afterward. This is evidence that you have made the necessary preparations for the next, higher-intensity level of marathon training.

Later, Train at Marathon Pace

While in aerobic training you dialed your pace down; now you will train at the higher lactate threshold level we described, which is also considered marathon race pace. (Such higher-intensity exercise also raises your anaerobic threshold.) At this level, you are also training your body to dispose of its waste products more efficiently. Running your marathon at this level gives you the greatest chance at a comfortable, faster, and efficient race. Another benefit of training at marathon pace is that you will become accustomed to the feeling of maintaining that level of intensity. As you approach race day, testing out your new marathon race pace on longer distances is an integral part of your training.

Runners who only train at race pace—that is, they never develop the aerobic base we have just described—usually can't increase their running pace significantly as they advance through their training. Without a strong aerobic base, even high heart rate work becomes less efficient in speeding them up. They must rely on a cooler day or a more downhill course to finish the marathon with a faster time. In other words, they will improve their personal best time only if they are lucky. Essentially, they rushed their training and have a false base, or an insufficient level of efficiency. They will never reach their maximal levels of ability due to this improper training. Now that you understand the "why" of aerobic and anaerobic threshold training, you will never make that mistake.

Tapering

Including tapering in your training program is absolutely critical. It may sound counter-intuitive to factor in periods of lower activity when you are working hard to build endurance, but incorporating tapered weeks will actually push your training ahead even further. Exercise more and you become tired. That is true for one work-out, but it's also true for a period of workouts that extend over a week or a month or longer. It's during periods of recovery that you have the most growth in endurance abilities. It's also essential for you to regain your energy following a period of hard work.

In addition, your body will use this opportunity to adapt to the increasing levels of stress you are placing on it by strengthening muscle tissue. Another important reason to taper is to allow time to replenish depleted hormones due to hard exercise. An increase in the production of red blood cells, which carry oxygen, is also found during periods of taper. (See Chapter 10 for more on tapering.)

Hormones Affected by Training

Hormones are natural substances produced by your body that regulate many bodily processes and can contribute to drive and energy levels—hence, they are vitally important in endurance training. The more work or exercise you do, the less energy and hormonal output you will have. You exercise, you get tired. Likewise, you exercise, and certain hormones are depleted. It's an inverse relationship: more exercise means less hormonal output. Hormones that can be depleted by long-distance running include testosterone for men, estrogen for women, and human growth hormone (HGH). HGH is critical in the process of repairing and reproducing muscle tissue. So without appropriate hormone levels, your body has a harder time building and healing your muscles, and an increased risk of injury can develop.

In this state, you can also experience a lack of drive and a waning interest in training. Some get to a point, usually late in training, when they have no motivation to run anymore. This is generally due to overtraining and not enough interval week-long tapers, and therefore a lack of testosterone. In Chapter 10, we show you how regular intervals of tapered training will counteract these cumulative effects and will help keep your hormones at optimal levels.

Waste Products from Muscular Activity

Lactic acid is a by-product, or waste product created by your muscles at higher levels of exercise intensity, when you are burning mostly glycogen. It's not a by-product of lower-intensity or fat-burning, aerobic activity. Since your body is always using some glycogen, even when utilizing fat, lactic acid is likewise always being produced. This is true even at a low, aerobic heart rate. However, as your heart rate increases, less oxygen is used, and at a certain point the creation of lactic acid skyrockets. At this point a build-up of lactic acid and other waste products in your blood will begin. At a higher heart rate, after a prolonged period of time, you may experience some discomfort in your muscles. This point is often referred to as "lactate threshold." Most of your marathon will be run at this threshold to take advantage of your high energy output without the downside of lactic acid build-up.

Most lactic acid is broken down by your body into lactate. About a quarter of this lactate will be sent to your liver for recycling. There it will be processed into glycogen again and sent back to your muscles for use as fuel. This is a good thing, as once this fuel is returned to your muscles, you can perform at a higher heart rate for longer periods of time. As you become more efficient, your ability to recycle lactic acid will improve.

Lactic acid is created on a one-to-one ratio with hydrogen. As lactic acid is built up, the same amount of hydrogen builds up as well. It's the additional volume of hydrogen that makes your legs feel swollen and uncomfortable during prolonged or intense periods of exercise. Hydrogen also plays a role in the associated burning sensation you may feel during intense exertion. Hydrogen is an element in all acids and it easily mixes with other compounds in your body to create a true acid in the muscles. Hence, more hydrogen equals more discomfort, unless you have the capillaries to get rid of it.

YELLOW LIGHT

Bodybuilders aim for the "burn" in their muscles caused by lactic acid and hydrogen build-up. In endurance sports, we train to avoid this debilitating state.

For an illustration of lactic acid and hydrogen build-up, try running up a set of stairs. Note the warming sensation in your leg muscles that grows into a burning feeling. With enough exertion, your legs will feel as if they are filling up like balloons, which they are. Many marathoners complain that their legs become heavier and that bending their knees becomes more difficult as the race progresses. This is often due to a build-up of lactic acid and hydrogen. Had these runners trained at an aerobic level (low heart rate), and built up additional capillary veins and arteries, they would have delayed or eliminated this discomfort. Additional capillaries would have transported the lactate to the liver and back into the muscles as glycogen, resulting in more fuel for prolonged intense work.

Fitness Tests

Sport-specific endurance tests help you quantify your improvements and fine-tune your training plan. Some of these tests can be quite expensive, as they provide very detailed information about your body's chemistry and athletic performance. They are certainly not necessary in your training but can be helpful. Some you can do by yourself, with reasonably accurate results.

YELLOW LIGHT

Insurance won't cover any of the lab tests discussed in the following sections, unless there is some illness requiring this type of test. Lung patients, for example, may need a VO_2 Max test.

Aerobic Capacity or VO_2 Max

VO_2 Max is the highest volume of oxygen you are capable of utilizing in your muscles at any given time. It's a good indicator of your aerobic capacity. The higher the aerobic capacity (VO_2 Max), the better the athlete can be expected to perform. VO_2 Max tests are administered by placing a runner, wearing a plastic mouthpiece, on a treadmill. The mouthpiece forms an airtight seal, and is connected to a machine that measures oxygen use. The test administrators will interpret your results. Repeated testing will track your progress over time. Don't forget, all your levels can change, at least slightly, over an eight to nine week period. Pricing for this test varies greatly, based on region and availability of the equipment. It can run between $50 and $200.

VO$_2$ Max is the volume of oxygen an individual is capable of using. The higher the VO$_2$ Max, the more efficient you are. It defines your aerobic and anaerobic levels. Your VO$_2$ Max is the maximum heart rate where you still use oxygen and fat as a source for ATP.

Lactate Testing

Tests to define lactate threshold are usually done in a lab for best results. However, there is portable test equipment now, for use out in the field. Equipment used in the lab or field for this test also show other important results besides lactate threshold, including aerobic and anaerobic thresholds. The price for this test is similar to VO$_2$ Max tests, often a few dollars less.

You can also find your approximate lactate threshold by performing the following test with a heart rate monitor. A good heart rate monitor can cost about $40 to $60, but the more sophisticated models can cost more than $300. Instead of a heart rate monitor, you could simply stop every 5 or 10 minutes and take your pulse. This self-test won't yield as accurate a result as a blood lactate test.

To find your marathon race pace or lactate threshold, follow these steps:

1. Run comfortably for about 10 minutes. At that point, continue running, and start your heart rate monitor.

2. Run for another 20 minutes at a slightly higher intensity. The average heart rate for this 20-minute period will probably fall within the lactate threshold range.

3. Do that a few times, and you will obtain a fairly accurate range. This heart rate range will vary between individuals. And after a period of time and training, it can change.

To take your own pulse, slide two fingers to the side of the tubelike hard area in the center of your throat. Push in gently, until you feel a pulse. Count the beats for 15 seconds and multiply by four. That is your beats per minute.

One question always asked is, what is a good or common lactate threshold? It varies greatly from individual to individual, and one person's results can even vary based on their level of training and efficiency. For this reason, it's best to test yourself frequently, especially before an important race. Then, you will know what your target heart rate is in order to avoid crossing your lactate threshold. After eight or nine weeks of training, threshold levels are likely to change. On average, older people often have lower beats-per-minute lactate and anaerobic threshold ranges than younger athletes.

Following are two classic examples of lactic acid test results. Both are from the same person performing two different exercises on two different pieces of equipment. In the first test, the subject is running on a treadmill. This person is an experienced runner. The second is performed while the subject is biking on a stationary trainer. He is a novice cyclist. To find your lactate threshold, look at the graph, and you will notice when the volume of lactate suddenly increases dramatically. Before this point, the line is flatter. Above the point of rapidly increasing lactate is also the heart rate level, where your body begins to use more glycogen, and less fat and oxygen. It's about where you want to remain at race pace.

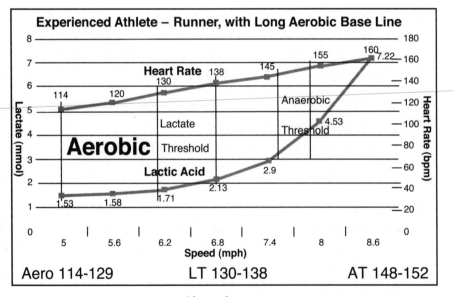

Advanced runner.

(Graph recreated based on work done at Phase IV, in Santa Monica, California.)

Notice that this person has a longer flatter line running on the treadmill, at lower heart rates, while aerobic. This is referred to as the base line. The volume of lactic acid isn't increasing as much as the heart rate is. In fact, lactic acid isn't increasing very much at all. This advanced runner remains at a comfortable state longer, even while the heart rate and/or speed is increasing. And since less lactic acid is produced with lower glycogen consumption, we can also conclude that this person is using a low volume of glycogen. He is aerobic, utilizing fat at a higher level of intensity. The runner can go faster longer, without depleting glycogen levels and hitting the wall.

The second chart shows the same person, a less experienced cyclist. The base line is much shorter. This person is accumulating blood lactate nearly immediately with exercise, while his heart rate is increasing as well. This means that glycogen is consumed at a lower level of intensity, so he isn't going to be able to perform at a high intensity level for very long. More aerobic, low heart rate exercise is required for this person on the bike to become more efficient. The aerobic work will cause that aerobic, nearly flat line to become significantly longer. Once that occurs, this cyclist can do his race pace and faster work with better results on the bike.

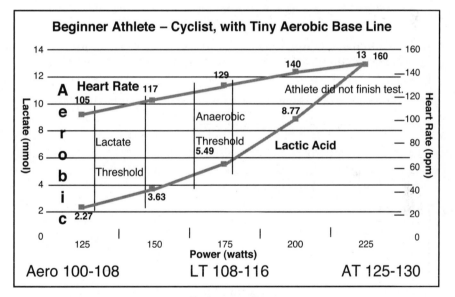

Beginner cyclist.
(Graph recreated based on work done at Phase IV, in Santa Monica, California.)

The tests were performed 24 hours apart, nearly to the minute. The technician and the lab were the same for both tests. The results make a valuable point. It proves that in order to be a good cyclist, you need to cycle. And to be a good runner, you need to run. There are benefits of cross-training (which are discussed in Chapter 7), but the lesson is clear.

st Heart Rate

Fortunately, this test requires no costly lab work, nor any equipment. The results will tell you if you are becoming more efficient or overtraining. For the most accurate and consistent results, perform this test at the same time every morning when you first wake up. When you take this test, your body must have been at rest for at least an hour. Take your pulse as described in the previous "Coach Says" sidebar. This gives you your heart rate in beats per minute. Because you were at rest, you have your at-rest heart rate.

> **MILE MARKER**
>
> The average at-rest heart rate is 65 to 80 beats per minute. It's common for marathoners to average well below this heart rate in training. Lower heart rates mean the heart is more efficient and needs to pump less often to get the job done.

You will need to take the test consistently for at least a week in order to establish your normal pattern. If your at-rest heart rate is lower than normal during training, you are becoming more efficient. This is a good sign that you are adapting to training properly. If, however, your at-rest heart rate is higher than normal, you are overtraining or injured. This may occur the morning after a tough workout. Your heart will work harder to send greater blood flow and more oxygen to injured or recovering muscle tissue. If at any time your at-rest heart rate goes up, your body probably needs more time to recover. Cutting back, more rest, or a taper period may be needed.

Heart Rate Max

Your body has a safeguard to keep your heart from exploding at the highest levels of exercise intensity. Beyond a certain high heart rate, your body will begin to shut down until your heart rate lowers. Light-headedness or dizziness can be associated with reaching your heart rate maximum. Often companies that do VO_2 Max tests or lactic acid tests will also give you your HR Max (Maximum Heart Rate) result. HR Max results from a lactic acid or VO_2 Max test shouldn't cost an additional fee. It's information that is part of the test.

The do-it-yourself method for testing HR Max is running at a high level of intensity for an extended period. Using a good heart rate monitor, download the test results to your computer and you will see your highest heart rate. Stopping to take your pulse with your fingers will also work, but it won't be completely accurate, as stopping will lower your heart rate. Running at high levels of intensity, however, is dangerous. You may not want to perform this test early in the season, especially if you are a beginner. Instead, check your heart rate toward the end of a short race or training run.

Some training programs will recommend levels of intensity for training runs, as a percentage of your HR Max. Knowing your approximate HR Max could be a plus in these instances, but it's a small part of your training plan. As you train, your level of intensity, before you hit HR Max, will go up. This indicates your increased performance efficiency.

Fat-to-Muscle Ratio

Among other methods, modern scales will often include fat, muscle, and even bone density measurements. This is useful in determining how much extra weight you are carrying as fat, which affects your running efficiency as well as your joints. Modern consumer scales can calculate your approximate percentage of fat by running a low-grade electrical signal through your body and calculating its resistance as it passes through fat versus muscle.

The Least You Need to Know

- The muscles you run with use more fat as fuel at a low heart rate, and more glycogen at a high heart rate.
- The final fuel used by muscles is ATP. Fat and/or glycogen are processed into ATP, depending on your level of exercise intensity (heart rate).
- Only aerobic training, using fat and oxygen for fuel, can increase your endurance. Training anaerobically, without oxygen and with glycogen as fuel, will make you faster.
- Hormones can be depleted by long-distance running; these include testosterone for men, estrogen for women, and human growth hormone.
- Until you become more efficient through training, waste products from running can accumulate in your muscles, causing discomfort and slowing you down.
- Fitness tests are available to aid in your training and track your progress.

Nutrition and Diet

In This Chapter

- How to match your diet to your training regimen
- Using carbohydrates, fats, protein, and electrolytes to your best advantage
- Making smart food choices
- When and what to eat and drink on long runs

For long-distance runners, nutrition and diet play a pivotal role in health and performance. Your knowledge of basic nutrition will become one of your most important and versatile tools in your running and in your general health. Not only do you need to know what to eat between training runs, you also have to plan what to eat on longer runs as well as during the marathon itself. Food and drink, when used appropriately, can unlock your potential and keep you healthy and strong throughout your training.

Vary Nutrition with Training

In Chapter 5, we discussed the types of nutritional resources you use when training at aerobic and anaerobic intensities, such as glycogen and fat. In Chapter 10, we discuss the specific benefits of both types of training as you prepare for the marathon. Hence, if your training is designed to change, then your diet must change as well. You will need to alter your nutritional plan to meet the demands you place upon yourself throughout your training. Likewise, during periods of taper, you will need to consume less. If you do it all the right way, you can build muscle, lose fat, and have increased energy on race day, not to mention throughout your entire season. First we discuss the role of different foods and then how to incorporate them into your training plan.

Energy from Carbohydrates

Carbohydrates are the quickest and easiest source of fuel to replace in high volume. They are also a key source of fuel for your entire body. Your brain requires 95 percent carbohydrates to function effectively. Your body, however, will only store approximately 1,600 to 1,800 calories of carbohydrates. Therefore, you need to replenish your store of carbohydrates, which reside in your muscles, liver, and blood, with regular meals. Once carbohydrates leave your small intestines, the nutrients travel through your bloodstream to your liver, where glycogen is produced. This is one of the key factors in ATP fuel production, which powers your muscles. Your body will use mostly fat in a marathon lasting longer than four hours. Running at that pace might be considered 65 percent of your maximum effort, and mostly aerobic. At 75 percent of your maximum effort, carbohydrates become your major source of fuel.

Much debate has gone on about low carbohydrate diets. The key factor in knowing how many carbohydrates to eat is to know how much you use:

- At rest, we utilize approximately 35 percent carbohydrates for energy, with 60 percent of that energy coming from fat and 2 to 5 percent from protein.

- Add a little light exercise, and carbohydrate consumption increases to 40 percent, with 55 percent from fat and 2 to 5 percent from protein.

- With intense high heart rate exercise, your carbohydrate use jumps to about 95 percent, with only 3 percent from fat and 2 percent from protein.

Of course, eating more carbohydrates than you use up or store as glycogen will cause your body to store the excess calories as fat. But it's also important to understand what happens if you utilize more energy than you take in as carbohydrates, or have stored as glycogen. If you fail to replenish carbs during high heart rate exercise, and you run out of glycogen, your body will begin to use fats and proteins to create carbohydrates. This comes about the time when you hit the wall, or bonk. And it's not a good situation at all, as fats take more energy to turn into carbohydrates, and proteins are needed elsewhere. In effect, you would be forcing your body to make fuel in any way it could at a time when it needs energy the most. Raising your activity intensity to an anaerobic level, and using up all your glycogen stores, will force your body to use fat for fuel in an inefficient and detrimental way. In other words, the more complex fuel creation will slow you down.

Carbohydrates are divided up into two basic categories:

- Simple carbohydrates are easily digested sugars such as fruits and honey, and are usually consumed during a race as gels or sports drinks.

- Complex carbohydrates are sugars that include starches and fibers. These carbohydrates go through a more complicated process to digest than simple carbohydrates. They include grains, beans, and vegetables.

Simple carbohydrates are broken down quickly by the body, while complex carbs take extra time to digest. Therefore, a mix of both will give you quick energy as well as a more sustained supply of fuel.

COACH SAYS ...

Generally, during most times of training—especially during high-intensity training and certainly during times of racing—athletes need to consume more carbohydrates than usual. They will need readily available energy to fuel their demanding workouts.

Good and Bad Fats

A diet in which less than 30 percent of calories come from fat is recommended by the American Heart Association. You use more fat while exercising at a low intensity such as in slow running than you do while training at a higher intensity. This means you need to slightly alter your diet to meet the demands of your training. But remember, if you don't use extra fat that you consume, you add it to your body. Too much stored fat will slow you down, and can lead to health issues, including heart disease.

Fat can come in forms which you want to avoid, including cholesterol, trans fats, and saturated fat. Trans fats are never healthy, and can raise bad cholesterol levels. They usually come in a form labeled as "partially hydrogenated oils," so read those labels carefully. Foods heavy in trans fats include certain margarines, fast foods, and fried foods like French fries. Unsaturated fats, on the other hand, are generally healthy, and are polyunsaturated or monounsaturated. Polyunsaturated fats are found in foods such as flaxseeds, safflower oil, walnuts, and fish. Monounsaturated fats are available in foods such as avocados, olive oil, and some nuts.

There are certain fats that your body can't produce and which must be obtained from the diet. These are known as essential fatty acids (EFAs). These EFAs can aid with the regulation of such things as blood pressure, blood clots, immune response, and inflammation. Omega-3 fatty acid, also called alpha-linolenic acid, can have positive effects, such as decreased formation of plaque in the arteries, decreased hypertension, proper brain development, decreased inflammatory disorders, higher healthy cholesterol levels, lowered triglycerides, and protection against stroke and heart attack. Omega-3 fats are found in cold-water fish such as salmon and sardines, as well as in flaxseed oil and walnuts. Health and grocery stores usually carry supplements of omega-3s in pill form. These typically contain fish oil derived from sardines. Make sure that you get a molecularly distilled version, the common form, to ensure that no pollutants are included, such as mercury. Eating fish twice a week is another way of getting your omega-3s. But don't go overboard, as too much omega-3 can be unhealthy.

In the right amount, omega-6 fatty acid (linoleic acid), another EFA, also plays a role in healthy skin and joints, as well as in proper brain function. The American diet generally provides an overload of omega-6 fats in the oils of seeds and nuts, such as soybean and peanut oil, which are used in many fast foods and snacks—and not enough omega-3 fats, which can lead to negative responses such as inflammation and cardiovascular and immunological diseases.

The Role of Protein

After stress has been put upon a muscle from exercise, muscle cell growth and repair, or *hypertrophy*, can occur under the right conditions. Proteins are an important part of this process, so consuming some protein within an hour following exercise is a good thing. Sadly, protein alone without the exercise won't build any muscles. That is, unless you are 18 years of age or younger and still growing. In addition, if you take in too much protein, and you haven't efficiently stressed the muscle, the extra protein won't be used in building muscle. Instead, it will be turned into fat, and stored in the body as such. For this reason, fad diets such as a high protein diet aren't the best choice for an endurance athlete.

DEFINITION

Hypertrophy, or cellular growth within the muscles, is what happens when stress is applied to the muscle, and proper rest and recovery follow.

Protein is made up of amino acids. Besides creating new muscle cells and fat, amino acids can create energy. This will occur when levels of other fuel sources become depleted, such as during a long run. However, protein isn't a good source of fuel for the distance runner, as it doesn't generate much fuel, and costs a lot of energy to create.

You must have essential proteins in your diet, which come only from food sources, as your body can't create them. These proteins are found in animal products, such as meat, dairy products, and fish. It's difficult for a vegetarian to find such essential proteins; however they are in soy products and some grains, such as quinoa. For this reason, some coaches find it a challenging experience to work efficiently with vegetarian or vegan athletes.

Soy is a good source of protein. It has been shown to improve glucose metabolism, lowering the risk of diabetes. It also boasts beneficial anti-inflammatory and *antioxidant* properties. However, soy also contains phytic acid, which can bind certain nutrients, making them more difficult to absorb. It may also affect men negatively, as it contains estrogenlike ingredients, which mimic the hormone more prevalent in women. For that reason, some men who eat soy can become moody, with depleted drive and determination. For these reasons, soy may not be the best choice for everyone.

DEFINITION

An **antioxidant** is a molecule that prevents certain damaging chemical reactions in your body. Antioxidants protect your cells against free radicals, which are rogue atoms and molecules that can cause mutations to your normally healthy cells.

Strategic Diet Choices

As we've discussed, the exercises you do must change according to where you are in your training, in order to fully develop your capacity. The same can be said for diet and nutrition. Early in the season, when you are doing more strength training and less race pace distance, for example, you need more protein. Later in the season, with more intense, higher heart rate running, you will need more carbohydrates. In other words, what you consume nutritionally must coincide with what you are using energy-wise. If your nutrition doesn't match your energy demands, you will store the excess as fat, or if you are using more fuel than you are consuming, you may be burning up important muscle tissue. Consider this: the body can utilize 1 gram of carbohydrate every minute, in moderately intense exercise. After an hour of exercise, that would be the equivalent of one 240-calorie energy bar, or a bit more than two carbohydrate gels.

Fat can inhibit the digestion of carbohydrates. You have a small window of time right after exercise, about 45 minutes, during which your body absorbs carbohydrates at a higher rate. If you miss this small window of opportunity to quickly replace needed carbohydrate levels, it can take up to 24 hours to completely replenish your full store of glycogen. This may impact your next exercise, if the next workout is done before your carbohydrate levels are back to full. Therefore, you may want to avoid eating foods such as pizza, which is high in fat, for two to four hours following exercise, to enable carbohydrate absorption.

Often the best food choices are found simply by imagining what food you crave. If you want salty pretzels, chances are you need salt and carbohydrates. If you crave something sweet, you probably just need carbohydrates. If you crave something unhealthy, simply exchange it for a healthy food, as discussed in "Best and Worst Foods" later in this chapter. For example, you could satisfy a craving for something sweet such as ice cream with a piece of fruit. Take in a variety of healthy foods, and chances are you are in the ball park for optimal energy output on race day.

Sample Meals

The following two tables from New Performance Nutrition list meals for a single day. The first table is designed for a male athlete early in the training season when he needs fewer calories. The second table is for a similar athlete later in the season when he needs more calories, because the volume of exercise he is performing is much higher and so are his caloric intake needs.

Some of the meals are small snacks, but they are important. For example, 0.1 cup of nuts would be the equivalent of just 4 to 6 almonds, and 0.1 cup of raisins would fill the middle of the palm of your hand.

Sample Daily Menu for Male Athlete, Day One (Early Season)

Daily Caloric Intake: 2,217 calories

Meal	Exchange	Amount	Example	Amount
1	Fruit	1	Apple	1 medium
	Fat	1	Peanut butter	1 tablespoon
2	Carb	2	Oatmeal	1 cup
	Meat	2	Whey shake	2 scoops
	Fat	1	Peanut butter	1 tablespoon
	Fruit	1	Strawberries	1½ cups

Meal	Exchange	Amount	Example	Amount
3	Fat	1	Almonds	0.1 cup
	Fruit	1	Banana	1 item
4	Carb	1½	Rice, brown	½ cup
	Meat	6	Chicken, white meat, skinless	6 ounces
	Vegetable	1	Broccoli	1 cup
	Vegetable	1	Green beans	1 cup
5	Fat	1	Peanut butter	1 tablespoon
	Fruit	1	Raisins	0.1 cup
6	Meat	10	White fish	10 ounces
	Vegetable	1	Lettuce, romaine	3 cups
	Vegetable	1	Summer squash	1 cup
	Carb	1½	Yams	½ cup
7	Meat	2	Whey shake	2 scoops
	Fruit	1	Strawberries	1½ cups

Sample Daily Menu for Male Athlete, Day One (Late Season)

Daily Caloric Intake: 2,620 calories

Meal	Exchange	Amount	Example	Amount
1	Carb	2	Oatmeal	1 cup
	Fat	1	Peanut butter	2 tablespoons
	Fruit	1	Banana	1 item
2	Meat	2	Whey shake	2 scoops
	Fruit	1	Strawberries	1½ cups
	Fat	1	Almond butter	1 tablespoon
3	Carb	3	Rice, brown	1 cup
	Meat	4	Turkey, white meat	4 ounces
	Vegetable	1	Asparagus	1 cup
	Vegetable	1	Green beans	1 cup

continues

continued

Meal	Exchange	Amount	Example	Amount
4	Carb	1½	Rice, white	½ cup
	Meat	4	Turkey, white meat	4 ounces
	Vegetable	1	Lettuce, romaine	3 cups
5	Fruit	1	Blueberries	1 cup
	Fat	1	Cashews	0.1 cup
6	Carb	3	Yams	1 cup
	Meat	6	White fish	6 cups
	Vegetable	1	Spinach, raw	2 cups
	Vegetable	1	Summer squash	1 cup
7	Meat	2	Whey shake	1 cup
	Fruit	1	Raspberries	1 cup
	Fat	1	Peanut butter	1 tablespoon

MILE MARKER

New Performance Nutrition (NPN) has provided custom nutrition programs and ultra-pure products to its clients for over 16 years. In 2010, they made NPN products and programs available online and at retail stores. NPN sells ultra-pure energy bars, supplements, vitamins and minerals, and custom nutrition programs. For details, visit their website: www.NewPFC.com.

Best and Worst Foods

Possibly the best diet tip ever has to do with the addiction which many have to cake, cookies, candy, and junk food. The next time you see that mound of chocolate triple layer cake, try this suggestion from sports dietitian Matt Mahowald, from New Performance Nutrition: instead of going for it, eat a piece of fruit and a small amount of nuts. The amount of nuts would only fill the middle of the palm of your hand. A good amount might be four to six almonds. More than that and you are probably going to store fat in your body. In most cases, the addiction to junk food comes from a need for carbohydrates and fats. The junk food may quickly satisfy the craving which you have for fats and carbs. Try the healthy stuff instead, and that craving will pass. With this plan, you will replace unhealthful carbs and fats with the healthful variety. In fact, try eating a piece of fruit and a few nuts every day as a snack. After about three months that craving will diminish greatly. Over time even the worst junk food addict will be able to walk past that table of warm, recently baked cookies, smile with confidence and honestly think, "No thanks."

COACH SAYS ...

Cardiac surgeon Mehmet Oz, M.D., reports eating two squares of 80 percent pure chocolate a day. Dark chocolate can be a good thing in moderation as it provides antioxidants and can lower blood pressure. Milk chocolate, however, can reverse those antioxidant benefits—too much could cause you to gain weight, which in turn can raise blood pressure, so eat it in moderation.

Having a proper diet and including certain foods can keep you healthy and add to your energy output. Likewise, eating processed foods can have negative effects. In general, the more processed a food is, the fewer nutrients it will have. For example, apples are rich in nutrients, but applesauce is processed with added sugar and contains fewer nutrients.

Vitamins

We do recommend vitamins for most people. However, vitamins don't increase energy or performance. Vegetable-based vitamins appear to be easily digestible, compared to the synthesized brands. Ask a clerk at your favorite health food store to help you decipher which is which. Many active people often seem too busy to take in all the vitamins, minerals, and antioxidants they need through diet alone. In addition, life in our modern society, with its stresses, pollution, and harsh rays from the sun, can lead to an increase in free radicals. These free radicals can mutate cells and lead to cancer. Antioxidants found in healthy foods like fruits and vegetables, and in certain vitamins like C and E, can combat free radicals. Hence, for many, there is a need for vitamins, if diet alone is not sufficient. So if you are not eating several helpings of unprocessed fruits and vegetables a day, it is a good idea to add a multivitamin to your diet.

Diabetic Concerns

The hormone insulin is needed to help glucose get into the muscles for energy and into the liver for storage as glycogen. Diabetics don't create enough insulin, or their cells are resistant to the insulin they do have. Exercise can benefit diabetics who have their glucose levels under control. The work load tends to deplete glucose levels in the blood, improve diabetic control, reduce the need for insulin, and reduce long-term health risks overall. Anyone engaging in an athletic endeavor, including those with diabetes, will benefit from a consistent focus on health, and everything that goes into it. However, if you are diabetic, don't exercise too soon after an insulin shot, as it can create *hypoglycemia*. At its most extreme, hypoglycemia can result in coma and even death.

DEFINITION

Hypoglycemia refers to low blood glucose levels. Glucose in the blood is essential for proper brain, kidney, and red blood cell function. Altered brain function can result in unconsciousness or abnormal or dangerous behavior. Diabetics in this condition have even been arrested for appearing drunk.

Although some diabetics can go on to complete extreme endurance events, such as ultra-triathlons and marathons, a few key components are required before a diabetic engages in any exercise. Approval from your doctor is mandatory, and obviously caution and medical support are also necessary. An automated blood glucose analyzer will give you the ability to monitor your levels. Maintain 3.5 mmol/l (millimoles per liter) during exercise. Test your blood every 20 minutes of exercise, as even short durations of exercise can cause hypoglycemia. Exercising the same time every day is important, as your insulin levels will likely be more predictable. When done properly, you should be able to decrease your insulin levels as you exercise more, and increase your carbohydrate intake following exercise. Take in, as needed, a rapidly absorbable carbohydrate, preferably a 20 percent glucose polymer solution.

Eating Before Running

Having a good meal before a run is important, so that you have enough fuel to expend. If you are running in the morning, when you may find your energy level at a peak, then breakfast becomes all the more important. Your body has been starving overnight and needs nutrition. There will be a trial and error process for everyone. What works for one person will not work for another. In general, however, heavy foods such as eggs with cheese, bacon, and sausage won't contain the carbohydrates needed to keep you going. That meal will probably leave you feeling heavy and less than energetic. Oatmeal, whole-grain cereal, and fresh fruit are all great breakfast options.

We estimate about 5 percent of all runners can't eat breakfast; there may be certain foods that cause them stomach distress (pain). This is an easy fix, as they can simply avoid those foods. However, some athletes can't eat anything at all prior to exercise.

They are the "quiet minority" as they rarely talk about it. Obviously, diarrhea and/ or terrible stomach distress is difficult to talk about, and somewhat embarrassing, but there is an answer for those of you who suffer from this. Try a small sampling of any food you are craving before a run. Then, if that goes well, try that food with something else that sounds good, or simply eat more of that same first food. Eventually, almost everyone who suffers from this condition will find something that works. Maybe it's simply finding a gel or something else during the race that can keep you going.

Many find eating a single piece of toast or an orange slice to be the ticket for breakfast, as fruit and natural carbohydrate-based foods tend to work well. The process of finding food(s) that work best for those with sensitive stomachs may be time-consuming, but don't give up—trial and error will eventually show you the answer. It is very much an individual thing. Unfortunately, for those of you who suffer from this dietary condition, there is no universal answer that works for everyone. If you don't suffer from stomach distress or diarrhea from eating before exercise, be thankful, and have a good, healthy breakfast.

COACH SAYS …

If you choose oatmeal, make sure you get the heartier, old-fashioned variety. The "quick cooking" variety has been processed to help it cook faster, which removes a lot of the nutrients. The heartier varieties also take longer to digest, ensuring a more steady supply of energy.

Managing Nutrition While Running

Since the average person uses approximately 100 calories per mile, depending on their height and weight, they are consuming a lot of calories over the 26.2-mile marathon distance. For most runners, that would amount to more than a day's worth of calories consumed. Similarly, for your long-distance training runs, you will also be using a good number of calories. As discussed in Chapter 5, you do store a fair volume of resources ready to use in your body. However, your glycogen store isn't enough to power an entire marathon, so you would benefit from some sort of energy supplementation while running. It can be unwieldy to carry fresh fruit or grains on a run, so the most efficient forms of carbohydrates are gels, bars, jelly beans, and other similar supplements. These modern conveniences contain a high volume of easily digestible carbohydrates for fast assimilation.

Your fat storage, on the other hand, is adequate for a marathon and beyond, if run at a low enough heart rate. Your body is actually designed to go long distances, like 26 miles, at relatively lower heart rates, without modern gels, mineral pills, and sports drinks. Our hunting ancestors could track an animal long distances, until it was exhausted and they could kill it. This ability enabled our species to prevail. So if you are able to run the marathon on a cool day at a really low heart rate (therefore using more fat to fuel your run), you might get by with just water. Of course, not many want to run a marathon at such a consistently low heart rate, so if you are one of the majority, you will need to use some glucose supplementation as well. Elite level athletes often deplete their bodies of nutrients and pile up waste product (hydrogen) until they reach levels of extreme discomfort. Although they can't afford the time and effort it takes to eat while running, even they will occasionally grab a bottle with some carbohydrates, minerals, and their own secret stuff.

Replenishing Minerals

Especially on longer distance workouts or during the marathon itself, you will need to take in minerals, or electrolytes, in addition to carbohydrates. You may recall from Chapter 4 that electrolytes are specific minerals that the body uses to regulate processes in the body and generate responses on the cellular level. Sodium, for instance, is used to generate a signal from the nerve to begin an action in the muscle. That action would ultimately be muscle contraction, which generates motion. Another important function of sodium is to regulate fluid volume, including plasma, which is the liquid component of blood. Low sodium levels can have devastating effects, including seizures, impaired body temperature regulation, and muscle spasms or weakness. In fact, many cases of overheating during a marathon can be traced back to low sodium levels.

YELLOW LIGHT

Hyponatremia is a severe reduction in sodium, in which fluids aren't effectively being absorbed by the body. Water gurgling in the stomach or a sensation of good water tasting terrible may be early warning signs of this condition. Taken to an extreme, hyponatremia can be lethal. Some mineral depletion can come from drinking, but the greater reason for sodium loss is through sweat. So keep drinking or risk dehydration, and add some mineral supplements to your nutrition plan. On a hot day, you will sweat more and will need to replenish even more electrolytes.

Sodium is a mineral found in salt and many other foods. Many people take in too much sodium, which can lead to high blood pressure. Distance athletes can use a lot more sodium than nonathletes and will lose a good bit of it through perspiration. Distance runners will benefit from taking in sodium during training or racing longer distances, especially on a hot day. However, finding a consistent balance is absolutely critical. Potassium, another mineral, aids with proper cellular function. These two minerals are probably the two most important within the electrolyte group. Calcium also has a part to play in the nerve-to-muscle cell impulse, as well as in bone formation. Other electrolytes include phosphorus, magnesium, sulfur, iron, and zinc. As with vitamins, some minerals taken to excess, such as iron and zinc, can become toxic. If you have questions, check with your physician.

Women can more easily become deficient in iron, which can cause anemia as well as destroy their energy output. Monitoring iron levels can be an important task for women and girls. A serum ferritin test, which measures the level of iron in your bone marrow, can be a good indicator of the onset of iron depletion, before it can seriously affect you. Iron in bone marrow can be leached by the body to replenish reduced levels of iron in the blood. Then, if your iron deficiency progresses, you will develop anemia, which is marked by weakness, fatigue, dizziness, and headaches. Federal standards (USDA) are often low for determining what is normal. Any serum ferritin levels below 12 nanograms should be considered as anemic, or depleted in iron. A normal level for women is 30 nanograms, and 40 nanograms is considered normal for men. If you are suffering from an iron depletion, the doctor who ran the serum ferritin test should be able to give you suggestions on iron supplements or a change in diet. Many high school, college, and pro coaches demand serum ferritin tests of their female athletes. It is a good preventive measure.

There are several products on the market to help you replenish electrolytes during long runs (some are pictured in Chapter 4). They can be purchased online, at some running stores, or in most triathlon shops.

Following your longer runs, after you have tested different products, create a game plan of race day nutrition. Calculate how many gels, energy drinks, and minerals you will consume and when. If you simply take in water, there is a great likelihood that you will get into trouble with energy loss or worse, before the en[...]. Success is simply careful planning.

When to Start Eating and Drinking

Most marathons will have water stations approximately every mile. With a large marathon, the first mile always tends to have a lot of traffic and congestion. Many opt to miss the first water station for this reason. However, if you are running at a pace of 10 minutes per mile or slower, we strongly suggest that you need to begin hydrating with the first mile water station. If you are running at a faster pace, you can occasionally miss a water stop, but keep this to a minimum, as you need to drink approximately once every 10 minutes. If you are taking in water and gels, the gels would begin at about 30 to 45 minutes into the race, and continue at that same time interval thereafter. Mineral pills are taken every 20 to 30 minutes and thereafter. But be careful to factor in the amount of minerals in the gels and/or energy drinks you are consuming. On a hot day, extra minerals may be needed in addition to the energy drinks.

Effects of Hunger and Dehydration

As exciting and rewarding as endurance exercise is, it also requires you to pay special attention to nutrition and hydration. At a resting heart rate, approximately 15 to 20 percent of your blood flow goes to your working muscles. Conversely, during exhaustive exercise, about 80 to 85 percent of your blood flow goes to working muscles. This additional blood flow comes from other major organs in your body, including your liver, kidneys, brain, and stomach. During high heart rate work, your stomach is receiving only about 1 percent of the available blood flow. This makes digestion rather difficult. And as dehydration and fatigue set in during the race, and raise your heart rate, you will also find it increasingly difficult to consume heavy foods, or often any foods at all. Unless you dramatically lower your intensity, which means a lower heart rate, you will do better consuming something easy like a gel or energy drink. That may be one reason that endurance athletes tend to eat better, with lighter foods. When we don't eat right, we really feel it, especially when exercising.

The symptoms that can result if you ignore hunger pangs or thirst can completely derail your training or your marathon experience. Symptoms of low blood sugar or glycogen include nausea, headache, weakness, and light-headedness. If your blood sugar dips low enough, you can also experience dizziness, palpitations, trembling, sweating, confusion, disorientation, and unconsciousness. Symptoms of dehydration similarly worsen as dehydration progresses. Dehydration of just 2 percent can result in fatigue, weakness, loss of appetite, flushing of the skin, and bouts of light-headedness. Just 5 percent dehydration can lead to a worsening of the above symptoms as well as muscle cramps, increased heart rate, headache, and decreased sweating and urination.

Severe dehydration can be fatal, and may entail vomiting, seizures, confusion, racing heartbeat, loss of vision, and unconsciousness. Obviously, with all the stresses you are already placing on your body, it's in your best interest to avoid low blood sugar and dehydration.

YELLOW LIGHT

A 3 percent loss in hydration can lead to a 10 percent loss in energy output. So start drinking *before* you are thirsty; if you wait until you're thirsty, you are already on your way toward becoming dehydrated.

Rehearse on Longer Runs

A good rule for marathoners, or any endurance athlete, is to never use a food or supplement without first trying it on a longer workout (run and/or walk). Most of you will find that some food may cause a little abdominal discomfort. On the other hand, a different gel or food or sports drink may work fine. What works for one person may not work for another. Even one brand of gel may be fine for one person, and leave another with abdominal distress. The only way to find out is by trying different foods and supplements during long periods of running, at marathon intensity.

In trying to find the right food for the actual marathon, again trial and error is the key. First imagine what food you want during a long marathon race paced workout. Try that food, and in many cases, it will probably work. During the actual marathon, if you are really dying out there, for whatever reason—severe heat or cold, or you went out too fast—try the same concept that helped you find your race nutrition plan in the first place. If some food is out on the course that you never tried, and you really need something, first imagine what you want. If it sounds good, it just might work. On the other hand, if you are feeling okay, just a little tired, you may want to play it safe and avoid untested foods.

The Least You Need to Know

- As you train at different levels of intensity (heart rate) and with changing volumes (time or distance), you need to change your diet to include the necessary amounts of fats, carbohydrates, and proteins.
- Smart food choices geared toward training and racing are critical.

- During training, learning to eat and drink before feeling hungry or thirsty is critical in maintaining optimum health and performance.

- Experimentation can help you find the best foods for a sensitive stomach.

- Iron deficiency, especially in women, is an important thing to monitor, and a serum ferritin test is the best method for early detection.

Get Ready, Get Set ...

In This Chapter

- Scheduling your running time
- To stretch or not to stretch?
- Cross-training options
- The importance of cultivating good habits

Consistent sleep cycles are important to maintain high levels of energy output. Also, establishing a routine each week, as well as at specific times during certain days of that week is important. You never want to do too many consecutive days of hard workouts. And if you are a beginner, you don't want to do more than one day at a time of harder workouts. Beginner distance runners need to sandwich a tough day in between easy days, or days off. More advanced athletes can do more days of tough work, before an easier day or day off. That would also depend on your ability.

So to best facilitate the most positive psychological outlook and the highest physical energy output, create both a daily and a similar weekly routine. Keep in mind, the weekly routine will change slowly, as the demands of your training change. And depending on what you are doing each day, at least the start times should remain fairly constant.

Schedule Running Time

We all benefit from regular schedules. Being able to calculate workout and recovery cycles is critical to the overall process. Therefore, it may benefit you to set the same time aside on each of your training days to start your workout session. However, if you can't keep to a regular schedule, you may find success with a random schedule.

This would allow you to fit in your workouts wherever you can, although a complete lack of structure can also work against you. Even if your days are full, you need to find some consistent time to train, whether it's at the same time each day or not. Structure makes you accountable. If you are training with friends or a group, then keeping a schedule is all the more important. This may be the best way to stay accountable and use your training time for some socializing as well.

Your Best Time of Day

After a good night of sleep, most people have the highest volume of energy output in the morning. Usually, it's a cooler time of the day, before the sun heats everything up, depending on where you live. Obviously climate is an important consideration. In a freezing climate, it may be warmer in the afternoon, which would be a better choice. However, most races are usually in the morning. Training at the same time of day as your race is also an important factor. Yet some people have more energy later in the day, after all the stresses of the day are over. If nighttime is when you have the most energy and it fits in your schedule, then that is the best choice. Our point is, this is entirely an individual thing, based on when you have the most energy, good climate, and when you simply have the time to train.

Frequency of Workouts

Professional and college level athletes often train as much as six and a half days a week. Many, especially those on the pro level, will run in the morning and then again at night. Obviously, amateur athletes may not have the time or energy to keep up these high-level amounts of running and exercising. On the other hand, maintaining a minimum of three days of marathon training per week is critical to a successful outcome.

The *frequency* of your weekly workouts is entirely dependent on a few things. Obviously, things such as the amount of free time each day that you have is critical, and so are your energy levels. Having enough time to sleep, eat, and recover is also essential to gauge how many days you can train. Stress levels also need to factor into your *volume* and frequency. When you run, you stress the body, and the same is true of emotional stress, which can also tire you out. Before you calculate the frequency of workouts each week, you need to factor in all of these other criteria, as well as personal obligations each day of the week. Do you have regular meetings on a specific day, or need to be home with the children certain days? It can all add up, making consistent frequency a difficult but important thing to achieve.

DEFINITION

Frequency means the number of days each week that you exercise. **Volume** refers to the length of time or distance that you perform a single exercise. It can also refer to how much you do over a longer period of time, such as volume per week.

An inconsistent week, where you have too much training work loaded in a few days in a row, won't lead to sufficient recovery. Overtraining occurs without sufficient recovery. That means a permanent reduction in energy on race day, until a substantial rest period can occur. With a period of overtraining, the substantial rest usually doesn't come until after the race, or race season. So do try to find a consistent pattern in the frequency of workouts each week, which also facilitates recovery. If that means you can only do three days a week, then that's all you can do. However, less than that and you may have trouble finishing a race.

Use a Treadmill When Necessary

If you live in an area with a high crime rate or extreme hot or cold conditions, or the weather is bad when you want to train, you may need to use a treadmill. Some pro athletes use treadmills and still have success. However, on a treadmill you do use slightly different muscle fibers in the act of running or walking, compared to doing the same on land. Since most treadmills move without any energy input from you, part of the work of running is being done for you. Conversely, on land, any forward motion must be generated by you. For that reason, if you do most of your work on a treadmill, you will find it more difficult to run on land.

The opposite also holds true; if you do most of your workouts on land, then you will find it more difficult to run on a treadmill. So if you are doing a race on land versus a treadmill (and almost all races do take place on land), you would benefit from doing most of your workouts on the open road. However, if it's a matter of not wanting to get mugged or get sick from extreme climates, then please, use a treadmill to train for your marathon. Just understand it won't be quite as effective if you are exclusively training on the treadmill. Besides, the loss of a little speed versus the risk of violent crime, dehydration in the desert, or frostbite in a cold environment is a small price to pay for health and safety.

The Importance of Stretching

To stretch or not to stretch? That may be the biggest question right now in the running and exercising community. With proper and gentle stretches, we only see benefits, not deficits. There are several benefits to stretching both before and after exercise. For those with tight muscles, there is a benefit from stretching on days off, even with no exercise.

The list of benefits to stretching is short but absolutely critical:

- **Reduces the risk of injury.** If a muscle is tight, it will be pulling as you engage it. The tighter the muscle and the longer the exercise, the greater the risk that there will be an injury at the weakest link. Often that tight muscle may be pulling on a weaker area like the tendon, ligament, or joint, and that's where the injury will occur.

- **Increases the ability to run with proper form, which also reduces the risk of injury.** If your muscles are too tight to allow you to lift your knee high enough in the front, for example, or kick your foot upward behind you, you will not have an efficient form and will use more energy needlessly.

How Your Muscles Work

Recently science has given us a new understanding regarding what a stretch actually does. We now can see the submicroscopic particles that make up our muscles. Way down inside the layers that make up muscle fibers are millions and millions of filaments made up of protein molecules. These include a barlike filament (myosin) and two separate strands containing six fibers each (actin fibers). Understanding how muscles work will help you appreciate how important stretching really is:

1. **Muscle contraction.** The six actin filaments slide across the myosin filament. There are two actin groups that start at either end of the myosin filament. When your muscles contract, the actin fibers are sliding together from either side toward the center of the myosin filament. Picture two curtains sliding together over a window; if the curtain is too short, it will pull on the outer sides of the curtain. Millions of these tiny fibers coming together create muscle contraction and your movement.

2. **Muscle relaxation.** After contracting, the muscle fibers must relax, or go back to their original positions, so they can contract again. There are spring-like devices (titin) holding the actin strands in place on either end. To relax the muscle, the actin strands are released, and the springlike titin holding those strands at either end automatically pull the strands back. That is how a muscle automatically expands back to a relaxed starting point. Returning to the curtain image, if there were springs on the outer edges of the short curtains, they could be pulled together in the center when some tension is applied. When the tension is released, the outer springs would pull the curtain back, and it would fly open. Titin are those springs.

If the springy titin at this submicroscopic level is not stretched out and able to expand to its fullest potential, the fibers won't close all the way over the myosin. In other words, your muscles won't be as efficient, nor will they be able to contract or expand to their fullest capacity. For this reason, we need to stretch, to expand those submicroscopic titin springs to their fullest potential. This entire submicroscopic device of actin, myosin, and titin, which is held together on either end by walls called the Z-lines, is called a sarcomere.

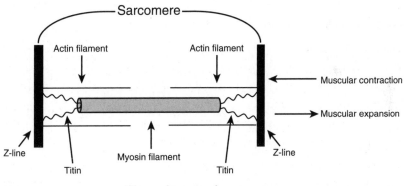

The working muscle—sarcomere.

As we get older, our muscles tend to become tighter and tighter, restricting power and energy output. It's extremely difficult to run when you are very tight and inflexible. And the risk of injury is much greater when you are tight. However, stretching consistently can reduce those effects of age and help you remain flexible and supple. When you include a routine of stretching and exercise in your life, you can avoid the stereotypical physique of old age, which is commonly thought of as hunched over and stiff.

"Cold" Stretching?

The concept of "cold" stretching is one of those old runner's ideas passed on, with no truth behind it. The idea has to do with your mistaken need to do a warm-up jog or active work to warm up muscles before you can stretch. If you don't "warm up" before stretching, you stand a great chance of being injured while stretching, or so the concept goes. And stretching is something you need to do before you can do the real workout, or you risk injury, which is true. If you stop and think about it, the idea of a stretch being cold makes no sense. True, if you haven't been jogging or doing some mild, limited exercise, your muscles may not be as supple or flexible. And yes, people do often injure themselves doing a stretch, but it has nothing to do with any of the above. Stretching before exercise is designed to loosen up the muscles to prepare it for running, as tightness can cause injury. Stretching after exercise is designed to stretch titin, which are submicroscopic filaments that expand the muscle, which makes the muscle more flexible and supple.

COACH SAYS ...

Stretching any time, with or without a warm-up, has benefits, suggests Robert Forster, a physical therapist who works with Olympic sprinters and elite athletes. Be gentle with your stretches and perform them with proper form. See Appendix E for a variety of pre- and postworkout stretches you can do.

Because humans are warm-blooded, at no time while you are alive is your body ever cold. Internally, you always have ATP firing off as fuel, electrical impulses racing down nerves, and chemical reactions taking place all over your body. We are a constant warehouse of electrical impulses and chemical reactions, all of which warm us humans up. The body is truly an amazing place, if you stop to think about it. Hence, the concept of "cold" stretching is a bit limited.

Stretching Gently

Stretching gently is important, as too many people injure themselves by stretching too hard. When you wake up in the morning, or have been at rest for a long period of time, your muscles tend to be tighter. But this tighter condition doesn't have to keep you from stretching gently. And a gentle stretch is more effective anyway. For an example of the danger inherent in hard stretching, ask a friend who trusts you to hold his arm out. Lunge at his outstretched arm, with both hands, as if you were going to rip his arm out of the socket. Before you touch him, he will probably have retracted his arm.

We have an automatic reflex that engages when something is pulling too hard. In the case of the outstretched arm, it's merely the suggestion of that action that engages this automatic reflex. When you pull too hard during a stretch, you engage this automatic reflex, and the muscle will actually contract, instead of elongate. In other words, by pulling a stretch too hard, you are actually tightening the muscle, not stretching it. Too often athletes are injured this way.

Try this: take your forefinger and pull it back as far as you can. Quickly, you will feel an increasingly achy feeling. This is actually caused by waste products (mostly hydrogen and lactic acid) building up. Now release the finger and take your other forefinger. (Hopefully, you have two.) Pull that finger back, but only go about half to three quarters as far. This level of tension probably feels comfortable, and is the correct intensity at which we benefit most from a stretch. Beyond that, and you may be tightening the muscle and possibly heading toward an injury. You don't ever want to stretch the muscle as far as it can go during stretching. Make sure that you can bend a fair amount more than you actually do during any stretch. That is, don't use your full range of motion while in a stretch.

Kinds of Stretches

Active stretches are simply a specialized type of movement that loosens up the muscles before a hard workout or race. Active stretches usually use some form of rotational movement, in which you generally rotate 10 times in each direction.

Progressive stretches are designed to elongate the muscle. They are the same as static stretches, except they are not held for 30 seconds, as static stretches are. Progressive stretches are held for 5 to 10 seconds. Studies show that the 5-second version is more effective than holding for 10 seconds. Some progressive stretches are beneficial to use with active stretches, generally before the run. They include the standing hamstring stretch, standing calf stretch, and standing quad stretch. Active stretches that can be done with these include ankle rolls, knee circles, hip circles, and rounds. The prerun stretch is simply designed to lessen the risk of injury by preparing the muscle to run.

Most postrun stretches are progressive stretches, mostly done on the ground with no weight on the legs, as they are more effective when performed that way. The postrun stretches are far more important than the prerun stretches. Both are designed to loosen up the muscle, but the postrun stretch is critical to relieve that tightness from the run so that it does not become more permanent. Muscles need to remain pliable and supple, to be functional and efficient. If you can't run with proper form due to inflexibility, you will waste a lot of energy, risk injury, and never reach your fullest potential.

Static stretches are the more traditional stretches, often the same as progressive stretches, but usually held for a period of 30 seconds. They do increase the risk of injury when pulled too hard, because you are holding them for a longer period than progressive stretches. Static and progressive stretches include knee to chest, pelvic rotation, pretzel, lying quad stretch, and adductor stretch. They can loosen up the muscle, but there is recent contradictory evidence regarding whether these stretches actually elongate the muscle.

COACH SAYS ...

See Appendix E for details on how to perform these recommended stretches, as well as many others.

Before and After a Workout

Much debate has gone on regarding the importance of stretching before and after a workout. Current theory continues to suggest that stretching before a workout prevents injury, while the stretch following helps to reset muscles back to their elongated state. Again, static stretches don't seem to achieve either the full benefits of stretching before or after. One additional benefit of progressive stretches comes from the number of times you stretch, release, and then stretch again, every 5 or 10 seconds. This repeated action helps to squeeze out waste products such as hydrogen and lactic acid. Remember, however, that waste product build-up is generally gone after about two hours anyway, so this benefit by itself isn't significant enough to demand stretching.

Yet, there does seem to be enough evidence that stretching of some kind does help before and after the workout. Most coaches and sports physical therapists believe that following the initial preworkout stretch, a period of warm-up is important. Some suggest possibly following the warm-up by another second stretch. Also, a period of cool-down work is beneficial following a workout, before the final stretch. The warm-up and cool-down usually both consist of easy jogging or walking, depending on what type of activity you have planned.

Cross-Training

We all benefit from a range of exercises and different sports. The running and jumping in beach volleyball, the varied running and directional changes in tennis, and many other aspects of other sports can benefit elements of our running, especially our cardiovascular abilities. Using other general approaches to exercise can help your training, especially early in the season. And let's face it, some people may become bored with endless runs and may need something else to make it fun again.

In fact, all of these other sports would best be kept to early in the season. As the season progresses, you want to become more run-specific. You only have so much time and energy, and as you build for an endurance run, you will want to spend more time and energy on running later in the season.

Bicycling

If you fear risking the pounding of hill runs, and need to build quad strength but hate the gym, then you have a great reason to cycle. Start at the bottom of a good-sized hill, in your lowest gear. After a short time, you will definitely feel the burn in your legs. Stop before you are exhausted, as you don't want to overtrain. If you get to the top of the hill and have the energy, do it again. This is a great strength-building exercise. Cycling is also a good cardiovascular exercise at any time of the season. But don't forget, cycling won't take the place of running in terms of marathon training. You are working slightly different muscles, so this can't completely take the place of run training.

Swimming

Swimming can be a wonderful workout to loosen up your entire body, and to strengthen your upper body as well. The twisting and turning creates a great series of stretches for the runner, especially for the hip and side. If you still have energy on your day off, or especially after a tough day, swimming can be a great workout. You can take a break from the pounding and still have a good cardiovascular exercise.

Running in water with an aqua-jogger floatation vest can be the best way to maintain your endurance base, if you are injured. Without the pounding of running on the ground, and with proper form in the water, you can use the same muscles you use on land. There is no other workout besides running in water that can match the same muscles as running. This isn't a method to build as a runner, but it's the best way to maintain. Running in water is usually done with a rubber floatation device, about an inch thick. Use the same run form as you would on land. Another benefit is the ability to look down and see your form, and feel any resistance from awkward arm or leg swings in the water.

YELLOW LIGHT

Be careful not to overtrain. If you are tired from the day before, you may want to take the entire day off and not do any cross-training—or, at the very least, keep the workout easy. You need to recover and adapt to your training. This is true for any cross-training you do during marathon training season—and don't forget to stretch, especially afterward.

Cultivate Good Habits

Maintaining good habits such as discipline, good nutrition, proper rest and recovery, and focusing on how you are feeling is essential to your overall marathon training program. Any good habits that enhance your health and fitness will also benefit your running. But your running demands its own set of habits and disciplines as well. The healthy habits you implement now will serve as a strong foundation for your running training. Habits, whether good or bad, do take some time to become second nature, so be patient with the process. Once you reap the rewards of good rest, good nutrition, and consistent training, you will find it easier to stay on the right track. Create a cycle of positive reinforcement: good habits equal healthy training.

One caution: while you may enjoy running with friends or with a personal musical device, you need to stay alert on a lot of levels during your training runs. Don't get so distracted by conversation or good music that you don't notice traffic, bumps in the road, or any other potentially harmful situation. You also need to pay attention to how you feel so you can run at the proper intensity for your training plan.

Consistency and Discipline

Consistency is important to build a stronger endurance base. Yet it's the discipline that makes you consistent. So sometimes you need to turn off the television, put down the phone, stop working, and go for a run. Chances are, your ability to focus and concentrate will be enhanced from the break.

Pay Attention to Diet

Your body won't run as well, meaning your energy will be reduced, when eating fried foods and sugary snacks such as cookies, cake, and candy. Likewise, you need to eat certain foods at the appropriate times. A heavy, protein-based meal before a long run may leave you without the additional carbohydrates that you need for fuel. Eating complex carbohydrates prior to a run is a good way to keep your energy up. On your days off, a well-rounded diet is essential. Adding vitamins to your daily regimen is also a good idea. (See Chapter 6 for more on diet and nutrition.)

Rest Is Part of Training

Just as it's important to take a day off to recover following a tough day or so, it's equally important to taper off for a full week now and then. Don't simply build and build in distance, but after a block of time cut your volume down for one entire week. You still need to maintain frequency and intensity, in order to build your endurance base. (We explain tapering in greater detail in Chapter 10.)

Focus on Yourself

Learn to pay attention to how you feel after a workout. If you are tired the next day after a training run, you are overtraining. Any aches or pains need to be dealt with. Also be aware of which training made you feel the best, so you can do that again, at appropriate times. Keeping a journal of distances and the way you felt afterward, including your energy levels the day after a workout, can give you a view of the bigger picture, illuminating where you benefited or where you needed to cut back.

The Least You Need to Know

- Setting up a consistent routine can help motivation, and for many, the morning is the time when they have the most energy.
- Stretching is important for flexibility, suppleness, and reduced injury.
- Cross-training options include strength training, swimming, and biking, but don't overdo it, or you will overtrain, which is counter-productive.
- Good habits such as discipline, good nutrition, proper rest and recovery, and focusing on how you feel are essential.

Strength and Hill Training

8

In This Chapter

- Why do strength and hill training exercises?
- A different way to build strength besides weights
- Suggested strength-building program
- Tips on proper form and intensity on hills
- Sample hill workout

When we talk about building strength in endurance athletics, it probably is not what you think. We are not interested in turning you into a weightlifter or bodybuilder. What we intend to do is make you stronger in ways that will specifically benefit your running. As a long-distance runner, you need to build strength on two fronts: in the muscles you use for running as well as in your cardiovascular system. One of the best ways to achieve both is to train intensely by running hills. Hills work out your legs and your heart, but there is also another, lesser-known way to build additional strength.

Thanks to thousands of years of evolution during periods of starvation and drought, your body's normal state is to use as little energy, and therefore, as little fuel as possible. One important way that your body uses less fuel is by not using all your muscles all the time. Certain types of muscle are used for some types of activity and not for others. Therefore, another way to build more strength is to teach more muscles to engage. The more muscles you use, the stronger you are, and the faster you are. This is called *muscle recruitment*, and in this chapter we show you how to achieve it.

The Importance of Strength Training

Of course, working out your muscles and building strength in your cardiovascular system is good for your health in general. But in endurance training, strength takes on new meaning. It gives you the power to run faster. And with targeted training, strength can also help you avoid injury and overcome imbalance issues that might lead to injury. You will also find that you have better coordination and control of your body when your muscles are engaged and powerful.

Improve Speed

Improving speed isn't just a question of going faster. It is also a matter of heightened endurance. When your legs are strong enough to push you along more rapidly, you also need the fuel to keep them going. That is, your heart and lungs need to provide enough blood, oxygen, and glycogen to fuel those powerful leg muscles. So teaching your body to run faster means you are strengthening both your muscular system and your cardiovascular system.

Avoid Injury

Strength training can also help you reduce the risk of injury. You can work certain muscles to even out various imbalance issues. Imbalance issues put greater stress on the joints and can stem from any of the following:

- A hip displacement (one side of the hip rides higher than the other)
- Weak muscles
- Poorly fitted or improper shoes
- Improper form
- Repeated running on uneven or slanted surfaces
- Over- or underpronation of the feet

The extra stress placed on the joints by these imbalance issues can be partially absorbed by stronger skeletal muscles and fascia. Skeletal muscles surround the skeleton, while fascia is a type of flexible connective tissue that binds muscles as well as other tissues. However, allowing these tissues to continually take the hit for misaligned joints or poor form will eventually take its toll and lead to additional problems. Simple strengthening of the muscles causing the imbalance can solve many problems for the runner.

For example, many runners wear an elastic band (patellar tendon strap) around their legs, just below the knee. This band can't absorb much of the stress from the pounding on your knee when you run, which is supposedly what the band is designed to do. With a little strength training, however, the muscles and fascia around your knee could effectively absorb much more stress than that band ever could. And stronger muscles would not inhibit movement as the patellar tendon strap does. The problem with the strap, besides not doing much, is that it rides just below your kneecap and tends to be rather tight. This can inhibit the full range of motion of the knee joint. A lack of full normal motion in the knee leads to improper form, which slows you down and could possibly create an imbalance issue. And the imbalance issue could lead to an injury.

Better strength usually means better alignment, and better alignment means fewer injuries. A sports medicine doctor or physical therapist can design an individualized strength-training plan for you to correct or at least mitigate any imbalance issues you may have.

Improve Balance and Coordination

Strengthening certain muscles which help with balance and stability will help you in your running in general, and especially when running hills. When you first start running hills, you may feel as if you're bouncing around and a bit out of control, especially on the downhill. Eventually, your improved strength will lead to a more coordinated effort, and the uphills and downhills will become more comfortable.

The downhill provides an additional coordinated benefit, which comes from *cadence* and *stride*. You benefit from shorter, faster strides on a downhill, which can translate into more efficient form or greater speed with the same energy output. Gravity naturally takes you down the hill faster. This is a perfect place to work on your stride or foot turnover. Focus on quicker cadence and shorter stride length. The problem with this form drill is that many runners don't increase their cadence and shorten their stride, due to the fear of falling forward. Additional strength in the leg muscles will help to negate this fear and improve confidence as well as ability.

DEFINITION

Cadence is the speed or rhythm in which your feet hit the ground; 180 steps per minute is an optimal cadence for marathon runners (3 per second). **Stride** is the distance your foot reaches forward and backward with each foot strike of the ground.

Recruiting More Muscles for Strength

Before we can explain how you recruit more muscles for additional strength and why this is important, you first need to understand the types of muscles you are working with. You have primarily two types of skeletal muscle, which is the type you use for running. These are known as *slow-twitch* and *fast-twitch* muscles. Everyone has some of each type, but your percentage of each is determined by genetics. Elite sprinters have more fast-twitch muscle fibers than a marathoner would have.

DEFINITION

Slow-twitch muscle fibers are aerobic and are used mostly for slower, longer distances. They are trainable. **Fast-twitch** muscles are mostly anaerobic and are used for shorter bursts of higher-intensity energy. They are not trainable. Fast-twitch muscles also break down into two types of intermediate muscles.

"Trainable" muscles engage when you run at the level of intensity at which those specific muscles are designed to perform. That is, slow-twitch, aerobic muscles will engage during low heart rate aerobic exercise. But if that muscle is trained consistently for a while, it will continue to engage, even at times of different intensities. Therefore, if trained properly, you may be able to get your aerobic, slow-twitch muscles to engage when you are doing high-intensity work. This would make you stronger and more efficient overall. Conversely, when a muscle is not "trainable," that means the only way it will engage is when you use it at its preprogrammed intensity. It cannot be taught to engage at other times.

Famous New Zealand coach Arthur Lydiard researched the idea of training his world-class athletes at different levels of intensity. What he and others found was that a certain type of fast-twitch muscles were more readily engaged when there were short but high-intensity workouts. Similarly, doing low-intensity training for longer periods of time saw more of the slow-twitch muscles engaged. By combining the two types of training, we can increase the use of the two types of muscle fibers, and the athlete can go faster throughout the marathon. The more muscles that fire (are recruited), the stronger the athlete, and the stronger the athlete, the faster he or she will go. This is the logic behind training at lower aerobic intensity as well as at the high intensities required for hill work. See Chapter 9 for more information on high-intensity training.

Strength-Building Program

A concept in strength building that we use today comes from studies performed on athletes in the former Soviet Bloc countries. The idea behind those training programs (which is similar to your training program) is to do different workouts at varying levels of intensity to continue to shock the body and build strength. This constant variety causes the body to constantly use new sets of muscles.

Always begin each strength workout with a short warm-up of jogging, biking, or some machine (such as an elliptical machine or stair climber) for about 20 to 25 minutes. Jogging would be the better choice for marathoners. This is followed by some gentle progressive stretches (see Appendix E). Then the strength workout begins. More advanced athletes could do a strength workout following a 5K or even a 10K aerobic run. Keep in mind you're trying to gain strength for running, not become a bodybuilder. Therefore, what you do for strength training will be different from what bodybuilders at the gym will be doing.

As a beginner, you will need to start with an "adaptation phase" where you prepare all your muscles, ligaments, and tendons for the stresses to come. During this phase you will even out any imbalances caused by weak muscles, begin to slowly increase weights, and begin to increase your endurance. This period or phase will take about six weeks and is best done before your marathon training season, or at least during the beginning weeks. Make sure you use proper form, especially with machines. When in doubt, always ask a trainer about proper form. We recommend only about two to three sets per movement (machine or exercise), although bodybuilders would do more.

This initial phase would use a circuit training concept:

1. Go from one machine or movement to the next, with only 60 to 90 seconds of rest between each machine or exercise.

2. After doing each exercise once and resting, move on to the next.

3. Once the full circuit has been completed, take one to three minutes of recovery and then do it all again.

4. Don't increase weights too quickly, as your tendons and ligaments also need time to adapt.

Following are some exercises to be performed over a six-week period (see the schedule that follows the exercises). These can be changed according to your needs, and one machine can be switched out for a movement you can do at home with no machines. This list has both home and gym versions. Do one movement from each group. More strength-training movements that you can do at home are found in Appendix E.

 COACH SAYS ...

Don't forget to stretch following each completed workout. See Chapter 7 for more on the importance of stretching.

Group One (quadriceps):

Leg Press (gym machine): Push on the plate with your feet, which pulls the weight up, as you sit. It is better to use a machine where you do not push the plate up, but your feet remain at shoulder level.

Squats (advanced—free weights): With the weight on your shoulders, squat down. Do not go down to where your knees are below 90 degrees.

Lunges (gym or home): With dumbbells in your hands or not, reach forward with your leg and go down only to where your knees are at 90 degrees.

Group Two (upper body—pectorals and triceps):

Bench Press (gym): Laying on your back, push the bar up with your arms.

Plank (home): Get in push-up position and hold it for as long as you can, while keeping your back straight.

Bridge: Same as the plank, but on your elbows.

Group Three (upper back—latissimus dorsi muscles):

Cable Pull-Downs (gym machine): While seated on the machine, grab the bar above with both hands and pull down.

Seated Cable Rows (gym): Pull the cable toward your chest.

Dumbbell Rows (gym or home): With one knee on a bench and your other foot on the floor, lift the dumbbell up while supporting your upper body with the other hand on the bench.

Group Four (hamstrings):

Leg Curls (gym machine): Push the round pad on the back of your ankle up. This machine can be designed in different orientations. Whether you are laying down or upright, it is the same movement.

Hip Raises (home): See Appendix E.

Group Five (calves):

Calf Raises (with or without machine): Lift your heels off the floor, or raise heels up, lifting the weight on the machine.

Group Six (core):

Dead Bug (at home or gym): See Appendix E.

For the following six weeks, if this is before the marathon training season, do two to three of the workouts each week. If it is during the beginning of the marathon training season, do only one or two each week, or follow the schedule in Appendix D. Beyond the first six weeks of marathon training, do only one strength workout each week. Taper off your strength workouts after you reach a long weekend run of about 16 miles, or maintain as needed, as long as you are not overtraining and tired the next day.

First week: Forty percent of the maximum you are capable of in one lift for each exercise with 15 repetitions, and Dead Bug at 12 repetitions, and all at two sets of everything.

Second week: Fifty percent with 12 repetitions. Keep Leg Curls at 40 percent with 15 reps, and Dead Bug at 15 reps, and all at two sets of everything.

Third week: Sixty percent with 8 reps, with Leg Curls at 50 percent and 12 reps, and Dead Bug at 15 reps, and all at two sets.

Fourth week: Drop back to 50 percent with 15 reps. Leg Curls are at 40 percent with 12 reps, and Dead Bug is 12 reps, and all with three sets.

Fifth week: Sixty percent with 12 reps, with Leg Curls at 50 percent and 12 reps, and Dead Bug at 15 reps, and all with three sets.

Sixth week: Seventy percent with 10 reps, with Leg Curls at 50 percent and 12 reps, Dead Bug at 15 reps, and all at three sets.

Follow the six weeks with a week of taper, where you do 50 percent with 15 reps and only one time around the circuit. For those who need to build muscle, use the next three weeks to bring all movements to the point of failure, at which you can't do one more repetition. This extreme effort needs to be done at a time of little or no running. It will also increase your weight (muscle density) and cause you to burn more calories on the marathon. So it's certainly not a phase that is necessary for most.

The better choice for endurance athletes who don't need more muscle bulk might be to do a program following the first six-week program and a taper. Use less recovery time between sets (four to five seconds rest), far more repetitions, and much lighter weights—30 percent to 50 percent of your one rep maximum. This strategy would build endurance and help burn that fat closest to the muscle (subcutaneous fat), which is difficult to get rid of.

Why Hill Training?

Here is the crossroads of strength and hill training: strength helps you run hills more efficiently, and hill training makes you stronger. Therefore, in addition to a traditional strength-training plan, hills can be wonderful training grounds for building strength and endurance. This is so important in your training that certain days should be dedicated specifically to hill training (described later in this chapter). The only way to get better at running hills is to run them over and over again.

Strengthen Muscles and Improve Endurance

Running as hard as you can up a hill can have two major benefits:

- It strengthens the muscles you use to push your body up the hill, predominantly your quadriceps muscles on the front of your thighs and your calf muscles. You're actually strengthening and training the specific muscles you use for running.

- It improves endurance. Whenever you race your heart for short periods of time, you raise the bar on your endurance ability. That point at which you no longer use oxygen in the muscles you run with, instead utilizing fat as fuel (VO_2 Max), goes higher. This switch allows you to go at a slightly higher level of intensity for longer, as you use more of the abundant fat fuel than the limited fuel source of glycogen.

With enough of this type of workout, you'll eventually find that your uphill speed increases, while your intensity level (heart rate) remains consistent on the same uphill. In other words, your efficiency increases with regard to hills. This is another benefit of hill training that you will appreciate on race day.

Every Marathon Includes Hills

Running hills in training isn't designed just to make you a better hill runner for the heck of it. It is also to prepare you for what will inevitably be a marathon course with at least a few hills. There are certainly some flat marathon courses, but most will include some hills, and some will even include dramatic elevation gains. For example, the most recent Los Angeles Marathon of 2010, which was the inaugural year of its new race course, saw a few big hills in the first quarter of the race. There are downhills in that section as well, but it is believed that runners needed to lose nearly 10 to 15 percent from their anticipated average goal finish pace in this first section of that particular race just to negotiate the hills. This would mean that in the first quarter of that race, a 10-minute-per-mile runner would drop nearly 10 minutes, at a distance of about 6½ miles. On the other hand, runners could make up some of that time at the end of this race, where there are about 4 miles of solid downhill with no uphill. (See Appendix C for more information about the Los Angeles Marathon and many others.)

Another marathon that is notorious for its hills is the fabled Boston Marathon. At about mile 20, the infamous Heartbreak Hill looms, with a gain of half a mile of elevation. This is an especially difficult hill not only because of its size, but because it is so near the end of the race when runners are already exhausted and may be on the verge of "hitting the wall." Those who make it, however, are rewarded with some picturesque scenery and another half mile of downhill on the other side of the peak.

MILE MARKER

Here's a secret: as a runner it's okay to walk part or most of a hill. When your heart rate begins to go up, you need to lower your intensity. If the slowest run (jogging) is still too high an intensity level, it's okay to walk.

How to Run Hills

Hills can be an exciting, enjoyable addition to any marathon or race, as long as you understand one simple idea: pace is meaningless. If you don't understand this concept, hills can be a gut-wrenching, nightmarish experience. So how can you turn hills into a gleeful rollercoaster ride instead of feeling squashed by a steamroller? Do the intense work now so that you can maintain even levels of intensity on both sides of the hills during the marathon.

Intensity on the Uphill

Understand that running or walking at a consistent pace when it comes to hills is completely self-destructive. Going up a hill raises your heart rate, and so does a hot day. If your heart rate goes up too high, you're depleting that limited reservoir of glycogen (fuel from carbs) too quickly. If you use up that reservoir of glycogen, then you "hit the wall." So running up a hill at too high a heart rate will cause you to crash and burn when you run out of fuel later in the race. You need to lower your level of intensity when running up a hill.

Likewise, if you are doing a run/walk, if your heart rate is still too high when you begin to slow down the run portion of your run/walk for a hill, you can make that run portion of the timed run/walk a walk as well. Walkers who raise their heart rate can stop for a moment. After a few seconds, your heart rate will drop down and you can continue. Although hills usually aren't steep enough to cause walkers to stop and take a break, understand that you have that option.

Downhill Intensity

Now that leaves the downhill. Again, remember that pace is meaningless. If you try to completely make up for the uphill with speed on the downhill, your level of intensity (heart rate) will be too high. As with the uphill, this can lead to using too much glycogen, which leads to a crash and burn later in the race. The problem is, because the unfortunate result of your intense actions on the hill comes so much later in the race, you might not realize that the hill early on was the culprit.

Don't try to make up entirely on the downhill for the time lost on the uphill. That is, when you're going over a hill with even uphill and downhill slopes, you should even out your levels of energy output. You can just as badly screw up by taking the downhill at too high a level of intensity as you can by going uphill at too high a level of intensity. Notice we try not to use terms such as "fast" or "slow" in this discussion. It's because pace is meaningless.

Uphill Running Form

Your form on hills will be a bit different than on flat ground, depending on how steep the hill is. On the uphill:

- Lean a bit forward from the hips. At no time do you bend your back. This is a slight lean forward, nothing remotely dramatic.

- Take short, quick steps ("baby steps") up the hill. If you take big steps, your ankle will be overextended, especially with the downward angle of the hill already extending your ankle. Pushing back too far in this way can easily lead to Achilles tendinitis. The symptom is achiness in the back of the ankle.

Downhill Running Form

Running down the hill is similar to the uphill form:

- Lean forward slightly at the hips, so your center of gravity is over your knees. If you lean back, this will slow you down, but it can cause greater stress on the knees due to the slight extension (sticking out) of the knees.

- Shorten and quicken your stride, especially if you're going too fast, and you will quickly regain control. The shorter, quicker stride on the downhill will also put less stress on the joints, especially the knee.

You can pick up a lot of speed from simply lifting your knee higher—90 degrees at the highest. However, not only will you find yourself dramatically speeding up, but also smashing into the ground much harder with every step. If you are near the end of a race and really want to risk the pounding in order to speed up, go for it. On the other hand, this isn't a good practice at other times. If you're in the first half of the race, the pounding could tire out your quads and feet and hurt the rest of your race. If you are on a training run, the additional pounding from raising your knees to pick up speed on the downhill can lead to an increased risk of injury. And that extra speed is simply not worth the risk.

Sample Hill Workout

In your hill training, you will raise your heartbeat on the uphills as a way of building strength and endurance and to push your anaerobic threshold up. This is different from your approach to the marathon, during which you must strive to keep your heart rate as level as possible. This high heart rate work will make that kind of control easier during the marathon.

Try running up a hill at 85 percent of your maximum effort, or heart rate. Don't start on too steep a hill, as you may become injured and the level of intensity to maintain any amount of time at a higher heart rate may be too much. If you're new to this, don't spend too much time with an elevated heart rate, and begin with sets of 30 seconds only. After that time, simply stop wherever you are, take a break, and then start again when you've recovered. As you progress, add time to the intense uphill training. For this, you may need to move to a larger hill. Or start out by running only partly up a larger hill. Do one to eight repetitions for these shorter-intensity workouts. When you finish this workout, you don't want to be exhausted. Fatigue is the litmus test as to when this workout is over. Please remember, if you're tired the next day from a workout the day before, you were overtraining.

When you can run up a hill for a period longer than six minutes at a high heart rate, you will have the greatest gains. Your heart rate needs to be at least 85 percent of your maximum heart rate (HR Max). At the six minute or more level, do four to six of these maximum, again at 85 percent of your HR Max. Make sure that you have enough time to recover. Start with four minutes of recovery time when training at high intensity for over six minutes. You can reduce recovery time to help quicken your recovery abilities. If you become light-headed or dizzy, you may have reached your maximum heart rate. Just back off the intensity slightly and your head will clear.

The Least You Need to Know

- You can gain strength by training at different levels of intensity to engage more muscles.
- You can improve running speed and avoid injury by building strength in a gym or at home, even with no equipment at all.
- You need to do different types of exercises with strength training and running to gain strength.
- Hill work strengthens your muscles and cardiovascular system and improves endurance.
- Running hills is a matter of evening out your energy levels, or slowing down a lot and speeding up a little accordingly.

Hitting the Road

In This Chapter

- Key points for your first runs
- The different types of running form
- Tips for improving your speed
- Doing shorter practice runs
- Using a pace chart
- Keeping a running journal

By now, you have your water bottles, the right shoes, clothes, and maybe a group or coach to help direct your training. To even out your strength and flexibility, you have hopefully been doing some strength training and a lot of gentle stretching. It's time to make the leap—you are ready to start running. So go outside (or go to an inside track) and get to it, and enjoy becoming a better athlete.

Remember that in early season, the lower heart rate runs will expand mitochondria and will increase capillary veins and arteries, making you more efficient. In addition, you will be engaging different slow muscle fibers at this low intensity. Later, you will build strength by engaging faster muscle fibers at higher intensities. This is critical for all levels of endurance training, from beginners to pros.

Your First Runs

Obviously, if this is your first run, or the first time you have run or exercised in years, you need to focus on a few key points. Your muscles are probably tight, weak, and inefficient. In other words, you are definitely not ready for high-intensity work, and you are especially not ready for speed work. For one thing, you won't have the fuel (glycogen) in your muscles to sustain exercise for very long, and you may get injured due to less strength. On the other hand, to experience the greatest gains, you want to maintain exercise as long as you can. So keep it all comfortable, at a low aerobic rate of intensity. And remember, you are going to speed up later on.

The pace that you are achieving now, or are able to achieve now, is going to increase. Remember, pace is meaningless; intensity is everything. Focus on building efficiency with low intensity, and not pace. Feel it. If you are breathing hard, then ease up. Hopefully, that will be an easy, comfortable, fun feeling, not a beat yourself senseless feeling. You're far better with a heart rate monitor right now than a pace/distance watch, though neither are a necessity for training or racing.

COACH SAYS ...

We want to build you up, not beat you up! This is an important axiom of training. If speed work is torture, you probably don't have the strength or base (aerobic) efficiency yet. Hold back and slow it down until you're ready. Rule number one, you need to have fun!

To best achieve this low level of comfortable intensity, you may want to find a track or open walkway. Bring a water bottle or something to drink, which you can leave on the side of the track or walkway. Running in a group can be a great thing. But for your first run, you may want to do it on your own, to allow you to really focus on the way it feels. Often, in groups, we can get pulled into a faster run than what we benefit from. That can be fun and occasionally good, but to start, learn your own levels. For proper running form, please see "Modern Form of Running" later in this chapter.

For the beginner on your first marathon training run, try these steps:

1. Get in the outermost lane of the track, to allow faster runners to speed by on the inner lanes. Try not to be intimidated by faster runners. You may be beating them soon.

2. Walk with proper form and complete two laps around the track. Note that on most tracks, each lap is a quarter mile, or 400 meters.

3. Take a break and do some stretches (see the preworkout stretches in Appendix E).

4. Walk another lap.

5. Jog the straightaway. This is 100 meters in length. The curves are also 100 meters in length.

6. Walk the curve, and jog the next 100 meters, with a walk on the last 100 meters. You have just completed 1 mile, and if you maintained a low enough intensity on the jogging, it probably felt easy.

7. Jog half of the straightaway and walk the second half of the straightaway. Do this with the curves as well. So every 50 meters (half the straightaway or half the curve) you are walking or switching to jogging. Continue this for four laps. You are now at 2 miles.

8. Walk a little more and find a comfortable place to lie down and give yourself a good postworkout stretch. If you have the energy, this would be a perfect time, before the stretch, to do some of the strength-training exercises found in Appendix E.

Hopefully, you won't be tired the next day. If you are, you did too much; do less next time. Regardless, take the next day off, and start with the same thing two days later. You should maintain about three days a week of this regimen, and try to go a little farther each week.

Eventually, the 50 meter runs will easily increase to 100 meter runs and then they will get even longer and longer. Again, focus on your low intensity and not pace. Feel your breathing, which is a great indicator of heart rate and intensity. If you are breathing hard, hold way back and take it easier. You can walk; be patient. You'll increase your efficiency dramatically, and then when it comes time for speed work, you will increase much more quickly, as you'll be able to maintain your training with high intensity for a greater period of time. But that is way down the road. And as you watch those fast intimidating runners fly by, just remember, you are training for a marathon. And someday, on a marathon, you may see them again, as you pass them by.

Where to Run

Because this is your very first run, or even just a run early in the new season, you need to keep it comfortable, easy, aerobic, and all things that mean low heart rate. In other words, you want to avoid doing big hills, which would raise your heart rate on the way up the incline. Obviously, in some neighborhoods, it's impossible to completely get away from hills. If you must go up a hill, make sure you slow it down significantly, or even walk it. Maintaining even levels of intensity is what is important, especially now. Remember that pace is meaningless. The bottom line is, avoid any hills, if possible, and try to stay on the flattest ground around. An occasional treadmill run is okay. But you would be utilizing slightly different muscle fibers, so this would probably be a benefit on occasion, but not a good thing for most of the time. However, if you must use a treadmill, then you must.

> **YELLOW FLAG**
>
> Security is a critical consideration. Running alone at night, early in the morning, or in a bad neighborhood can be dangerous. Likewise, running in the wilderness on your own can be a danger. You never know what animals you may run into. Or if you injure yourself, it may take a long time before someone finds you. The best choices for running outdoors are in familiar neighborhoods during daylight hours or at a public track. If necessary, join a training group or run with a friend for added safety. Or, as a last resort, join a gym with treadmills and/or an indoor track.

Many but not all high school or college tracks are accessible and open for public use, especially in the evening and when not in use by the school. At night, however, the lack of lighting may be an issue.

Intersperse Running and Walking

Using both running and walking in a workout can be a plus for beginning runners. Walking usually forces you to lower your heart rate. On a hot day, the walking portion of a workout can be critical. This keeps you going longer and farther, which is always a plus in marathon training and racing. Spending a portion of time walking also switches the primary energy consumption from the muscles you run with, to muscles you walk with, which helps rest the running muscles.

It appears that the slower athlete benefits the most from doing a run/walk program. However, many inexperienced but faster run/walkers often run too fast to make up for the slower walk. Instead of maintaining even levels of low energy output, which would maximize glycogen consumption, they end up racing their heart rates on the run and then bringing it down on the walk. This isn't an efficient pattern, as they use glycogen faster than they can replenish it and never really achieve those critical, consistently low heart rate aerobic runs. Training in a group with a pace leader or running with a heart monitor may help you keep your intensity at the right level.

Build Distance Slowly

A huge mistake would be to build distance too quickly. Wanting to "get ahead of the game" is a critical error that is often made by highly motivated runners, and it can lead to injury and overtraining. Any energy output leads to a decrease in hormonal output, which includes human growth hormone (HGH), and others, which help to repair muscle tissue.

YELLOW FLAG

You never want to increase volume by much more than 10 percent per week. In other words, if your long run one week is 10 miles, the next week's long run shouldn't exceed 11 miles.

Also, you don't want to peak too early, meaning you don't want to get to your longest run at race pace too early in the season. Staying up there at a high level of intensity for a long period of time could lead to overtraining. This includes depleted hormonal output, and therefore, greater risk of injury and less energy on race day. Overtraining can also lead to several other problems including decreased red blood cell count and a depleted immune system, which can leave you susceptible to illness. The build and taper of a schedule has a delicate balance between too much and too little, and too soon and too late. This is where the art of creating a schedule comes into play, for everyone adapts to training at different rates. In addition, everyone recovers from the stresses of exercise at a different rate. Some athletes, especially the young, can handle much higher volumes of stress for longer periods of time. From this, we can conclude with certainty that the one-size-fits-all schedule doesn't fit all. However, building reasonably slowly is important for all.

Preparatory Schedule

There are different types of preparatory segments or phases of a schedule. A college or pro athlete would spend a few weeks doing general preparatory work. This would include building up the aerobic (low heart rate) mileage, strength training, core work, and possibly some work not specific to the marathon. Long hikes up a tall mountain would be a general preparatory thing to do, for anyone in training for a marathon. In fact, the women on the Japanese Olympic marathon team have gone mountain hiking during early preparatory marathon training. For us *age grouper* athletes, little time is spent with general work other than building mileage. Rarely is an untrained age grouper building mileage at an aerobic level in the early season, which is a mistake that is often based on ignorance. However, running and building mileage isn't general work. Running is running. It's absolutely specific. Hiking, strength training, stretching, and yoga are all examples of general preparatory work. This is a major deficiency in most nonprofessional, noncompetitive athletic training, and can't be emphasized enough. So if you want to get faster by being more efficient, take a look at adding some general preparatory work to your schedule, early in the training season.

> **DEFINITION**
>
> An **age grouper** is any nonprofessional marathon runner. As the name implies, age groupers usually run in races competing against times of those in their age group.

Following the general prep work is the specific preparatory work. For the marathon this would include more aerobic distance work, and things that are more specific to the marathon, such as hill and speed work. This is where you may drop the mountain hikes, or bike rides, and other work nonspecific to the marathon.

Different Running Forms

There are several theories on how one should run, or one's running form. Walking form can be quite similar. It includes the same arm swing, and same quick, short stride. The major difference is that the walker must have one foot on the ground at all times, and the walker must land with a straight leg. For the race walker, any bending of the leg, as it goes under you, would be labeled as "creeping." You could be disqualified in a race walking competition for this infraction in form. Hips are also turned much more forward in race walking to help gain ground quicker. It maximizes the distance gained by each step, compensating for not being able to leave the ground and flying, while running.

Modern Form of Running

A common, modern-day, efficient form of running includes the following steps:

1. Keep your back straight, relax your shoulders, and lean forward from the hips slightly. The pelvis is tilted forward slightly so as to not extend your lower back. You want to create a cylindrical flow with the foot, not simply up and down.

2. *Starting position:* Raise your knee up to the point at which your thigh makes a 45-degree angle with your torso, as your foot comes forward slightly. The front of your foot raises slightly, as a lion raises its paws, before grabbing the ground and pushing back (dorsiflexion).

3. *Stance phase:* Your foot will land on the ground (foot strike or foot plant), about 2 to 3 inches in front of your hip. In fact, you want to land with your foot as close to being under your hip as possible. The knee is bent slightly. With your leg firmly under you, your push-off is short.

4. *Recovery phase:* Your calf, from the knee to foot, will naturally fly back and up, with your foot coming up to knee height, and your calf parallel to the ground. Pull your knee back to the starting position.

When your calf is raised behind you and is parallel to the ground, you are effectively shortening the length of the leg you are pulling through. If your leg remained extended, with your foot closer to the ground, it would create a longer pendulum, and more wind resistance. The shorter the leg, the shorter the pendulum you are pulling through. And the shorter the pendulum, the less energy it takes to bring your leg forward. At this point, your position is known as a "four-point stance" because your legs are making the number four, if you look at it from the side. Empirical studies have shown that faster runners run with greater efficiency at a rate of about 180 steps a minute (3 per second), or slightly faster. This is a good stride rate to shoot for. And it works with proper form at any pace or level of intensity.

COACH SAYS ...

To speed up dramatically, raise your arm swing, so your hand comes up to your chin, and knees come up higher as well (a float). This is a great, short-term way to go faster without a dramatic increase in energy output. But you will need strong hip flexor muscles.

Arm swing is also a critical component to proper form. Proper arm swing is identical for running or walking:

• Your elbow is bent and locked the entire time. If you had a cast over your bent elbow, you would still be able to run or walk. It remains open a bit more than 90 degrees. Let's say about 100 degrees is a good position for your forearm and upper arm to meet at the elbow.

• With your elbow at that angle, drop your shoulders and keep them relaxed. If you don't, you will probably start getting a pain just below your neck after a few miles.

- You will notice that your forearms are a bit angled across your stomach. They don't go straight out, perpendicular from your shoulders. You want your arm swing to be natural, and go across your stomach a bit. If your arms don't cross your stomach a bit, and arm swing does go straight out, you will undoubtedly get a pain in your lower back. However, if you were to draw an imaginary line from your nose to your belly button, or the center line of your body, you never want a hand to cross that center line while running or walking. This will throw off your center of balance, making you feel wobbly.

- Rock your arms from the shoulder socket only. Avoid twisting your body, or moving your shoulders forward. This will also throw off your center of balance, and will detract from the stored energy in your core, which is released with each arm swing.

- Swing your hands from the front of your hip to just below your chest. You can even stick your thumbs out to touch your hip, so you know your limit. Glancing down a bit, you can see your hands come up to just below your chest. Try to bring your hands up to the same height with each stride. Often, someone with an imbalance issue will unknowingly run with one hand going up higher than the other. This could indicate an issue which might lead to an injury.

- Hold your wrists straight with your hands relaxed. Your thumb and forefinger may be touching lightly, as if you are gently holding a potato chip. Never clench your hands and make a fist. Tight hands can affect circulation and waste energy. Keep your hands and entire body relaxed.

The Traditional Approach

There are both benefits and drawbacks to the traditional or "old school" approach to marathon running form. This method of form doesn't use a forward lean from the hips. Instead, it uses an upright posture. Jeff Galloway (former pro athlete, running theorist, writer, and coach), a proponent of this concept of run form, also suggests keeping your feet close to the ground while running. He recommends pushing your body forward and not up. This is an important idea. The benefit to this form is that everyone can do it. No matter how inflexible or weak (within reason), everyone can pick their feet off the ground a little. Galloway also urges the majority of runners to avoid most stretches and strength training. He does, however, condone strength training for the advanced competitive runner only.

Understandably, most nonpro athletes generally utilize this approach to marathon running, both with regard to form and not strength training or stretching much. Ironically, the nonpro form may largely have to do with less flexibility and weakness in certain muscle groups. However, most professional athletes and faster nonpro athletes naturally don't use this traditional form of running. The use of this more traditional approach, instead of a more current approach, stems from one major fact: nonpro, age grouper athletes rarely stretch or strengthen their *hip flexor* muscles. In fact, this may be the most overlooked, weak element in running training. Runners might strengthen their quads in front, their hamstrings in the back, and their calves, but rarely does anyone on a nonpro level consider the hip flexors. This is the only muscle which allows you to raise your legs up off the ground. And it is common to injure this muscle group due to weakness. In other words, a runner may benefit from strengthening this muscle group to reduce the risk of injury.

DEFINITION

The **hip flexor** is the muscle group that begins about halfway between the hip and knee, in the front of the leg. It wraps around the side of the hip and connects in the lower back.

In fact, in some cases, runners can have lower back pain from simply having tight hip flexors. The tight muscle group pulls on the lower back, where it connects. This is right where the pain occurs, in a spot at the belt line, on either side, between the spine and hip. The Pelvic Rotation stretch (see Appendix E) will help alleviate this condition.

A major reason people don't have stronger hip flexors, besides the fact that they don't strengthen them, is that most people don't use them effectively in the first place. We learn to run when we are children. First we stand up and take our first steps. Then we try to walk, but realize quickly that if we pick up our knees too high, we fall over. At that point we learn to keep our feet close to the ground in a kind of waddle. As we begin to run, we maintain similar form by simply waddling faster. As we maintain this form, our muscles develop. This causes certain muscles to become stronger, while unused muscles, like the hip flexors, remain weak. That weakness can remain permanent for life, preventing you from raising your knee to a 45-degree angle as you should in running. Running with your feet low to the ground is an easier way to learn to run, but it's inefficient and takes more energy, as it robs you of power and leverage. Getting your knee up to about a 45-degree angle gives you greater leverage, enabling more force in the stance phase (with your foot under you). This allows you to cover more ground with less exertion than running with your feet close to the ground. But you must strengthen those hip flexors first.

You can, over a few weeks, quickly strengthen your hip flexors. This would enable you to pick up your knees, and run more efficiently, with less energy output. The High Knee exercise in Appendix E is the critical movement. This can also be done with ankle weights or a low cable machine and an ankle attachment.

Pose Method

Nicholas Romanov, a running coach and theorist, created a form of running called the "pose method." It's nearly identical to the first method described in the previous section. Romanov suggests many important theories about running form. Possibly the most essential of his theories on form is that gravity must interact with body weight. Proper form will best engage gravity, for the most efficient run. If you could freeze a runner, or take a picture of a runner in action, that runner would create a "key pose." At the end of the recovery phase, when the hand and knee are at the highest levels, this is the major pose he focuses on. The knee should be higher, with the foot clearly off the ground. The upper body should be leaning slightly forward, bending at the hips only. No bend will be found in the back. It will remain straight and relaxed, for fear of injury, and inefficient use of energy.

The only significant difference between the pose method and the modern method described in the previous section is the foot plant. Romanov suggests landing on the front of your foot. Most runners usually land on the heel or back of the foot. He does point to studies indicating far more stress being placed on the knee, from landing on the heel or even the midfoot. Thus, landing on the front part of your foot creates less risk of knee injury, as Romanov concludes. That makes sense, in part, because the foot is able to reduce more of the stress, or absorb more of the shock, of the foot strike. In addition, there is greater emphasis on pushing back, facilitated in part by the knee height.

A simple law of physics states, any action creates an opposite and equal reaction. When you are pushing back with proper form, there is greater forward thrust. When you run with less efficient form, a low knee height creates more downward motion, therefore equal force coming back up at you, and greater risk of injury. Low knee height can come from weak hip flexor muscles, which are the only muscles which raises your knees. Try the High Knee exercise in Appendix E.

One problem, however, is that although there is less stress on the knee from landing more forefoot, there is greater stress on the lower part of the leg. The bulge in your calf is the gastrocnemius muscle. Just below that is the soleus muscle. Your soleus and Achilles will sustain a greater risk of injury if you land toward the front half of your foot, around the ball of your foot and toes (forefoot). If you want to run in this style, doing calf raises on a machine in the gym or raising your heels off the ground can give added strength to this area and lessen the risk of injury. Start by raising both heels, then progress to raising one heel at a time, holding the other foot off the ground, for a set. Try to slowly build to three sets of 30. Building strength and flexibility can take weeks, so be patient.

Changing form takes time. You need to stretch and strengthen muscles that you have not been using. Some simply naturally land forefoot, which is fine. Others would need to develop that ability slowly, or they will have a greater risk of injury from landing in an unnatural way. Occasionally, trying this method for short distances is a good thing. But don't do too much of a good thing without proper work beforehand. This form can make you faster, but it can also cause injuries over long distances if not performed properly.

There are certified coaches who specialize in all of these different forms of running, and they can help you define your own individual best form. Ask around a local running club or running store, or check online.

Chi Running

This form of running is similar to the pose method. It takes the philosophy of T'ai Chi, which stems from the theory of inner power or energy that runs through your entire body. T'ai Chi translates roughly as "supreme ultimate fist," and uses leverage through the joints based on coordination and relaxation rather than muscular tension.

Created by Danny and Katherine Dreyer, Chi running gets its name and concept from T'ai Chi. It starts from the center or your core and radiates outward. The overall concept is similar to the pose method's focus on gravity and your center of balance. Both require a slight forward lean and similar overall form. Working your arms and legs properly causes normal hip rotation. This tugs on certain muscles, creating a rubber band effect. This is where your upper body stores energy, which is released with the next forward arm swing.

The major difference for Chi running comes from the emphasis on the beginning of the recovery phase. Your legs are considered "passive," in that they don't push off, but simply support the rest of your body. The forward lean and use of gravity, in falling forward, allows you to move forward. Your entire body is considered an aligned "column." Your head, shoulders, back, hips, and feet are all aligned, even with the forward lean. This, too, is similar to the pose method. However, Chi running focuses on a midfoot strike or foot plant.

COACH SAYS ...

If you were running on sand, "leaving clean prints" is an important attribute of Chi running. You see the entire shoe evenly imprinted in the sand, showing a midfoot strike and no push off. Practicing on sand is recommended.

Assuming that there are no stones or broken glass on the beach, running barefoot on the sand can be a fun, effective workout. Unless the sand is packed down, you will find it a bit more challenging to run, as your foot will sink in a bit. Make sure you leave "clean prints," landing with your entire foot (midfoot), and don't allow your heels to sink in. Otherwise, you can injure the back of your ankle (Achilles and soleus). Also, beaches are usually angled toward the water. With or without shoes, try to run where it is flatter, as the angle can cause an imbalance and possibly an injury. Angled street surfaces will have the same effect.

Chi also focuses on your leg bending at the knee, swinging back and up behind you. This is said to counter-balance your forward upper body movement with lower movement behind you. This is an important thing to focus on. With the modern form of running that we described earlier in this chapter, this leg backswing occurs naturally from the backward thrust of the leg, which is a slightly different focus than Chi running recommends. However, there are enormous similarities among this form and pose and Chi running forms.

There is an important psychological component to Chi running as well. Simply, you need to focus internally and not externally. Feel your emotional and physical balance as you run. Blocking out external stresses is critical. The Chi psychological focus on balance can also be used in everyday life.

Improving Speed

We've already talked about some different components of running faster, such as achieving flexibility (see Chapter 7) and using strength training (see Chapter 8). However, there is another way to become faster. Greater muscle recruitment or simply getting more muscles to fire makes you faster. In Chapter 8, we discussed fast- and slow-twitch muscle fibers. Fast twitch make you go faster, and slow twitch make you go farther. The fast oxidative glycolytic muscle fibers make you go faster and farther. Though you can't train more fast-twitch fibers (speed) to engage, you can train more fast oxidative glycolytic (speed and distance) and slow-twitch (distance) muscle fibers to engage. The more muscles firing, the stronger you are, and the faster you can go.

We highlighted the benefits of aerobic running, meaning low heart rate or slow runs, earlier in the chapter. Those engage your slow-twitch muscle fibers. The more you fire those specific slow-twitch muscles, the more they will fire at a higher intensity as well. However, we have yet to cover speed work, or higher heart rate work, which helps to raise the anaerobic threshold and train the fast oxidative glycolytic muscles to engage. Engaging these faster muscles regularly later in the season with higher-intensity work (speed work, etc.) will cause them to engage, even when going slower (low intensity). And the more muscles that fire, the stronger you are; and the stronger you are, the faster you can run. That's the idea of "muscle recruitment."

Track Work

Track workouts are usually done at a high level of intensity, so there is greater risk of injury. Make sure that you have a strong aerobic base, and significant strength and flexibility before beginning high-intensity track work.

Track workouts make you faster in several ways. These higher-intensity workouts engage more of the faster muscle fibers, making you stronger. You will also teach your body to remove waste products more efficiently, allowing you to run faster and/ or longer without muscle discomfort. These high-intensity workouts also raise your heart rate to the point at which you stop burning fat as fuel (anaerobic threshold). In doing this, your body will learn to burn more fat and less glycogen at a higher heart rate, allowing you to go faster longer.

MILE MARKER

Using a track for higher-intensity sessions can help you control the workout by enabling you to see how far you have gone and how fast. However, modern pace/ distance watches can do the same.

These threshold runs are higher heart rate runs, perfect for marathon training. They can be performed on a track or not. There are generally two types of threshold runs that are designed to train your body to run longer at higher levels of intensity:

- "Tempo" runs are generally about 20 minutes at an intensity which you can maintain for about an hour. Going for longer than that can also be beneficial, but you have to build up to it.

- "Cruise intervals" are shorter, but slightly more intense forms of tempo runs. These can vary from about 3 to 15 minutes per interval, with 1 minute of recovery following each.

If you are doing mile repeats, take a minute break. For 2-mile intervals, take two minutes, etc. Try not to do the same workout too often or your benefits will diminish. (These general track workouts can be attributed to Jack Daniels, Ph.D.; see Chapter 10.)

Simply stated, running faster teaches you to run faster. Do you need track workouts or any high-intensity work to run a marathon? No. Marathoners don't benefit from doing a track workout that is tailored for a sprinter. Sprinting for distances of 100 meters or less doesn't do a whole lot for marathoners. That is too high an intensity to work the energy systems that will benefit us. You may recruit, or engage, more muscle fibers at this intensity, but you won't raise your anaerobic threshold.

Speed Play ("Fartlek")

Fartlek means "speed play" in Swedish. It's the perfect method, especially for a beginner, to train to get faster. In fartlek, you are engaging different muscle fibers all the time, and learning to shift gears rather quickly. In addition, you completely control what you do on the workout. Someone else's track workout won't be running you into the ground because it's beyond your ability. To perform this workout, pick an object that you can see. Next, pick a level of intensity (high, low, or in between) at which to run to that object. Now do it. Before you reach that object, pick another object and level of intensity. Now continue on, without stopping, to that next object. Continue this for a period of scheduled time, and you have completed a fartlek workout.

Shorter "Practice" Races and Runs

Let's face it: too much of a good thing is too much. The same can be said for all races, both short and long. They can be fun ways to get used to the longer marathon race, if you don't put too much pressure on yourself to perform. Races like 5Ks and 10Ks can help you become more efficient and better able to handle the higher speeds at which these shorter races are usually run. These races are too long for sprinting, so they keep your intensity level high, but not too high. The excitement can also motivate you to go faster and farther. Just organize them into your schedule, so you have a bit of a taper before and after. But don't do too many of them, especially in your early training season.

Remember, racing your training isn't appropriate and can lead to injury. Often faster runners will want to compete with each other throughout training, but you cannot speed up your training. You can't race through it or get through it any faster. Slower aerobic runs are critical, and so is completing the scheduled training plan without burnout. So please don't race too much of your training, and keep most of it at the prescribed level.

Half Marathon Races

Half marathons are now becoming popular and respected entities all by themselves, often with huge turnouts. Many half marathons can boast registration numbers approaching those of full marathons. The inaugural Los Angeles Rock 'n' Roll Half Marathon had 14,000 participants. Given that so many factors are similar to a full marathon, these can be fun experiences to get you ready for the full marathon event. They can be a good test of how you are doing with your training and can train you to focus on your own race, not everyone else's. You can also confront the very common desire to start out too fast. If it falls in the right time frame in your training schedule, you can use a half marathon as a real-world training run.

Fun Runs

The number one rule of running is to have fun. Focused, specific work is important, especially later in the training season. However, you still need to enjoy yourself. Fun runs are generally organized group runs in which people run together in the mountains, or around a lake, or simply through a neighborhood. No one really takes notice of a winner, but often these can become competitive, especially at the end. For this reason, they can also be motivating to get you to go faster and increase your overall speed.

YELLOW LIGHT

Because there's no supervision or coaching, fun runs can be a bit reckless. Be careful not to beat yourself up too much.

How to Use Pace Charts

Obviously, hills and heat alter your pace. Pace in itself is meaningless, and maintaining a steady pace can be destructive with heat and hilly conditions. Therefore, a pace chart can give you perspective, but you need not follow it exactly, especially on hilly terrain or in warm climates. In fact, we discuss several reasons to alter your pace in our race strategy section in Chapter 15. There is little reason at this stage to try to hit every mile at the exact time listed, but knowing the per-mile goal pace could keep you on track. You might create a paper wrist band with the numbers.

In the chart on page 131, the first column of numbers on the left represent each mile of the marathon. The top line going across lists average pace times in 30-second increments from 7 minutes per mile to 13:30 per mile. If you find your per-mile average pace at the top and follow it down, you will find the average time needed to stay on pace.

For example, if your pace is 9 minutes per mile, you should expect to hit the 3-mile mark in 27 minutes. If you stay on pace (follow the column of numbers to the bottom), you will finish the marathon in 3:56. You may want start out a bit slower than that during the first few miles of the marathon, but this gives you an idea of where you stand with respect to finish time. Similarly, someone who keeps to a 12:30 average pace will finish a marathon in a little under five and a half hours.

You can also use the chart to interpret your progress. That is, if you plan to run a 10–minute-per-mile pace but you cross the 5-mile marker in 55 minutes, you know you have actually averaged 11 minutes per mile. (Pace strategy is described in detail in Chapter 15.) Don't forget, with hills and heat, sticking exactly to this chart is ill-advised and can be dangerous.

Keep a Running Journal

Keeping a daily running journal to track how you are doing can show you patterns in your training performance and may allow you to draw conclusions you wouldn't otherwise see. For example, if you feel tired for a long period, you need to taper down or take a day off. If you go too long without enough sleep and constantly feel fatigued, you will know that a lack of sleep is the real problem. Often marathoners don't think they have the ability to do better, but when they look at a journal they can see patterns and better understand where they went wrong.

In your journal, include notes on the following:

- Distance or time (workload)
- Intensity
- Enjoyment or attitude/mood
- Waking heart rate
- Exercise heart rate

- Early morning weight
- Hours of sleep
- Climate and altitude

Miles	7:00	7:30	8:00	8:30	9:00	9:30	10:00	10:30	11:00	11:30	12:00	12:30	13:00	13:30
1	7:00	7:30	8:00	8:30	9:00	9:30	10:00	10:30	11:00	11:30	12:00	12:30	13:00	13:30
2	14:00	15:00	16:00	17:00	18:00	19:00	20:00	21:00	22:00	23:00	24:00	25:00	26:00	27:00
3	21:00	22:30	24:00	25:30	27:00	28:30	30:00	31:30	33:00	34:30	36:00	37:30	39:00	40:30
4	28:00	30:00	32:00	34:00	36:00	38:00	40:00	42:00	44:00	46:00	48:00	50:00	52:00	54:00
5	35:00	37:30	40:00	42:30	45:00	47:30	50:00	52:30	55:00	57:30	1:00:00	1:02:30	1:05:00	1:07:30
6	42:00	45:00	48:00	51:00	54:00	57:00	1:00:00	1:03:00	1:06:00	1:09:00	1:12:00	1:15:00	1:18:00	1:21:00
7	49:00	52:30	56:00	59:30	1:03:00	1:06:30	1:10:00	1:13:30	1:17:00	1:20:30	1:24:00	1:27:30	1:31:00	1:34:30
8	56:00	1:00:00	1:04:00	1:08:00	1:12:00	1:16:00	1:20:00	1:24:00	1:28:00	1:32:00	1:36:00	1:40:00	1:44:00	1:48:00
9	1:03:00	1:07:30	1:12:00	1:16:30	1:21:00	1:25:30	1:30:00	1:34:30	1:39:00	1:43:30	1:48:00	1:52:30	1:57:00	2:01:30
10	1:10:00	1:15:00	1:20:00	1:25:00	1:30:00	1:35:00	1:40:00	1:45:00	1:50:00	1:55:00	2:00:00	2:05:00	2:10:00	2:15:00
11	1:17:00	1:22:30	1:28:00	1:33:30	1:39:00	1:44:30	1:50:00	1:55:30	2:01:00	2:06:30	2:12:00	2:17:30	2:23:00	2:28:30
12	1:24:00	1:30:00	1:36:00	1:42:00	1:48:00	1:54:00	2:00:00	2:06:00	2:12:00	2:18:00	2:24:00	2:30:00	2:36:00	2:42:00
13	1:31:00	1:37:30	1:44:00	1:50:30	1:57:00	2:03:30	2:10:00	2:16:30	2:23:00	2:29:30	2:36:00	2:42:30	2:49:00	2:55:30
14	1:38:00	1:45:00	1:52:00	1:59:00	2:06:00	2:13:00	2:20:00	2:27:00	2:34:00	2:41:00	2:48:00	2:55:00	3:02:00	3:09:00
15	1:45:00	1:52:30	2:00:00	2:07:30	2:15:00	2:22:30	2:30:00	2:37:30	2:45:00	2:52:30	3:00:00	3:07:30	3:15:00	3:22:30
16	1:52:00	2:00:00	2:08:00	2:16:00	2:24:00	2:32:00	2:40:00	2:48:00	2:56:00	3:04:00	3:12:00	3:20:00	3:28:00	3:36:00
17	1:59:00	2:07:30	2:16:00	2:24:30	2:33:00	2:41:30	2:50:00	2:58:30	3:07:00	3:15:30	3:24:00	3:32:30	3:41:00	3:49:30
18	2:06:00	2:15:00	2:24:00	2:33:00	2:42:00	2:51:00	3:00:00	3:09:00	3:18:00	3:27:00	3:36:00	3:45:00	3:54:00	4:03:00
19	2:13:00	2:22:30	2:32:00	2:41:30	2:51:00	3:00:30	3:10:00	3:19:30	3:29:00	3:38:30	3:48:00	3:57:30	4:07:00	4:16:30
20	2:20:00	2:30:00	2:40:00	2:50:00	3:00:00	3:10:00	3:20:00	3:30:00	3:40:00	3:50:00	4:00:00	4:10:00	4:20:00	4:30:00
21	2:27:00	2:37:30	2:48:00	2:58:30	3:09:00	3:19:30	3:30:00	3:40:30	3:51:00	4:01:30	4:12:00	4:22:30	4:33:00	4:43:30
22	2:34:00	2:45:00	2:56:00	3:07:00	3:18:00	3:29:00	3:40:00	3:51:00	4:02:00	4:13:00	4:24:00	4:35:00	4:46:00	4:57:00
23	2:41:00	2:52:30	3:04:00	3:15:30	3:27:00	3:38:30	3:50:00	4:01:30	4:13:00	4:24:30	4:36:00	4:47:30	4:59:00	5:10:30
24	2:48:00	3:00:00	3:12:00	3:24:00	3:36:00	3:48:00	4:00:00	4:12:00	4:24:00	4:36:00	4:48:00	5:00:00	5:12:00	5:24:00
25	2:55:00	3:07:30	3:20:00	3:32:30	3:45:00	3:57:30	4:10:00	4:22:30	4:35:00	4:47:30	5:00:00	5:12:30	5:25:00	5:37:30
26	3:02:00	3:15:00	3:28:00	3:41:00	3:54:00	4:07:00	4:20:00	4:33:00	4:46:00	4:59:00	5:12:00	5:25:00	5:38:00	5:51:00
26.22	3:03:32	3:16:39	3:29:45	3:42:52	3:55:58	4:09:05	4:22:12	4:35:18	4:48:25	5:01:31	5:14:38	5:27:45	5:40:51	5:53:58

If your waking heart rate is higher, or morning weight gets too low, you are probably overtraining. If you keep good notes, you will see patterns in your performance and how it relates to the other factors you record. This helps you tailor your future training runs so that you improve your efficiency and stay as healthy as possible.

The Least You Need to Know

- For your first runs of the season, find a flat area such as a track and intersperse running with walking.
- Different running forms exist, which can lead to greater or less efficiency depending on your individual needs. Coaches and resources are available to help you choose.
- To improve your speed, build efficiency with low heart rate work, and then do high-intensity speed work on a track or flat route.
- Shorter practice runs—such as a 5K, 10K, or half marathon—can be a good experience. But don't overdo a good thing, and don't race others on your training runs.
- When using a pace chart, remember that intensity is more important than pace, and it must constantly be tailored to your running environment.
- A running journal can help you see patterns in your training so you can improve and also stay as healthy as possible.

Choosing a Training Program

Chapter 10

In This Chapter

- The simplest of training programs: random training
- What's involved in organized training
- Creating a training program tailored for you
- The importance of peaking and tapering

You need to choose a training program that suits your ability. A pro athlete, or even a semi-pro or college-level athlete, could be running 80 to 100 miles a week or more for a few weeks. Most of that would be at low intensity. Later in the season they would be doing more speed work on a track, threshold runs (higher intensity than a marathon), and strength training. A first-time marathoner wouldn't be doing any kind of mileage remotely close to 100 miles per week. That would mean a guaranteed injury for the beginner. Similarly, the beginner would probably not be doing steady speed work on a track. A beginner's intensity level would not be that high, also for fear of injury.

However, there are similarities that all athletes share, all marathon theorists share, and all training programs share. For the most part, healthy athletes all respond to training in similar and predictable ways. Marathon theorists and training programs all recommend building to a peak, and a final taper before the actual marathon event. Beyond that, there are numerous differences. Some athletes will require individualized training plans, and some training concepts and programs are more efficient than others. However, any schedule or training plan demands that you're able to do it without injury. In other words, you need to pick a program that is appropriate for you and tailored to your athletic ability.

Random Training

There are primarily two types of marathon training programs. The first is referred to as random training. This is the simplest of training programs, because there really is no set schedule at all. A person training this way might simply wake up and decide what they are going to do that day in terms of exercise. You could choose a 6-mile faster-than-marathon race pace tempo run, with some strength training afterward. Or it could be a 15-mile aerobic run, or you could simply stay home and get more sleep. The choice would depend on your level of energy.

Pros of random training include the following:

- It is flexible for people with variable, unpredictable, or stressful schedules.

- It is changeable for those who do not like to be tied to a specific routine.

- It is adaptable to varying levels of energy.

- It offers better protection against overtraining—if you are tired the day after a workout (a sign of overtraining), you can cut back.

As you might expect, there are some pitfalls to avoid with this training plan.

Cons of random training include the following:

- It can be difficult to track your improvement precisely.

- A novice may not yet understand how much is too much (or too little).

- If you miss too many training runs, you lose your endurance base and have to slowly build back up again.

- Less accountability can mean less discipline.

- Cutting back too much can cause you to lose the physiological benefits of consistent training such as greater strength, energy, and VO_2 Max.

- Your confidence may be affected if you fall too far behind.

Although random training can be the secret to success for those with difficult schedules, it requires more dedication and management than a structured training plan. Those who are successful at random training have a strong sense of what they need to do to peak or build to the farthest distance or intensity necessary in training.

Most of what they do exercise-wise is done with that peak in mind. In addition, to use this plan successfully you need to be attuned to your own body. If you are tired or stressed out, you need to recognize that. And you need to know what your body would experience with a specific workout. Would you be taking on too much? Would you be exhausted the next day? If so, you're overtraining. If you were not experienced enough or didn't know how exercises would affect you, you would not know how much to do when.

As with any training program, random training is not for everyone, and is generally more appropriate for more experienced athletes. A novice marathoner would benefit from an organized daily training schedule. That schedule may have to change from time to time to meet shifting demands, but the structure would help the inexperienced novice.

Organized Training Plans

As we've mentioned, the organized training approach is a better choice for beginners because it gives some needed structure and guidance to their training. There is a lot of variety with organized training. In fact, scientific research and general knowledge have altered the face of training quite a bit in recent years. Some training programs can be quite complex, built upon complicated ideas. On the other hand, some training, as with the Three Day a Week plan described later in the chapter, can be simple, with a focus on greater time for recovery. The key is to pick a plan that is right for you and your current level of ability, but is also strongly founded in science.

One caveat: training has changed enormously over the years, and continues to change, as science figures out new ways to make people more efficient athletes. Be aware of this and don't pick an antiquated, ineffective program.

COACH SAYS …

Kenyan runners' success is probably based on several factors. They train harder than Americans with speed work, and go longer distances at high elevations, running in small groups. They live for free in training camps down in the Rift Valley, at low elevation, where everything is provided for them. Their lives are all about organized training. If U.S. runners had their lifestyle, we would win marathons, too. Proper training and lifestyle is the key to success.

Traditional Schedules

Many nonprofessional athletes use this system to train for their marathons. It is an antiquated training system that does not use modern science to the fullest. It includes a *lateral build* without regular week-long tapers throughout. (We cannot recommend this system, but we explain it here due to its persistent popularity.) This type of schedule will increase the risk of injury due to depleted hormone levels such as human growth hormone (HGH). It will also decrease your ability to reach your maximum potential due to a less efficient aerobic system, general overtraining, and less effective taper.

DEFINITION

A **lateral build** is a training theory that uses a straight, linear increase in weekly mileage. Each week the runner's energy output goes up a bit. There is no tapering until the end of the training season.

Currently, we can't calculate the energy output by a single runner. Cyclists, thanks to the mechanical motion of their bicycles, have that ability with power meters, which measure their power output at any given moment, or as an average. Unfortunately, runners do not have any such device. However, if you could create a bar graph with a single runner's energy output each week, in this type of training you would see a steadily increasing total. That is, you could draw a straight line from lower left to upper right, connecting the total energy output for each week.

This lateral build makes up the basic training for most nonpro athletes today and breaks down weekly training as follows:

- Generally utilizes increasingly longer runs at marathon race pace intensity, usually done on the weekend.

- All other mid-week, shorter runs are also at marathon race pace.

- Often includes some mid-week speed work of different types, based on the level of the athlete and the different coaches' choices.

- Ends training season with some taper, nearly always a three-week step taper. That is where you step down the volume each week by a similar percentage. See "Types of Final Taper" later in this chapter.

This training method has brought nearly all who use it successfully to the finish line. Sadly, the athlete can't become significantly faster or more efficient by using this lateral build type of schedule. For one reason, the athlete has no interval week-long taper to increase hormonal levels and decrease cortisol levels. Cortisol, often called the "stress hormone," can decrease glucose (fuel) use in the cells, making the runner less efficient. Emotional and physical stresses can increase cortisol levels, tiring the athlete. Many such athletes, after long weeks of training without week-long interval tapers describe feeling tired all the time, or worse, not even wanting to run for a few weeks at the end of the training season. In this case, a reduction in hormones has occurred and testosterone has plummeted, leaving the runner without motivation. This is severe overtraining, and leads to a permanent reduction in ability for that season.

Also with a lateral build, there is little true controlled aerobic intensity (slower than marathon pace) training. At higher mileage there is a significant build-up of lactic acid, hydrogen, and general waste products. This is due to the fewer capillary veins and arteries, a result of the complete lack of less intense aerobic runs.

Recently, a pace group from the LA Roadrunners training program was polled. Years previously, they had done all of their runs at race pace, with a traditional lateral build. Nearly all of the 80 nonprofessionals polled said that by a mile 18 water station stop, they found it extremely difficult to get started. Their legs felt as if they were turning to rocks if they stopped running for too long. Conversely, after their current season with nearly 12 weeks of those much-needed aerobic runs, almost none of them had anything close to that feeling at the same mile 18 water station. They were clearly more efficient at ridding their bodies of waste product. This improvement had occurred during the same overall period of months of training. All other elements of training conditions were the same. Training was done on the same course, with similar weather conditions, and at the same time of day. You could not deny the dramatic change within the group that utilized the less intense aerobic runs absent in the lateral build method.

Variable Intensity Training

Variable intensity training is a training method for nonpro (age grouper) athletes that incorporates many of the ideas used by professional and semi-pro athletes, theorized by coach Dr. Jack Daniels, Arthur Lydiard, and others (discussed a bit later in the chapter). Yet, the nonpro isn't going to be able to log the kind of mileage the pro or even college athlete is expected to do. What follows, therefore, is a training plan based on their theories which is tailored to the nonpro athlete.

It all begins with about 12 weeks of aerobic work for the marathon, also referred to as "base training." Our example in Appendix D shows eight weeks of aerobic work for the half marathon training. This aerobic work would include all distances run, run/walked, or walked, mid-week and weekends for nearly all of that period. For the marathon, this aerobic work builds to a 20-mile training run. Volume (time or distance) is then cut to less than half of the 20 miles. However, now the intensity is increased across the board. Mid-week runs now include higher than marathon intensity efforts, including speed work, tempo runs, threshold runs, and hill training. Although the weekend long runs begin at less than half the distance or time of the last 20-mile aerobic run, now efforts will be at race pace. This build in race pace mileage with less distance but higher intensity mid-week, will build for the rest of the season until the final taper. Then the exponential taper is used, which is described later in the chapter. Incremental or interval tapers are also used throughout this training program. Every fourth week is considered a "cut back week." This means a significant reduction of volume for one week, once every fourth week of training. Intensity and frequency of workouts remain the same during these week-long tapers while volume is cut. Such tapers are explained in greater detail later in this chapter.

The City Of Angels Half Marathon used these same concepts, and a schedule similar to the half marathon schedule in Appendix D, in their training program for two years. During that time, about 60 of the 85+ sized group were polled on their results. About half of those polled had done a half marathon previously. From that experienced segment, there was a *P.R. (Personal Record)* reported by better than 90 percent of that group that had used this training program. The same statistic held for both years, and included a few who had a P.R. both years. In other words, they performed better during both progressive years of training for the same race course. That half marathon has become the new Los Angeles Rock 'n' Roll Half Marathon, and hopefully the training model will return. However, the Los Angeles Marathon's training program, the Roadrunners, currently uses this method, and so does USA Marathon Training.

DEFINITION

P.R. or **Personal Record** (or P.B. or Personal Best) describes the fastest race finish ever, by an individual athlete, at a specific distance.

Jeff Galloway Method

Since his days as an Olympic athlete in the early 1970s, Jeff Galloway has motivated countless "ordinary" people to run. He has also created a sensible training system supported by volumes of books, training groups in over 90 different cities, running schools and retreats, free newsletters, and blogs. Possibly more than any other single coach, he has enabled the nonprofessional to finish marathons and endurance races, with an up to 98 percent success rate, as he claims. Thousands of those have become fast enough to qualify for Boston.

His walk/run approach to distance training is the cornerstone of many a successful training group, and it is most beneficial for slower marathoners. He claims walk breaks allow people with bad joints to run, with increased energy, less fatigue, and better results. This method erases fatigue even on very long runs and has improved average marathon times by over 13 minutes for runners who previously used other training methods, claims Galloway. This is achieved by having the runner walk for a certain amount of time each mile, which gets the heart rate down and maintains that reservoir of glycogen. The run-walk-run ratios are guided by the runner's pace per mile. An example of a run-walk-run ratio is run 3 minutes and then walk 1 minute, which equals a 3:1 ratio.

Base training ("relaxed, easy, and comfortable" runs) make up 50 percent of Galloway's training plans. The idea of feeling-based runs, as opposed to using mechanical devices such as heart rate monitors, is central to this system. Repetition and threshold intensity work is also recommended. Speed work should be 35 percent of total training time, with hill training 15 percent.

Starting slow during the race is important. For every second you run too fast in the first 3 miles, Galloway suggests, you will lose approximately 10 seconds at the end. Based on his research, he doesn't advocate stretching or leg-strengthening exercises. He uses a three- or four-day-a-week plan, and promotes a general do-less methodology, especially for older runners. He doesn't recommend pushing for more on race day, but to enjoy the psychological and health benefits of a running lifestyle. For more information on Galloway's training system, check out *Galloway's Book on Running* (see Appendix B). His free newsletter is available at www.jeffgalloway.com.

Jack Daniels and Arthur Lydiard Methods

Sorry, this section has absolutely nothing to do with drinking the famous Tennessee whiskey. Jack Daniels, Ph.D., is considered by many top coaches to be the best training theorist today for the longer distances, 800 meters (half mile) to the marathon and beyond.

Some of his guidance can be attributed to the work of previous coaches, such as Tudor Bompa. Many important scientific discoveries about training and physiology came from the last few decades of the Soviet Bloc countries. When Soviet trainers wanted a tissue or blood sample from one of their athletes, that athlete submitted or could opt to live in Siberia. Not exactly fair ways to collect data, but many modern training ideas were born under this athletic program. The idea of peaking and utilizing different stimuli (different workouts) came from the Soviet Bloc. Around the same time, Arthur Lydiard, a coach in New Zealand, was working with distance runners specifically. Lydiard's ideas and teaching went on to build some of the top Olympic and pro runners in his day.

> **MILE MARKER**
>
> Tudor Bompa, Ph.D., brought "periodization" to the west using different exercises during certain periods or phases of training. Arthur Lydiard began to use this concept of periodization for distance runners, building them aerobically, then adding intensity, with tapered intervals in between.

Lydiard and Daniels share many key concepts. Among them, both theorized that you can't do all your training at race level intensity. Or "don't race your training," as coach and marathon world record holder Rod Dixon preaches. Dixon's coach, his brother, was trained by Lydiard, who came to their town once a year. The idea is you do not want to leave your best race on the training track, as Daniels warned. Training too hard leaves the athlete exhausted, overtrained, and unable to perform at peak level. Dixon reminds us of how many in his area would run track mid-week faster than he. Or outrun him on training runs. But when it came time for the actual race, they were exhausted and he beat them. A consistent violator of this rule, and a runner who Dixon beat often, was Steve Prefontaine. "Pre" also went out too fast at the beginning of his races, which also caused him to slow down and fall behind. The more, more, more approach to training, in which you beat yourself senseless as often as possible, really doesn't work. Sadly, there seems to be an epidemic of this type of training among nonpro, age groupers.

Lydiard suggested his male pro athletes run 100 miles a week, but at a lower level of intensity. Each easy (aerobic) run was "more money in the bank," suggested Lydiard. This would work out to 20 miles one day and 10 miles the next, he theorized. Daniels suggests similarly training hard on one day and easy the next. A plan such as this provides some recovery on the easy in between days. In fact, Daniels recommends, if you're still tired, you may need to take the entire day off. Again, please do not run 100 miles in a week, unless you're at a pro or semi-professional level and have built up to it slowly.

Daniels suggests that the runner can improve with intensity training workouts such as "repetition training" and "threshold training." Briefly, repetition training would be shorter, intense intervals, which are repeated after a brief recovery period. Threshold training would usually be longer than repetition runs, performed at higher than race intensity, but nowhere near the distance. These aren't considered long-distance runs. A more in-depth explanation of intensity training is found in Chapter 9.

In a nutshell, both coaches generally suggest building, peaking, and tapering at an appropriate level for the individual athlete. Both tended to gear their training levels to the pro or semi-professional athlete, who competed to win. Those of us who are nonpros can still benefit from these training concepts.

Possibly one of the best advancements in training attributed to Daniels may be his VDOT (based on VO_2 Max) assessments. His VDOT charts can be found in his book, *Daniels' Running Formula* (see Appendix B). The genius of his VDOT chart is that you do not have to spend a lot of money to get blood testing or VO_2 Max testing. With his work you can know how fast to run on flat ground, or average pace, at appropriate intensity levels, for specific training. His calculations are surprisingly accurate. He has created a chart on which you can look up your single 1-mile best time, or 5K best, or other distance, and see what you can be expected to do on several other distances, up to marathon distance. He is using the variable intensity training described earlier, but assigns average paces to everyone for his or her different levels of intensity training. For instance, if you can run a 4:49 marathon or 1-mile best at 9:11, you have a VDOT of 30. This VDOT translates to an "easy" or aerobic run at an 10:23 per mile pace. That would mean doing longer aerobic runs at about 1:23 slower (10:23) than marathon race pace (8:57), for this level of ability. And your threshold mile pace would be at 8:22. A "Threshold Run" is done above anaerobic threshold, which is also referred to as VO_2 Max. VO_2 Max is the term which Daniels uses consistently.

A 4:22 best marathon, for another example, would be a VDOT of 34. This would translate to an "easy" or aerobic run pace of 11:32 per mile, and a threshold run at 9:20. That's about a minute and a half slower for that level's aerobic runs. Unfortunately, Daniels didn't continue his chart of calculations slower than a 9:11 single best mile. For that reason, many of us nonpros will not be able to benefit from his calculations. However, they do give us a good idea of where our training could be, and what we can expect from longer or shorter races. In addition, Daniels' work shows us at which pace to train for different intensities. He continues to be considered one of the top distance running coaches in the United States.

Training Three Days a Week

Falling under some of the theories of Daniels and his predecessors, a three-day-a-week training plan has emerged. This would be used by us nonpro athletes only. It suggests that you only train three days a week. As with Daniels' plans, your run days would be split up with an easy day in between. Though in this case, that easy day would be a day completely off. Two of those days would be intensity training, and the third run day each week would be going for longer distances.

This plan has had some successful statistics, which make sense. However, it doesn't really allow for a consistent aerobic or base training period, early on. In addition, with two days off in a row, a standing theory is that you lose 1 percent off your endurance base during that two-day-off period. In other words, your muscles and additional capillaries begin to atrophy, and mitochondria shrink, among other things. Keep in mind that this is an insignificant percentage of loss. A 30-minute aerobic run would essentially keep that loss from occurring. Yet, there are some who need more recovery time and would benefit from the extra day off. With the additional rest provided for in this training plan, they would have increased energy and would have restored their depleted hormonal levels. So it's all a balance based on your individual needs. This plan is touted as being appropriate for all nonpros. However, the three-day-a-week plan is probably best for beginners and older people, both of which may not recover as quickly.

Creating Your Own Training Program

Before creating your own training schedule for a marathon, you need to honestly assess where you are in your running ability. Ask yourself two critical questions:

- What was the last long run you did within the last few weeks?

- Have you ever done a marathon before?

Your answers determine how much preparation time you will need, including how much general and run-specific work you will need. For general training, do you need more strength training before you even begin running? Are there other things you need to do before running, such as walking longer walks, or hiking up hills? You will absolutely need to build an aerobic base, with its benefits of increased numbers of capillaries and mitochondria. This can be done with weeks of aerobic or low heart rate work. Generally, that can take approximately 12 weeks.

However, if, for example, you have spent the entire summer doing aerobic work and strength training, you may be able to jump into the Building Phases. This is where you build with intensity. A common mistake is to build to a peak too early in the season. If you're capable of doing a few longer 20 milers, then possibly jumping into high mileage early on could work. However, if you don't have the ability to do a few 20 milers over a few weeks without enormous fatigue, this could be a disaster. You have to have done the type of mileage recently that you want to start with. You cannot simply jump up into higher mileage. This would be a textbook case of risking injury. We all need to build up slowly, with an approximate 10 percent increase each week.

Build each week with a longer aerobic run. In other words, you're building volume at low heart rate, generally to about 20 miles. All mid-week runs at this base phase are also entirely aerobic. More than the weekend longer runs, knowing your ability, and how much you can take, will determine how much you can do mid-week.

Once you have your strength, flexibility, and aerobic base down, then you can begin to build with intensity. In order to do this, you will need to cut way back in volume (distance or time), and begin again with your increasing longer runs at race pace intensity. Usually these are the longer runs done on the weekend. Mid-week runs are often at higher levels of intensity than race pace, but shorter. And they aren't performed as fast as you can go (maximal level). Keep in mind, you still don't know your actual minutes-per-mile marathon race pace. If you label yourself as a specific pace, you're limiting the outcome of your race. Pace is meaningless and you can only begin to estimate what that pace on race day will be. To make things worse, if you have a hot race day, you need to slow it all down anyway. So even then, pace is quite relative to temperature and terrain, and is not specific. Heart rate, and knowing (with blood testing) your thresholds of lactate threshold and anaerobic threshold is a better indicator. Daniels' VDOT, which helps calculate pace at each level of intensity and distance, is another good indicator.

Finally, you will need an interval taper, once every fourth week, for one full week, and you will need an exponential taper at the end for at least two weeks, if not three. Tapers are discussed later in this chapter.

Schedule to Fit Your Lifestyle

The one-size-fits-all schedule does not fit all. And once you find or create a schedule that works, it'll not work all the time. This is the great truth about schedules. But at least start with something that will fit your lifestyle. If you know Fridays are stressful at work, keep that as a day off from all exercise. If Wednesdays are stressful, but you have time, keep that as an easy run day. Build or alter a schedule where every other day is an easy or off day. Or try to compromise with your partner, that one day you'll train hard, and the next day you'll be home cleaning up and watching the children. Sometimes you have to create a schedule with your partner to make your own schedule work. Remember, every fourth week is a taper week. This might be a week when you can take a vacation and do less exercise. Maybe even stay out a bit late and have some fun, kicking up your heels. However, once you have organized everything, and made everyone around you happy and in sync, there is still one unfathomable truth to deal with: stuff happens. Flexibility is key.

COACH SAYS ...

If you feel fatigued the day after a hard workout, cut back on the time or distance of your workout. If you are still tired a day later, cut back on that day, too. If you can run 30 minutes every other day, you'll maintain your entire endurance base.

Change Your Program as Needed

You need to be able to recover after every workout, before the next. If you are tired the next day, you did too much the day before. That is the key litmus test for overtraining. And acting upon the way you feel each day may be the key to making a schedule work on a daily basis. Remember, no one schedule fits all. And the schedule that is right for you will still need regular assessments and change. That is what coaches do constantly with clients. They ask how they feel, and then they change that athlete's schedule accordingly.

Besides the vigilance against overtraining, things happen in life. Added stress at home or at work, a cold or sickness, business conflicts, bad weather that makes training outside impossible, or any number of issues can mean a schedule change. Remember Daniels' concept: never put two tough workouts back to back. Obviously, what is tough for one athlete may be easy for a different athlete. A 10-mile aerobic run may be easy for one person, but longer than the other athlete has ever gone. Unless they are different workouts, and you can recover from each completely, don't put two possibly tough workouts back to back. In other words, you might have a repetition workout with intense intervals one day, and a hill run at tempo pace the next. That would be only if you recovered from the first and there would be a recovery day after the second. Even then it would still probably be ill advised. A day off or easy run in between would be a better choice.

Some pro athletes will do three tough days in a row, but they will all be different, and recovery after each is still critical. It might be something like an intense tempo run the first day, with an aerobic 10 miler the second day, and an intense repetition workout the third. Again, you need to know your capacity for training and recovery. And when you exceed that to a point of fatigue the next day, then things need to change—this is critical.

Tapering and Peaking

The key to a good schedule requires a well-timed *peak*, followed by an effective *taper*. Regardless of the training program or schedule you end up using, you want to reach your peak in volume (time or distance) and intensity work (heart rate) just before your final taper for your race. If you time it wrong and hit your peak too early or late, you will have less energy on race day. You benefit from a well-designed taper. Building to a peak can deplete several important biological factors in your body. These can include depleted or damaged muscle tissue, depleted hormones, and an increase in cortisol, which is detrimental. When you taper, you recover and alter those factors, which makes you more efficient on race day. You can determine the amount of taper you need by analyzing how quickly you recover after your second-longest race pace run. This can give you a general idea for your first marathon of how long you need for a final taper. The more you do distance running, the more you will know your body and how long a period it needs to taper.

DEFINITION

Peak is the point in training where you reach your longest and most intense runs in time or distance. **Taper** immediately follows the peak in your schedule. It's a recovery period with less volume, usually just before a race, unless it is a shorter-interval taper during training.

During normal training there are several factors you can develop that make you stronger or more efficient. These include red blood cell count, and the amount of oxygen being transported to the muscles. Red blood cell count can actually be depleted temporarily with overtraining. The volume of blood pumped out of the heart increases with proper training. Even the left ventricle of the heart can have an increase in size. This is the chamber of the heart which pumps blood throughout the entire body. More nerves are activating more muscles. With marathon training, you also become more efficient at buffering waste product (hydrogen), along with several other physiological benefits.

However, you have also temporarily depleted several hormones, including testosterone and human growth hormone (HGH). The first has to do with motivation and the latter is one of a few hormones dealing with muscle regeneration. Often just before the final peak, when someone has overtrained, they may feel as if they do not want to run any more. This is a sure sign that their testosterone is severely depleted. Immune system function has been temporarily lessened. Especially, if the athlete has been overtraining, there is a risk of upper-respiratory infection, at the point immediately following the peak in training. A proper taper readjusts all of these levels back to normal or above normal, depending on the hormone or system. This is why taper is so critical to the training program.

Interval Tapers

Exercise + rest = growth. This may be the simplest version of training. You can't have growth without exercise and rest in combination. As we saw with the schedule that simply builds without any taper, the lateral build, there is depletion in hormonal output, and fatigue sets in. This limits the results on race day. To allow for full recovery from exercise, you need an interval taper. These are absolutely critical to the overall process, says Inigo Mujika, Ph.D. He has made a career out of studying taper. For one thing the one week interval taper, once every fourth week, allows for muscle regeneration and for your hormone levels to come back up to normal or higher. Fatigue for weeks on end is not a normal function of marathon training. It is a function of overtraining and the need for an interval week-long taper.

Regardless of the period or phase of training you're in, each week needs to build with some kind of volume. Do that for three weeks, and then cut that volume down significantly during the entire fourth week. As long as you maintain at least 30-minute runs nearly every other day, you're okay. With that in mind, you may want to cut the volume by as much as half the volume of the previous week. Frequency of workouts each week, and intensity of those workouts needs to remain the same. If not, "detraining" (loss in ability) occurs. Women need a bit less of a taper, and some individuals also need more or less of an interval fourth week taper. But that is the essence of what it is and why.

The following graph shows each bar as the total volume of energy output (work load) in one week. There are three weeks of building volume, followed by one week of taper at 50 percent.

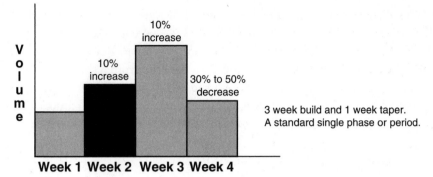

Build and taper phases of a typical four-week period.

Types of Final Taper

There are three different types of taper: gradual taper, step taper, and exponential taper. The first two are the more traditional forms of taper. A gradual taper begins with the volume at your final peak. Slowly, day after day—usually for three weeks or so—the volume comes down gradually.

The step taper also brings down the volume from the peak, by cutting everything by a big percentage each week. This is the more commonly used marathon taper. The peak longest run may have been 20 or 22 miles. The next weekend it may have been cut down to 12 miles, with the next at 8 miles, and then the marathon race after that. Mid-week runs are similarly cut by percentages each week.

Mujika and others have found that in most cases, these two more traditional tapers aren't as effective as an exponential taper. Three things are critical in an exponential taper, or in any taper:

- Intensity needs to remain constant. In other words, maintain your average pace.

- Frequency needs to remain constant. That means the amount of workouts each week needs to remain the same. Work out on the same days during taper week, as you did on a build week. And do a similar type of workout that you did the previous week.

- The volume needs to drop exponentially. Instead of slowly dropping in distance or time, you plummet to as little as possible, for two to four weeks, while maintaining that endurance base. Doing nothing leads to "detraining" (less energy on race day).

The exponential taper can be found in the schedule in Appendix D, for a final three-week taper. That schedule only has a two-week taper for the "Advanced" runners. Everyone benefits from a two-week taper, and not everyone needs a three-week taper.

A rare case could require a four-week taper. However, after a period of extended taper, instead of increased strength and energy on race day, you could end up with less. So there is a fine line between too much and too little taper. Beyond that, you begin to detrain. Every individual is unique, and each benefits from a specific amount of taper. However, there is a hump, beyond which the benefits from taper begin to fade, and detraining begins. Trial and error is the best method. You can gain 0.5 to 7 percent increased energy output from an exponential taper on race day; 3 percent is average.

MILE MARKER

Recent studies indicate women don't do as well with as big a reduction in work-load as men. That's because women do not carry much testosterone to begin with. When they get too much of a taper or rest, they tend to lose what little they have. This is in contrast to the effects of taper on male runners, whose depleted testosterone levels increase and return to normal or higher during taper. Therefore, to maintain drive and aggression on the race course, women benefit from maintaining higher workloads than their male counterparts during the final taper and all tapers. Though everyone is different, for most women we generally recommend 10 to 15 minutes of additional training each day during the exponential taper.

Incidentally, the last three days of the schedules are structured with a small benefit in mind. Note the training schedules in Appendix D. You want to take your training to zero just before race day. That's why we only do 20 minutes on Thursday with a day off on Friday. Then increase training slightly the day before to 10 minutes on Saturday. From this, you will receive another 0.05 percent increase of energy on race day. Not worth worrying about, but hey, every little bit helps.

The Least You Need to Know

- Random training is probably most effective for experienced athletes.
- A novice marathoner would benefit from an organized daily training schedule.
- There are several different training concepts to choose from, but building aerobic ability (base) should be the cornerstone. Then if you want to get faster, you need to train faster.
- Whatever training schedule you pick should be one that fits your lifestyle, factoring in personal and work obligations.
- For the taper following the peak in your training, you need to maintain intensity (heart rate), maintain frequency (same workouts on the same days), but exponentially cut volume (time or distance).

Staying Motivated in Training

In This Chapter

- Tips on how to train your mind
- Facing your fears
- What the finish line really means
- Proven strategies to keep you focused and inspired
- How to recruit support systems to reinforce your commitment

Long-distance running can be as much of a mental challenge as a physical one. Just as you have to train your body to run 26.2 miles, you must also train your mind to pilot the engines that keep you going. It's a good idea, therefore, to define what those engines are. What keeps you going? What inspires you? And how can you obtain more of it, whatever it is?

Getting philosophical or psychological about running may seem silly to some, but there is good medicine behind the concept of "sound mind, sound body." After all, it seems to be a big part of human nature to challenge ourselves. Some of the greatest minds of ancient Greece are believed to have participated in the first Olympic Games (believed to have been held in 776 B.C.E. in Olympia, Greece), including Aristotle, Plato, Herodotus, Sophocles, Euripides, Hippocrates, and Pythagoras. There must be something about physical competition and challenge that speaks to the greatest minds in history. It has also spoken to millions of athletes throughout the centuries. Why should you be any different?

Mind-Body Connection

When it comes to marathon training, you already have everything you will need: a mind and a body. And how you use these two assets will spell your destiny in your running career. The rigors of training will simply develop and fine-tune what you already have and what you already are. You will learn to better visualize your goals and make structured plans to achieve them. You will discover new reserves of discipline and focus. Your body will slowly learn to run for longer and longer distances. It will become more efficient and healthier. The seeds of these abilities are already within you. But all of this doesn't just happen on its own. You also need to figure out how to stay inspired and dedicated to your training. You must become your own best friend, and figure out how best to motivate yourself. Take all the strategic thinking you learn in your physical training and use it to strategize about your own motivation.

MILE MARKER

We can take a lesson from the mythological Icarus, who said, "All limits are self-imposed." Icarus should know, as he's the fellow who flew too close to the sun, melting his wings of wax. The limitations he placed on himself were: he ignored sage advice about avoiding the sun, and he also didn't prepare well for the challenge ahead. His equipment was inappropriate and inadequate. As a marathon runner, you need the faith of Icarus as well as the wisdom and experience he didn't implement.

Finding Motivation and Reinforcement

So how do you train your mind to train you? As you begin your marathon training, you will need to draw upon your inner strengths as well as your physical capabilities. A good quality to develop is the ability to focus on the positive. You will need this during the marathon as well. Another powerful tool you have is your ability to shift your perspective. You may not feel like running on a particular day, but at the same time you can focus on all the reasons you should run. You are building a marathon runner, brick by brick, and every run counts. You will feel better and have more energy afterward. It's good for you. After a long day of sitting at a desk, you can recognize that it's your mind that's tired, not your body, and you actually can make it through your training run. Whatever it takes to keep your eye on the prize, say it or do it.

Perhaps you work well with rewards. In that case, define your reward system. Do you reward yourself after your weekend long run? Or should it be something small after every run? And if so, what exactly will be your reward? What carrot can you hold in front of your own nose to keep you literally running? It can be anything from a date night with a spouse to a new pair of running shoes, or a pedicure, or a piece of chocolate, taking a nap, sleeping late …. Only you can say what will work best.

Sometimes a simple pep talk can get you back on the road. Tell yourself how well you're coming along compared to where you were before you started running. Tell yourself you're stronger than anything life can throw at you. Throughout history, humans have consistently broken through barriers and set records. You're doing well at breaking your own barriers and setting your own records. Or cheer yourself up with a run to a specific place, like an errand you need to complete. That way, you can get two things done at once. Or, if you need a pep talk on the road, think about your evening plans and how good it will feel to have your run out of the way. Or plan your next meal or social gathering. Imagine that you are one step closer to your goal.

Remember that even elite runners need some reinforcement now and then, and often resort to *mantras* or rituals just like beginners. Paula Radcliffe, a marathon world record holder, counts her steps when she's struggling. She knows that a certain number of steps equal a mile, and by distracting herself with counting, the miles pile on. You can also memorize and repeat inspirational or humorous lines you enjoy from songs or movies. Remember how Tom Hanks' character in *A League of Their Own* (1992) berates one of his team members by yelling at her when she quits the team? He tells her that of course it's hard, and if it weren't, everyone would be doing it. He tells her that that's what makes it good.

DEFINITION

A **mantra** is a word, phrase, or sound you repeat in your mind that aids in concentration and spiritual centering.

Is it Physiological?

Finding ways to motivate yourself throughout the training season is important. However, if it ever does become exceedingly difficult to motivate yourself to run, there may be something going on with the training itself that needs to be addressed. It may not be all psychological, but it might be a physiological issue regarding training. For example, if you find you hate intensity work on a track or hills, you may need to go back and get more aerobic (low heart rate) work to build efficiency. If you are burning out and hitting the wall after 90 minutes, you are almost assuredly going a bit too fast and need to lower your intensity (speed). You may simply need to rest more or taper, as your testosterone levels could be too low, causing you to not be motivated to run. All these things are critical to reaching your optimal levels of performance, and can affect your desire to train. If you experience any of these issues, motivation alone is not the answer. You require alteration in your training. See Chapter 5 for the science of how your body runs, and Chapter 10 for training programs.

Define and Defeat Your Fears

Many thoughts and emotions can keep people from starting something new like a training plan, and can also trip them up after they begin. One of the most powerful of these emotions is fear. Just about all beginning runners experience it. Not only fear of the unknown, but fear of injury and fear of failure, too. Those who fear failure often place "all their eggs in one basket." Too much of their identity is wrapped up in the performance of this one event. They often fear that they will be perceived as lacking discipline if they do badly. Symptoms of this include a person who has excuses before, during, and after performance. They are preoccupied with what others around them think. Often they break down with an injury or illness, seemingly out of the blue, or due to stress. And they have fears of being out of control and unable to perform with the needed skills.

Fear of success also plagues a lot of people. They fear the results of success, and the pressure to perform that it brings. Performance anxiety is a form of fear as well. However, education and preparation are the best ways to conquer these fears. Forget about the unknown, because you're uncovering it right now. You are educating yourself about what to expect and how to handle it. Look at your specific weaknesses and focus on how to improve. Imagine that you win that race, and it's okay to do so. Try to accept the idea that what people think about you or your actions doesn't matter or affect you much as you think. Developing a goal, such as completing a marathon, and following the structured progress of getting there can help with any performance anxiety. Don't find a way to fail, find a way to succeed. Remember this equation: success = effort × ability × preparation × will.

COACH SAYS …

Always evaluate what you're telling yourself. If you're thinking any negative or irrational thoughts, recognize them and get rid of them. A single negative thought can take root and kill your chances in a marathon. Positive athletes generally get to the finish line faster—and they certainly enjoy the race more.

You can mitigate your fear of injury by recognizing that most injuries can be prevented with education and preparation. A good training plan prepares your body slowly so the likelihood of injury is minimized. If you're afraid of failure, ask yourself what your definition of success is. If you cannot complete one marathon for whatever reason, there are countless others from which to choose. This is no one-strike game, and you are the captain of the team. You may be afraid to start a long training program because you fear you may not want to finish it. There is nothing wrong with trying something new and stopping if it doesn't suit you. Any performance anxiety you may feel will likely dissipate as your training progresses and your confidence grows. After all, to what standard are you holding yourself? You're not going out on stage. The only person you should be competing with is yourself. You're just going to run and do your best, whatever that is. That's all there is to it.

More Than a Finish Line

Another way of thinking that can strengthen your resolve is to focus on the larger picture. You're not just striving for a finish line after all, are you? Training for a marathon, and running the race itself, are both such unique and rich experiences that they really can't be boiled down to that one small goal. In your training, you're going to be triumphing over yourself. You'll be testing yourself and pushing beyond any limits you thought you had. By the time you get to the finish line, you'll have set and achieved countless goals. Your fitness will improve, your confidence will reach new heights, and you will become a bona fide, long-distance runner.

Training for a marathon requires something of a lifestyle change. If you let it, it can change your life after the finish line as well. Throughout your training, you will learn a great deal about nutrition and diet, and you will also come to understand how to best manage your energy. These are indispensible tools that can benefit you throughout your life, no matter your age or activity level. Not to mention, the sheer joy of improving, of developing your running abilities, is an inspiration in itself. Going a little further every week is exciting and shows you what focus and determination can do—or, rather, what you can do. During your training, you will also be benefitting from the various health improvements offered by long-distance running. Your heart will grow stronger, as will your bones and your muscles. You will have more energy, and many runners report increased alertness as well. The glory of the finish line is but a small piece of the mosaic of benefits that marathon training can provide.

Strategies for Success

Of all the tricks and tips out there to help keep you going, it's up to you to stitch together the plan that works best for you. But no matter how you strategize for success, there are some constants that you should be sure to include. For example, getting enough rest between runs is a huge factor in keeping you feeling good and ready to run. If you feel physically and mentally spent, you will have a much harder time staying motivated and focused. If you find the thought of your long runs to be intimidating, try thinking of them in smaller pieces. That is, your 10-mile run is really only equal to about a 5K and a 10K put together, and those aren't so hard on their own. This kind of imagery can help during the marathon, too. After all, a marathon is really only about four and a quarter 10Ks.

If your schedule is unmanageable, don't throw up your hands. A half-hour a day is better than nothing if that's all you can manage. Every training run you can log literally gets you one step closer to your goal of completing a marathon.

You can fit in your training runs and stay motivated in creative ways:

- If you have a treadmill at home, you can run in between doing laundry or other chores.
- Try focusing on an object or person in particular to take your mind off of your running.
- Pick out a landmark and run to it.
- Run a new route to enjoy some new scenery.
- Use a mantra while running.
- Talk to a fellow runner if you're in a training group.

MILE MARKER

Competitive runners are said to "associate" or focus inward during long runs to help manage negative thoughts. They pay attention to heart rate, nutrition, and pace. Noncompetitive runners tend to "dissociate" or focus outward on things like mile markers and fellow runners. Marathon runners do best by alternating between the two.

Another important strategy is to build slow weeks into your training plan. If you're not training with a group, you should be sure to allow your body time to recover in the big picture so to speak. That is, you may do shorter runs during the week and a long run on weekends, but this same pattern should apply to your training on a larger scale to allow your body time to recover and rebuild more deeply. This recovery time also helps with your morale and general sense of well-being. (We discuss the value of tapering in Chapter 10.) To keep yourself motivated, you can also choose to run shorter races as part of your training. Find 5Ks, 10Ks, and half marathons that coincide with your long runs of similar distances. The preparation and excitement of a new challenge may breathe new life into your training regimen. Similarly, running to music can keep you focused and inspired. Many runners create running-specific mixes to help set their pace and keep them motivated. Another helpful tactic is to pick a running hero who you can emulate. After all, they were beginners once, too.

Stay Focused

A critical factor in creating success is the ability to focus. This requires a certain mental toughness and resiliency, which can be achieved in the following ways. When you arrive at your training location, or at the marathon itself, learn to expect the unexpected. Something may go wrong, but if you decide ahead of time how you will handle it, or you decide that you will not let it stop you, you already have the upper hand. Anger can destroy focus, and generally comes from feeling out of control. By preparing as thoroughly as you can, both physically and mentally, you avoid that out-of-control feeling.

You can also take steps to keep your anger or frustration under control such as deep breathing, counting, or distracting yourself in some way. To help dissipate any stress you might be feeling at the start of a training run or race, you can also develop mental and physical routines, such as stretching and then jogging a bit to warm up. Retying your shoes before the event or wiping your forehead three or four times can be consistent routines that help you focus. However, don't obsess about routines. They will not make or break your day. They are simply a part of your coping strategy. Rehearse your training run or race before you begin. How fast are you going out? Where are the big hills? See it, feel it, trust it, then stop thinking and start performing.

Add Variety to Your Workouts

Endurance runners come up with infinite ways to combat the long hours and monotony of training. One effective approach is to add variety to your workouts. You can vary your running locations to help you maintain a sense of discovery and exploration. On your long runs, you will have a lot of ground to cover, and it may as well be an adventure. Your spirits will also benefit from a variety of types of workouts.

Your training plan will include speed work and hill challenges, which can shake it up enough to keep you interested.

Cross-training can also help you avoid feeling like you're in a rut. Try to stay focused on activities that will benefit your running or endurance in some way, however, such as bicycling or aerobic sports. If much of your training must be completed on a treadmill, you can also use it for speed and hill work. Sprinting for short distances, interspersed with slower running to cool down, can make the miles fly by much quicker. And setting your treadmill to differing degrees of incline to approximate hill work will help you use your muscles differently and will strengthen your cardiovascular system as well.

YELLOW LIGHT

Cross-training can help prevent overuse injuries and can develop muscles not used much in running, but its usefulness in distance running is limited. Building endurance in other sports will certainly help your endurance overall, but you can only improve in running by following a comprehensive running training plan.

Buddy Up

Even the most experienced runners may occasionally feel burned out and uninspired. One of the most popular ways to combat running burnout is to find a running buddy. You can help motivate each other when the chips are down. A buddy also adds friendly accountability, in that you are more likely to show up for your workout if someone is waiting for you. You can get this same effect by joining a group training plan. In most plans, runners are divided by average pace, so you will be matched with runners of similar abilities. Many runners look forward to group runs as social events, and the camaraderie is inspiring. The cumulative energy of a large number of people pursuing the same goal can help carry you along.

If you prefer a less structured running plan, you can most likely find a running club or two in your area. Many such clubs host weekly runs a couple of times a week, and they are often broken up into shorter- and longer-distance contingents. Either of these options gives you a large pool of resources in that you can share experiences with fellow runners and learn from those who are more practiced than you. There are even running clubs for those who like to drink beer or search for extraterrestrials.

A good way to find local running clubs is by checking the Internet. Most groups have a website and are easy to find. For example, www.meetup.com is a good way to find groups sponsored by running shops or a few individuals that are often free.

MILE MARKER

On average, there are 9 running clubs per state in the United States. Leading the pack is California with 163, followed by Texas with 83 and New York with 73. Tied for second-to-last place are Hawaii, Nebraska, and Wyoming, with 5 each. Bringing up the rear is North Dakota with 4.

Alternatively, you can also sign up to run for a charitable cause that inspires you. Many charity organizations offer structured training plans in return for a guaranteed minimum contribution. It's up to you to secure sponsors and donations for your run, which can often be structured in dollars per mile. It's also your responsibility to pay for your own travel to and from the race. This kind of commitment helps to keep some runners focused on their training. It also offers all the benefits of group training. Quite often, the training program will also feature special events like motivational talks or visits from medical specialists.

Keep Track of Progress

Sometimes the best way to keep your eyes on your future goal is to look backward at how far you have already come. Keeping a running journal helps you keep track of dates, mileage, time, and course details. It's also a good way to track your food intake and weather variations, as these can affect your performance for better or worse. Especially make note of your energy levels and how you feel. If you were tired consistently during a period in which the training load was high, you will know how a certain training load affected you, and you can see where you might have been overtraining. In addition, were you happy and having fun during a period of training, or simply toughing it out? The latter can also indicate overtraining. By keeping good notes, you can recognize what internal things you're telling yourself and work to improve your inner dialogue. What you learn from your own running history can help you grow as a runner. Detailed notes will make it easy to look back and analyze what you did right and what you did wrong.

Classes and Lectures

Knowledge is power, especially when you're learning something new. Therefore, it's wise to seek out classes and lectures on running and related topics such as sports nutrition, sports medicine, and exercise physiology. When you understand how your body works, and why training is structured as it is, it'll be easier to understand how the entire experience fits together. And when you understand something, you learn to work within its parameters. The science of running is always evolving, so it's in your best interest to stay informed. This is also the best way for you to ask questions and receive personal instruction or advice. You can find classes and running-specific talks through your local gym, via word of mouth, or even through some sports supply stores. Some clothing and running shoe manufacturers sponsor running clubs in larger cities. Sports physical therapists often have lectures and demonstrations.

Identify Support Systems

While running may seem to be a solitary sport, it pretty much takes a village to create a well-rounded runner. Running takes a good deal of time, which means it leaves less time for other pursuits, be they hobbies or relationships or social activities. However, it's time you are taking for yourself, to improve your health and well-being, and that's a very constructive use of your time.

This means, however, that you'll need to get your family and friends on board to support you. You'll need to define who or what your support systems are in daily life. Is it your spouse? Your best friend? In either case, you may need to make extra time for that person in other ways so that you can take the time you need for running. And you'll have to be upfront with the person so they don't feel neglected or cheated. Help them help you, and be clear about what you need and what you're willing to give in return. Sadly, not all relationships, including family and friends, are always supportive in ways that you need. Often well-meaning people in your life can question the idea of running a marathon or your ability to do so, which could cause you to question yourself and lose confidence. Confidence is critical and shouldn't come from outside sources. It should develop from within, from trusting your body and your abilities, and by taking note of the improvements you are gaining through your training.

You should also be aware that coaches and trainers are people, too, with their own worries and concerns. They may betray a fear or negative thought they may have. This can cause you to worry as well, but you shouldn't take on their concerns as your own. In the best of all possible worlds, the closest people in your life will join you in your running training. In that case, you won't have to fight for the time alone that you need, and you can enjoy your most precious relationships at the same time.

If good rest is one of your support systems, you should be aware that quite often external sources can affect your ability to relax enough to recover from training. These can include your family and work. Don't forget, stress is stress, whether it comes from exercise or a psychological source. Learn good relaxation techniques. Deep breathing, and stretching one's arms above one's head, can help deal with stress and create relaxation. Plan periods of rest, even while managing busy work and training schedules. These periods can include vacation, or even just extra time to sleep. Most adult athletes need at least seven to eight hours of sleep. Children need more than that. Stay focused on the end result, and your ability to achieve it, and any negative stresses from family, friends, and work can be overcome.

Defined in another way, support systems can also be nonhuman. You may find inspiration in running with your dog, for instance. Or you may find that your place of employment offers a gym membership for free or at a discount. Some company gyms even offer rewards for various achievements such as running the most miles in a set amount of time or logging the most time at the gym. Some people find support in group running activities or clubs. Or you may find sustenance in completely unrelated activities. The key is to spend your down time in a way that ultimately helps you develop into a healthier and better runner.

The Least You Need to Know

- To maintain discipline and focus, you must train your mind at the same time you train your body.
- Combat fear of failure and success by keeping your focus, planning for the unexpected, and setting goals.
- Physiological issues such as overtraining can alter your mood and affect motivation.
- Crossing the finish line is only the beginning to realizing that you're now empowered to do anything you set your mind to.
- Use different strategies, such as adding variety to your training and keeping track of your progress, to help you stay motivated.
- Having a support system in place keeps you motivated and helps you to maintain balance between training and other aspects of your life.

Training Injuries

In This Chapter

- The three basic causes of runners' injuries
- Types of common injuries
- RICE: rest, ice, compression, elevation
- Getting physical therapy
- Treating blisters and other minor complaints
- Your best plan for a safe return to running after injury

During your evolution from little or no running experience to the long distances you will tackle during your marathon training, you may experience various types of injuries. Proper preparation, the right equipment, and a structured running plan help to prevent many common complaints.

Always check with your doctor to ensure that you are in good health before starting any kind of exercise plan. It's also a good idea to resolve any injuries or chronic complaints you might have so that you don't aggravate an existing condition. Then, if you do become injured, be sure to ask your doctor what the reason might have been. Without knowing the reason, and fixing it, athletes are often injured again fairly quickly.

Causes of Injuries

Running injuries generally stem from the following three basic causes:

- Ill-fitting or worn-out shoes and equipment
- Poor running form
- Muscular imbalances

These simple root issues can result in a wide variety of problems. Of course, accidents can also play a big role in causing injuries, so stay aware and use caution when choosing your running locations. Injuries sustained in other sports such as skiing or biking can also limit your mobility and flexibility, so be strategic in your choice of activities while in training.

YELLOW LIGHT

Pain is a sign that something is wrong. Don't ignore your aches and pains, as they could grow into much larger problems. With a little investigation, you may find a simple solution that will keep you running safely and pain free.

Shoes and Equipment

Perhaps the simplest yet most persistent causes of running injuries are problems with shoes or equipment. Ill-fitting or worn-out shoes can result in a host of problems starting with the feet, ranging all the way up through the legs to the back. Were your shoes purchased at a running specialty store, with a knowledgeable salesperson? Did you get a chance to run in them before purchasing them? How old is the shoe? Shoes that have begun to break down, offering less and less support, can be an important but hidden culprit.

Similarly, shoes that cause your feet to strike the ground at the wrong angle, or that do not support your feet appropriately, are often a cause of unexplained soreness or injury. Any shoes or equipment that don't fit well or that change your running posture can lead to muscle and/or joint pain. Quite often a simple change of shoes can alleviate nagging ankle or knee pain. You may also have a physical condition that could easily be corrected with shoes or orthotics, such as a leg length discrepancy. A thorough physical examination is an important first step in finding and diagnosing such conditions so that you can use the appropriate equipment. We offer tips on buying the right shoes and equipment in Chapter 4.

Running Form

A great deal of your training is aimed at improving your running form. Good posture and alignment are crucial in preventing injury and maintaining strength and endurance in long-distance running. Slouching or leaning too far forward, which are common when fatigue sets in, can affect your lower back and the angle at which you must lift your legs. This causes you to use an unnatural range of motion throughout your hips and legs, which will lead to additional fatigue and pain. Similarly, leaning too far back, or taking too small or too large steps will also add up to pain or fatigue. Your stride length can also contribute to injuries. Is your foot landing, ideally, about 2 to 3 inches in front of your hip, or further in front of you? Likewise, are you pushing back too far, or leaving your rear foot on the ground too long? This can put additional stress on the Achilles tendon, leading to inflammation or tendinitis. Short strides are best. Be aware of topographical irregularities that can affect your form, such as hills or angled surfaces. Many streets are angled for water runoff. This causes an imbalance, placing more stress on one side than the other.

Lastly, correcting any over- or underpronation of the feet will help to keep your ankles, knees, and hips aligned, which means more efficient and pain-free running. This may require professionally fit shoes as well as orthotics. Often simple corrections in form, such as bringing your knee up a little higher with each step, to a 45-degree angle from your torso, can correct for an issue like a hip displacement. The correction is accomplished because when the knee comes up higher, certain muscles are engaged, and the hip discrepancy is evened out. This correction can take some strength training of the hip flexors in order to enable the athlete to make such a change.

Muscular Imbalances

It may be hard to believe, but your own muscular system can work against you if certain muscles develop more than others. For example, the quadriceps muscles on the front of your thighs are each made up of four individual muscles which connect to your kneecaps. It is quite common for the muscles on the outer sides of the thighs to develop more than those on the inner sides of the thighs. This can result in the kneecap being pulled to the outside of the knee by the stronger outside muscles. In this case, the outside edge of the kneecap may start rubbing on the leg bones beneath, rather than floating above the knee joint as it should—and this can cause debilitating pain. The remedy for this condition is commonly a regimen of lower leg-lifts in the gym, with the knees pointing outward in order to isolate and strengthen the inner quadriceps.

Similarly, stronger muscles can pull on joints or bones creating an unnatural alignment or range of motion. Endurance runners should be mindful of such possibilities and take time to exercise and develop the muscles that are used less in running. Yoga, *Pilates*, strength training (with or without weights), and active and progressive stretches can all aid in stretching and strengthening the muscles. This can help to ensure years of injury-free running, not to mention healthier day-to-day life.

> **DEFINITION**
>
> **Pilates** is a form of exercise that strengthens the muscles of your torso by using your body weight for resistance. It's named after the inventor, Joseph Pilates.

Muscle tightness can also contribute to imbalances. While stretching, do you find one side is tighter than the other? It's common to feel more resistance on one side of the body, so you will have to spend extra time stretching that side. Do you stretch before and after every workout? As Robert Forster, an Olympic and pro-level physical therapist suggests, "If you don't have time to stretch, you don't have time to run." He adds that he never saw an Olympic or pro-level runner who maintained their abilities without a consistent program of stretching and strength training. Marathon world record holder Rod Dixon says that when he plans an hour run, he runs for 45 minutes and stretches for 15 minutes afterward. Before the run, Dixon also performs some loosening-up exercises. These consist of active leg movement to warm up the muscles. Rolling the ankle, rolling the hips around, and gently stretching different muscles for intervals of a few seconds only, are all part of his prerun work. You can find more details on pre- and postworkout stretches in Appendix E.

Types of Injuries

Endurance running increases your chances of injuring your feet and legs. Repetitive-use injuries are common, and can cause additional trouble if you continue to run through the pain. A small pain in your ankle, for example, can cause you to favor the other foot, and after a few hundred or thousand unbalanced steps you may end up injuring your "good" foot as a result. Hence, it is best to understand the most common types of injuries and how to handle them so that you do not cause additional damage.

Most minor injuries resolve with rest, anti-inflammatory medication, and some targeted therapy. The most commonly prescribed course of rehabilitation for minor injuries is called by its acronym, RICE (see the section later in this chapter). Be sure to consult your doctor if an injury doesn't respond to treatment.

Soreness

Many runners complete their training and their marathons without any major complaints, though the majority will experience significant soreness from time to time. This is normal and does not mean that any serious injuries are lurking. The key, however, is to know the difference between soreness and true injury. Muscle soreness is caused by overuse which results in tiny tears throughout the muscle tissue. Resting the affected muscles and allowing them to heal is an important part of the process that heals and strengthens the muscles. In this case, the pain should resolve within a day or two, allowing you to challenge those same muscles again.

Muscle soreness or burning while running may also result from lactic acid and waste build-up. This can occur if you have not built up an adequate aerobic base or if you run too fast for too long. Slowing down or walking will usually allow your body to catch up and remove the lingering waste products, which should alleviate the soreness. Waste product is generally expelled by the body within a few hours. If you're sore or in pain the next day, it isn't due to lactic acid, hydrogen, or waste product build-up. It is due to the fact that you are overworked or injured. Sore joints can result from overuse but may also point to issues with your shoes, muscular imbalances, or even minor cartilage damage. Any soreness that lasts longer than two days, becomes chronic, or suddenly gets worse should be addressed by a doctor. A good rule of thumb is that any pain that persists for two workouts should be considered an injury.

Shin Splints

Shin splints are one of the most pervasive injuries suffered by distance runners. Symptoms of shin splints are pain and possible swelling along the shinbone at the front of each of your lower legs which worsens with continued running or walking. The pain generally diminishes with rest. This condition is caused by overworking the tissue that connects your muscles to the bone. Quite often this issue is caused by a tight calf muscle, or tight muscle in that area. A tight muscle can pull on the shin with every step, causing the injury. It's common among those who are just starting a running routine as well as in activities that demand repeated starting and stopping.

As with any injury, it is important to give your body the time it needs to heal. Continually aggravating a condition like shin splints can turn a minor issue into a major problem. You can avoid this problem by running on even surfaces, increasing mileage gradually, allowing sufficient rest between workouts, and stretching and strengthening the surrounding muscles.

Sprains and Strains

Sprains and strains can occur in almost any connective tissue in your body such as in *tendons, ligaments,* and bones. You can pull or strain muscle tissue as well. Generally this type of injury occurs when you force a body part to move or twist in an unnatural way, resulting in inflammation and soreness. You can even strain your bones, which can lead to microcracks in the surface of the bone.

> **DEFINITION**
>
> **Tendons** and **ligaments** are classified as connective tissue because they bind one type of tissue to another. Tendons connect bone to muscle, while ligaments connect bone to bone or support organs within the body. Neither tendons nor ligaments can stretch.

Sprains generally result from twisting a joint, such as the ankle or knee, without breaking or dislocating the bones. Stretching or wrenching the ligaments can cause small tears and bleeding into the tissue resulting in pain, stiffness, swelling, and discoloration. A strain occurs when tissue, such as muscle, is stretched to its furthest point without breaking. To a lesser extent, this too can result in tiny tears and bruising accompanied by pain, swelling, and stiffness.

Torn Ligaments, Tendons, and Muscles

When a sprain or strain progresses past the point of causing tiny microscopic breaks in the tissue, major tearing can occur. This is extremely painful and debilitating. Because tendons and ligaments are so inelastic, they may "give" a minimal amount, but past that point they fail catastrophically. Muscles may seem more pliable and forgiving, but they too have their breaking point. Quite often, these types of injuries are caused by falls or collisions. Treatment for these injuries may consist of RICE, physical therapy, and even surgery.

Broken Bones

Of course, the most debilitating injury for any runner is a broken bone. While complete fractures are uncommon in running, stress fractures can occur unexpectedly. A stress fracture occurs when relatively low-grade force is applied to the bone over and over again. This can be caused by improper support (such as in worn-out shoes), a sudden increase in activity intensity, or running on very hard surfaces. The majority of stress fractures occur below the knee, but they can also affect the thigh bone and hip. Keep your bones healthy with a proper diet that is rich in calcium and make sure to rest between workouts. You should also avoid a sudden spike in exercise intensity or volume to help prevent stress fractures.

Cross-training such as cycling or swimming can also help to vary the stresses on your bones. However, be aware that cycling is not a load-bearing exercise and therefore doesn't maintain or increase bone density. Using cycling as your only exercise for a long period of time can lead to or worsen osteoporosis, or thinning of the bones.

Strength training, a load-bearing exercise, can maintain and sometimes increase bone density. Therefore, a combination of cross-training and strength training can be an effective strategy to prevent bone injuries.

Rest, Ice, Compression, Elevation (RICE)

For all but the worst injuries, rest, ice, compression, and elevation together make up a time-tested therapy known by the acronym RICE. This regimen is aimed at protecting the injured area and preventing as much swelling as possible. Heat and inflammation, or swelling, are important parts of your immune system's response to injury, but if allowed to continue unabated they can cause additional damage and pain. Many minor injuries such as sprains, strains, soreness, and shin splints can be treated effectively by following these four steps in the first days or week following the injury. Then, as healing continues, the therapy can be tailored to your particular needs.

1. **Rest.** First you must cease or cut back on the activity that caused your injury. Your body needs time to heal without the stress of incurring additional injuries. You may be able to cross-train or engage in other activities that don't use your injured body part. Keep in mind, your body is always working to heal itself, no matter what you're doing at the same time. Therefore, getting enough sleep will also help speed up your recovery. The greatest volume of cellular regeneration, or healing, takes place during sleep.

2. **Ice.** Use ice as soon as possible after the injury to control swelling and relieve pain. Do not apply ice directly to the skin as it can cause damage after a few minutes. Wrap it in a thin piece of cloth, such as an old T-shirt or a dish towel. Depending on the extent of your injury, ice should be applied for 10 to 20 minutes at a time, several times a day. Often the biggest mistake injured athletes make is to use ice for far too long. You don't want to freeze the muscle, as this will slow down the healing process and can also make it more susceptible to injury.

   If you need to use a lot of ice, for a sizable injury for example, try this. Take a rubber-lined ice bag with a screw-on cover, or a simple zip-lock freezer bag. Fill it with ice, then water, and squeeze as much air out as possible. Close the bag. Wrap the bag in a soft cloth and place it on the injury for 10 to 20 minutes and no longer. Then use warm water in a bag, or sit in a warm tub, for another 10 to 15 minutes. Be careful not to use hot water—you will need gentle heat at this point. The warm water gets your circulation going again, which brings more oxygen to the injury. This keeps the healing process going. Then you can ice again, with the same bag of ice. After a second 10 to 15 minutes or so of ice, your swelling and/or soreness can be substantially reduced. By the fourth day following your injury, ice may become ineffective, and heat becomes more important in order to maintain greater circulation.

> **YELLOW LIGHT**
>
> A popular practice is to use a bag of frozen vegetables such as peas to ice down an injury. A bag of frozen vegetables or a freezer pack can thaw too quickly, and is less effective than ice and water. Water is a far better conductor of temperature.

3. **Compression.** Wrapping the injury in an elastic bandage is another way to control swelling in between your applications of ice. This stabilizes the injured area and also prevents additional swelling. You shouldn't feel any throbbing when the area is bandaged, but it should be wrapped tightly.

4. **Elevation.** Ideally, an injured body part should be elevated above the level of the heart to reduce the pooling of fluids in the area. If this isn't feasible, try to elevate the injured area as much as possible such as sitting down and placing an injured foot on an ottoman.

The RICE method is used by professional athletes and is proven to help speed healing of minor injuries and prevent further damage. Once the injury has begun healing, and pain and swelling are no longer acute, heat compresses may help improve circulation and speed recovery. Gentle massage and stretching can relieve stiffness and can help you regain your range of motion. If pain and swelling do not decrease after two days, you should see your doctor.

Physical Therapy

An important component of rehabilitation after injury is physical therapy. Quite often, physical therapy will be prescribed by a doctor for minor and major injuries. The type of injury you have dictates which type of physical therapy is right for you. It's carried out by licensed physical therapists in specialized facilities. Your therapist fashions an individualized plan of rehabilitation for you based on your injury, your goals, and your level of fitness.

Physical therapy usually doesn't begin until an injury has moved past the acute stage. However, receiving treatment as soon as possible helps lessen the risk of more permanent damage. It's targeted at regaining strength, movement, and flexibility in the injured body part. Common therapies include the following:

- Gentle massage
- Stretching
- Gentle electric muscle stimulation

- Ultrasound
- Light weight-bearing exercises
- Ice or heat

Generally lasting several weeks, physical therapy evolves as healing progresses.

Therapeutic Equipment

Your physical therapist has a host of tools at his or her disposal. In addition to the weight machines, treadmills, and exercise balls that you might see in any modern gym, you'll find equipment that is tailored to certain therapy regimens. Pilates machines, which exercise the body's core muscles in the torso, can help stabilize the spine. Electrotherapy, a gentle current applied to the skin, can be used to work muscles, stimulate repair, and prevent atrophy. Ultrasound is often used to improve circulation and generate heat deep inside the tissue. Both electrotherapy and ultrasound are gently applied through the skin and do not cause any pain. Of course, crutches, canes, and braces can also help you keep the weight off of your affected area while it heals.

Water Therapy

Water is useful in physical therapy in many ways. Warm water heats tissue much more efficiently than warm air, and it can also create a gentle massaging effect. This type of heat increases circulation and thereby speeds healing. Aquatic physical therapy involves complete submersion in water, which relieves stress on joints and can allow a more full range of motion. Gentle exercises are performed underwater to improve strength and flexibility.

Minor Complaints

In addition to minor injuries like sprains and strains, long-distance runners can face painful challenges from unexpected quarters. The very nature of endurance athletics means that your body has to literally endure long periods of activity and repetitive movement. While you prime your cardiovascular system and your muscles for these challenges during your marathon training, other parts of your body may not yet be up to the task. Without appropriate preparation, you can experience trouble with your skin and toenails, for instance, that can literally trip you up and derail your training regimen.

Blisters

Everyone knows the pain of breaking in new shoes and the annoying blisters that can result. When it comes to long-distance running, however, blisters can develop quickly and deeply, causing bleeding and debilitating pain. Not only do you need to break in your running shoes, you also have to choose the right socks (see Chapter 4) and keep your skin as dry and healthy as possible. At first, wear new shoes only on shorter runs, and keep a comfortable pair available to alternate with your new shoes. Talcum powder can help absorb moisture, and skin lubricants such as petroleum jelly can prevent friction in vulnerable spots. Moisture-wicking socks can also help to prevent blisters. Conversely, cotton socks absorb moisture and hold it against the skin. This softens the skin and makes it more susceptible to blistering. Blisters are often an individual matter, where trial and error lead you to an effective solution.

Black Toenails

An unusual problem you might face is blackened toenails. Your nail beds can develop painful, swollen, blood-filled blisters for a few reasons, and if the problem progresses you can actually lose your nails. Blood may pool under your nails in response to impact, prolonged pressure, or crowding of the toes. This can be caused by too-small shoes or not enough room in the toe-box, or front of the shoe. Your feet will swell while you run, so extra room is essential. *Centrifugal force*, caused by the constant rotation of your foot with each step, can worsen the condition, pushing more blood into the injured nail beds. It can take months for a new nail to grow in. If the swelling doesn't go down within a day, you may need to drain the blister with a sterile pin. You can prevent this problem by wearing proper footwear and by keeping your nails cut short to reduce their contact with the shoe.

DEFINITION

Any object in rotation around a central point will experience **centrifugal force.** This is outward pressure that moves away from the central point, such as when you are thrown against the door in a car speeding around a curve. It can also affect the circulation in your hands and fingers during long-distance runs.

Chafing and Abrasions

While the skin on your feet generally develops blisters in response to friction, other parts of your body may react differently. For example, the elastic bands in your underwear can lodge in the crease between your leg and your groin. The repeated rubbing of your skin against the elastic will eventually wear away the top layers of your skin, resulting in a painful, raw abrasion. Just like in a blister, your skin will exude moisture to help reduce friction, and this can add to your discomfort. Skin rubbing on skin can also cause chafing, such as on the inner thighs or between the toes. After allowing the skin to heal, you can reduce friction with talcum powder or a gentle lubricant like petroleum jelly. Sticks of anti-chafing gel, in a package looking like deodorant, can be purchased from any running store (see Chapter 4 for more information).

When Can You Run Again?

With complaints like blisters and chafing, it's relatively easy to figure out when you can start running again. But with injuries below the skin, it gets a little trickier. For major injuries like broken bones or torn muscles, ask for your doctor's recommendation. A broken bone can take six to eight weeks to heal, but even then you will have to return to your previous level of activity very slowly. Spending any time immobilized in a cast seriously affects your strength and flexibility. Torn muscles and ligaments likewise require a prolonged period of rest followed by physical therapy and a very gradual resumption of activity.

Mild sprains and strains can take several weeks to heal. Your barometer in these cases is your level of comfort and flexibility. After a period of rest and light activity, you should be able to slowly challenge yourself with longer and longer walks and then runs. You can also combine short runs with a period of walking in between. As you start to build up some mileage, you need a plan to take you back up to your previous level of activity.

If you're injured in the middle of training season and don't want to lose your endurance base, try this (with the approval of your doctor): run in water. Some public pools even have running-in-water lanes and aqua-joggers. An aqua-jogger is found at many large sports supply or medical, rehab, or fitness stores. It is a rubber vestlike contraption that keeps you upright, with your head above the water line. While wearing an aqua-jogger, you simply run in water, with your feet off the ground and no pounding or stress on the injured area. Maintain proper form, and don't exaggerate movement, as in bringing your knees up too high, or using too great an arm swing. It's the only way to exercise the muscles you use for running with no stress.

Running in water will not allow you to make gains in your endurance ability, but it's the only truly effective way to maintain it if you can't actually run. With proper running form, you will improve slowly, so this tends to be a rather tedious workout. It's also not an intense workout, and may feel too easy. On the other hand, besides maintaining all that work you did previous to the injury, you can benefit from looking down and seeing your running form. Obviously, as with anything you do, if you feel any pain, discontinue immediately, until you can run in water without pain.

YELLOW LIGHT

If you can't swim, you may choose not to use an aqua-jogger. If the clasp on the front of the vest breaks or opens accidentally, you could find yourself over your head in water. A rare occurrence, but caution is advised for you nonswimmers.

Structured Return to Running

Once you have addressed the cause of your injury and you have completed your rehabilitation plan, you should be ready to start running again. When coming back from an injury, remember the first rule, which is *stop immediately* if you feel any pain. The biggest mistake many athletes make is coming back too soon. Quite often athletes will heal a little and then run and become a bit more injured. This is followed by more healing and more injury. A yo-yo scenario can continue through race day, with devastating consequences. Heal first and then train. You will be much stronger and more capable once fully healed.

If allowed by your doctor, you can remain active while you are healing. Perhaps swimming, aqua-jogging, or a stationary bike can keep your cardiovascular system in shape during your recuperation without aggravating your injury. This is almost half the battle in staying prepared for training. During physical therapy, you will likely also use light weights to slowly build up your strength, as well as stretching to maintain pliable, flexible muscles. In these gently constructive ways, you can maintain some fitness, which will make your return to training much easier.

Your First Weeks After Recovery

Once your doctor signs off on your return to running, start with some easy walks or runs to get your body used to running again. Choose level surfaces and avoid hills until later in your training, when you're sure you can handle them.

- **Week 1:** Run or walk at a pace that is up to 50 percent of your preinjury pace. Even though it may be difficult emotionally, holding back right now is critical. You want to avoid that yo-yo injury, heal, injury cycle. Start with a 10-minute run. If that goes well, two days later, do a little more. You could go for another 10-minute run, and if you still feel good, follow that with a 10-minute walk. Then, if all is still well, continue with another 10-minute run. Two days after that, you may want to repeat this one more time, depending on how it feels. At this point, you should assess your performance as objectively as possible. If you experience any pain or lingering stiffness, cut back during the next week and progress from there.

- **Week 2:** If all went well last week, continue to progress. Your pace and distance can increase slightly from your previous amounts. Again, keep track of how you feel and allow extra time if you need it.

Each week, you can add approximately 10 percent to your pace and distance if you feel well enough. This is partially dependent upon how much aqua-jogging, strength training, and gentle stretching you were able to complete during your rehabilitation.

If you're in the middle or late stages of your marathon training plan, you might consider taking a bit more risk. A physical therapist or coach knowledgeable in injuries can be a good tool at this point. Working with your unique needs and goals, they can help you plot an individualized return to training.

YELLOW LIGHT

Never increase distance or intensity by more than 10 percent at a time, especially while recovering from an injury. Too much stress on your body will halt or reverse your recuperation.

Estimate Your Remaining Endurance

Once you have become comfortable with easy levels of activity, what is the best way to actually resume your training? First, you need to figure out how much conditioning you have lost before you can understand where you are in your training plan. It's believed that you lose 10 percent of your conditioning for every week that you're not training at all. Therefore, your return to running should be structured to help you regain that lost ground. To calculate your remaining endurance base after your period of recuperation, take the longest race pace distance you achieved in your training before the injury. At about a 10 percent loss in endurance ability per week of inactivity, subtract that amount from your preinjury longest distance. (Don't count any week in which you were able to run 30 minutes every other day. In that case you maintained your endurance ability, and lost nothing for that week.) In the following table, we use 20 miles as the preinjury endurance base. All numbers are rounded off.

How to Calculate Percentage of Endurance Lost

Period of No Training	% Endurance Lost	% Remaining Endurance	Remaining Mileage Base
Prior to injury	0%	100%	20.0 miles
Week 1	10%	90%	18.0 miles
Week 2	10%	81%	16.2 miles
Week 3	10%	73%	14.6 miles
Week 4	10%	66%	13.2 miles
Week 5	10%	59%	11.8 miles
Week 6	10%	53%	10.6 miles
Week 7	10%	48%	9.6 miles
Week 8	10%	43%	8.6 miles
Week 9	10%	39%	7.8 miles
Week 10	10%	35%	7.0 miles

Of course, these measurements are approximate. As you can see, since most minor injuries take one to six weeks to heal completely, you may lose about 10 percent to 47 percent of your endurance base while you are laid up. For example, if you had a 20-mile base when you were injured, and you were laid up for four weeks, your recalculated endurance base will be approximately equal to 13 miles. If you have some weeks of training left, after the first two or three weeks of building back up with really short runs and maybe a little strength training and stretching, you can again begin to build up the 13-mile base. Listen to your body and make sure there is no pain as you build in distance. Because your endurance ability after these four weeks of injury is already at 13 miles, you can jump back up to 13 miles after running shorter distances with no pain. However, you need to heal first before you even begin to consider picking up where you left off. Then, after you get back to your old endurance level, increase your mileage by about 10 percent each week. Remember the rule: if you feel any pain, stop immediately.

Calculate Run/Walk Proportion

Do not feel as if you have to finish that all-mighty 20-mile training run at race pace. It may cause more harm than good, especially if you've had a recent injury. If you don't have time left in your training schedule to finish the longest distances in your regimen, or even if you don't come close, there is always a solution.

Figure that recalculated distance as your current endurance ability, and calculate its percentage of the entire marathon. To use our previous example, 13 miles is about half of the 26.2-mile marathon distance. Therefore, you have the ability to run half of the marathon. However, if you simply went out and ran half the marathon distance all at once, that would be it, and you would run out of steam. Because of your reduced endurance level (reduced strength and lung capacity, less muscle recruitment, and fewer mitochondria), you only have half the energy resources you would need to run the full marathon at your original pace. You don't want to "hit the wall" and run out of glycogen. Therefore, you need to slow your running pace way down and walk for about half the time spent out on the marathon course. In other words, if you run for one minute and walk for one minute (50 percent running and 50 percent walking), you will have the fuel you need to take you to the end. However, this scenario assumes that you run the entire way. If you're training as a run/walker or walker, you still have to cut your intensity levels by 50 percent to play it safe.

The shorter your final preinjury training run, the more you need to walk at a comfortable pace on race day. Based on your energy level throughout the race, you may have to adjust your race run/walk percentage accordingly. If in the last few miles you find that you have energy left, speed up to your old race pace, whatever that was, and be thankful you held back. (You should continue with the walking breaks, however.) If you're already a slow run/walker or walker, you need to keep it comfortable, and focus on keeping your heart rate low by averaging a much slower pace. Similarly, you can speed up a bit in the last few miles if you still have energy left. So fear not, all isn't necessarily lost, even with an injury a few weeks before a race. You simply have to change your game plan and strategy to finish.

Keep in mind, this plan for returning to running only works if you are healed. As you progress, always take the time you need to adjust to the added mileage. Consider it an investment in your future wellness. You do no good by rushing this part of your rehabilitation. Indeed, you're most vulnerable to additional injury during this time, so do whatever it takes to remain patient with the process. A well-healed injury with no lingering complications will be your reward.

The Least You Need to Know

- Most running injuries are caused by ill-fitting or worn-out shoes and equipment, poor running form, or muscular imbalances.
- Common injuries during training include soreness; shin splints; strains and sprains; torn ligaments, tendons, and muscles; blisters; and broken bones.

- Rest, ice, compression, and elevation (RICE) are used by professional athletes to treat many common injuries.
- Physical therapy can help speed healing, maintain strength, and restore pre-injury range of motion.
- Your return to running must be slow and strategic, only increasing your pace and distance by 10 percent each week.
- A long recovery doesn't have to destroy your marathon dreams.

The Main Event

In the last part, we show you how to wrap it all together—mind, body, and spirit—and how to prepare for the marathon during your last three weeks of training. We give you mental tricks to help you stay focused and inspired. And we describe the role of sleep in your marathon training.

As you get closer to race day, your physical training will taper, but your anxiety level will likely increase. We show you proven ways to manage anxiety, and we also describe what to expect when you get to the marathon. When you get to the finish line, you'll need to collect your finisher's medal and check yourself for injuries. We describe what your recovery should be like, and when you can run again. What? Run again? Yes, if you've followed our directions, you've had a wonderful time and you will definitely want to do it again!

Preparing for Race Day

In This Chapter

- What to do three weeks before the marathon
- How your final taper works
- Preparations one week before race day
- Last-minute details the day before the race
- Getting a good night's sleep

What you do during the last few weeks before the marathon is just as important as what you did for the entire four to six months of training that came before. Staying on track with your training is now more crucial than ever. In the last few weeks before race day, you will run approximately 20 miles in your longest training run, your mileage will taper off, and you will start making your final preparations for the race. Your longest training run will serve as a prerun test or dress rehearsal before the race.

Then, you will really need to trust your training during the final weeks of taper before the marathon. Additional mileage during this time will not help, and you will focus on resting and getting organized before the race. Often, athletes destroy months of training by doing too much during the final weeks of taper. This reduced volume is critical.

Three Weeks Before Race Day

Now that your months of prerace training are coming to a close, your focus will shift more and more toward the marathon race itself. Your training never really ends, of course, but three weeks before the race you enter a unique phase in your regimen.

Three weeks before race day, you will run your longest training run, which will answer a lot of questions for you. Then you will start your final taper and will need to adjust your nutrition to match. If you would like to run in relatively new running shoes for the race, this is your last chance to start breaking in a new pair. At this point you should also be finalizing your transportation to the race as well as your strategy in running the race itself.

During these last few weeks you will need to focus heavily on staying injury free and getting plenty of rest, too. Now it's more important than ever that you don't start anything new until after race day. In various ways, the last few weeks before the race will serve as your "dress rehearsal" during which you can test all of your preparations for your first marathon.

Getting There

Hopefully you started thinking about your transportation to the race when you signed up several months ago. Whether your race is large or small, one thing is true: a lot of people will be trying to get to the same place at the same time before the race starts. And if you haven't already made your final arrangements, now is the time to get them settled. Hopefully you've already purchased any airline tickets and made hotel reservations months ago. The last thing you need now is to stress out about logistics. If you are going to drive or be driven, finalize those plans now. With any luck you'll be staying at a hotel that is near both the start and finish lines—if you reserved one of the choicest hotels several months ago before it sold out. But if you weren't that forward-thinking, you can consult with the marathon organizers for suggestions. Some municipalities will even support the race with increased public transportation or special shuttles.

Keep in mind, there are sure to be road closures for the race which can also add to last-minute headaches if you aren't prepared. And, if you are flying to a different state or country, it can take up to a week to become acclimated to a new time zone or elevation. If you cannot make it a week early, try to arrive at least three days early, if possible. It's also a benefit to have a day away from your busy life to simply relax, find your way around, and get used to a new bed.

Prerun Test

Your training plan will culminate with your longest run about three weeks before the marathon. Some plans take you up to 20 miles while others will send you out for up to 26 miles or even more before the race. We don't recommend a single run longer than 20 miles. The benefits of a longer single run do not outweigh the losses.

Whatever gains you may experience in your endurance or strength at this point by running more than 20 miles is negligible compared to the increased chance of getting injured on such a long run. Ultra-marathoners, who do 100-mile races, only train to about 20 or 30 miles. It is not about the distance. It is about all that you do to become efficient.

If you feel strongly about completing additional mileage, you could run 20 miles in the morning, eat, nap, and do more miles in the evening. But we aren't recommending that for most runners either. In either case, your last long run can serve as your prerun test. You should treat this run like it is the actual marathon, using clothing, equipment, nutrition, and hydration that you expect to use in the race. Pay attention to how much rest you get in the days leading up to the run, and how you feel during the run. Make mental notes about what is working for you, what isn't, and why. You can also check your running journal for your 18- and 16-mile runs to compare notes. This is your chance to tweak your plans in response to your results during this run. It will also help you get used to running such long distances. You don't want any surprises on race day, and this is the perfect opportunity to suss them out.

There is one last item which we have not yet mentioned, with which you can experiment during your last long runs before the race. If you have high blood pressure, heart disease of any kind, or if you suffer from hypertension, please don't try this. However, if you do not have those health risks, this can give you as much as 12 percent greater energy output on race day—and it's legal. It's called caffeine. New findings show that caffeine is not as dehydrating as once thought and that it also stimulates adrenaline, which tricks the body into believing it isn't tired. The volume of caffeine found in certain carbohydrate gels can help, but is nowhere near enough to be highly effective. The volume of caffeine needed to help improve athletic performance is dependent upon the athlete's weight and size, and previous usage is important, too. U.S. Olympic triathlon team of 2008 nutritionist Bob Seebohar suggests "3–9 milligrams (mg) per kilogram (kg) of body weight" consumed about an hour before the race. To translate pounds into kilograms, divide your weight in pounds by 2.2. If you figure about 75 mg of caffeine per cup of coffee, that works out to three to five cups of coffee for an average-sized man. That is a lot of fluid to drink at once, so there are products on the market that contain higher volumes of caffeine than coffee. They come in pill or powder form. If you want to use caffeine on race day, make sure you test it out on your last, or your last few longest training runs. Those who do not drink caffeinated drinks regularly would likely be more sensitive to caffeine's effects than those who do.

COACH SAYS ...

This last, usually peak run of the season, just before taper, is the first time you can really begin to estimate your average marathon race pace. Before this, it was all about becoming more efficient and stronger. You will have more energy after tapering, but use that for the last few miles of the marathon.

If your final peak training run goes badly, or if you are not as fast as you thought, fear not. We all have bad days. Take a look at everything:

- Hydration for the week

- Mineral consumption during the week and during the peak workout

- Sleep and stress during the week

- Diet

- Whether you started out too fast during the actual workout

Due to dehydration and fatigue, your heart rate will continue to rise throughout the full marathon. Eventually, you will become anaerobic or no longer using fat to create fuel. When this happens it's all about glycogen consumption, which is the less abundant source of fuel. And when the glycogen runs out, you hit the wall, and that's it for any kind of normal pace. But if you start out at a lower heart rate, or slower average pace, you can maintain that lower heart rate longer. That way, you are less apt to hit the wall, and will have a faster overall race, because of your conservative start. This is something you can now begin to calculate and fine-tune on your last, longest training runs.

Tapering and Trusting Your Training

All good training plans will include interval tapered weeks throughout, as well as a more drastic final taper before race day. Many new runners get nervous around this time, as it seems counter-intuitive to run less when you are about to run more. However, there are decades of training experience behind this plan. Not only does your body need short-term rest, it also needs longer cycles of rest to allow you to recuperate from the additional, cumulative stresses of longer distances. Your body will understand this even if you don't. Don't forget, most of your improvement occurs during times of rest when your body is repairing, building muscle, and creating new mitochondria to help power your runs. Also during periods of taper or rest, levels of key hormones increase (testosterone for motivation, human growth hormone for muscle growth), red blood cell count increases, your immune system becomes stronger, and many other critical factors improve.

There is a long list of benefits to tapering. Without the chance to do all of this, your body won't meet the challenge of endurance training with as great a level of efficiency. So when your coach or training plan tells you to cut back on your mileage drastically before race day, listen. You will still continue to run, but your focus will be on maintenance rather than building distance. Be careful, as you can screw up an entire training season by doing too much exercise during a final period of scheduled taper. If you taper properly, you will actually become *more* efficient on race day, increasing your energy output by up to 6 percent or slightly more. Now what is there to argue with about that?

As you may recall from Chapter 10, the faster drop or decay in volume of an exponential taper is going to be more efficient than the slower drop or decay of a traditional step or gradual taper. Women benefit from less of a drop and may want to do 10 to 15 minutes more than the men. That might mean a 40- to 45-minute workout for women during most of taper. The men, on the other hand, are averaging about 30 minutes. Check out the end of the marathon schedule in Appendix D to see this theory applied in an actual schedule.

Here is one last note on training during the final taper. Marathon athletes are notorious for not feeling they have done enough. When the final taper arrives, many still have the desire to push for more. Keep this in mind: it can take at least 10 to 14 days for an exercise to affect your system to make you more efficient. In other words, during the last two weeks, if you went out and did more, it would probably not benefit you till after the race was over. Unfortunately, it would also deplete all of those critical elements we mentioned earlier (hormones, red blood cell count, and more), which make you more efficient. So if there were any greater truth right now, it would be that "more," especially during the last two weeks of taper, really does mean "less" on race day.

Finalize Race Day Strategy

Now that you have finalized your plan to get to the starting line, and have accepted the logic of your final taper, it's time to turn your mind to what happens after the starting line. During your training, you have learned how to regulate your energy output, with even levels throughout, including hills. You learned how to use nutrition and rest to your best advantage, and what clothing and equipment work best for you. Now is the time to put all this together and think through the race itself. How will you use all of this valuable knowledge to power yourself through your first marathon?

Ideally, you have familiarized yourself with the race course and all of its attendant supports and resources. You have analyzed the *elevation map* and noted the locations of bathrooms and water stops. You know you must start out slowly and maintain a consistent energy output throughout the marathon. But what if things don't quite turn out as you expect? What if it's a hot day, or you're simply not feeling your best? What if the hills are bigger than you expected? You need to keep some strategies in the back of your mind to draw upon at times like these. If the hills seem bigger, dial down your intensity. Don't ever pick up so much speed on the downhills that you raise your heart rate. (See Chapter 8 for a more detailed discussion of running hills.) If it's a hot day, slow your pace and take in additional water and electrolytes. Think about how you will handle any possible challenges, and come race day, nothing will ruffle you.

> **DEFINITION**
>
> An **elevation map** is a cross-section of the entire race course, illustrating the altitude gained and lost along the route. It shows you where the hills are, and how big they are. Most races will provide elevation maps. It is a crucial tool in planning your race strategy.

Get Plenty of Rest

Rest is an integral part of your training. In fact, your training would be useless without it. During the last three weeks before the race, you should be concentrating only on what it takes to be at your best. Based on your training plan, you should be taking it easy on your days off. Your body has come through many months of hard training and deserves to recuperate and repair itself. Don't cheat it out of that opportunity by starting any challenging new sports or cross-training. We can't say it enough: don't start anything new. Aim for eight solid hours of sleep every night.

Similarly, your mind has also been challenged by your months of training. Use proven techniques such as meditation or positive visualization to calm your body and your mind as you near the date of your race. During the first hour of sleep is when the greatest volume of cellular growth takes place. Therefore, just before sleep would be a good time to gently stretch. Generating greater flexibility is always a plus, especially before a race. Just keep it gentle, as your muscles will have been at rest, and not as flexible to begin with.

One Week Before Race Day

Race day is just around the corner. In your final week, your mileage will drop off even more than in previous weeks of your taper, and you will only run very short distances, at marathon race pace. You are in the last phase of tapering, and you should adjust your diet and rest accordingly. Now you also have a preliminary idea of what the weather will be on race day, so you can begin to tailor both your preparations and your race strategy as well.

As the days tick down to race day, you may begin to feel more and more anxious. This is natural, but you should take pains to keep your mind in check. The excitement and adrenaline of anticipation can wear you out, so you should try to distract yourself and engage in light, enjoyable activities such as spending time with friends and family or any other hobbies that give you pleasure. You may have trouble sleeping on the night before the marathon, so during the latter part of this week, strive to get plenty of rest. Remember, your extensive preparations have brought you this far, and you are as ready as you can be for a marathon. On a lighter note, this is also a good time to trim your toenails if you haven't done so already, so that any mistakes have a chance to heal.

YELLOW LIGHT

Try to avoid alcoholic beverages while you are enjoying the final countdown to race day. Alcohol can dehydrate you and is also metabolized as a carbohydrate. Therefore, it can disturb the delicate hydration and nutrition balance you need to maintain in order to run a healthy and enjoyable race.

Final Taper

You are already at a low volume in your exponential taper going into this final week. During your final full taper you will run your 30 minutes or so at marathon race pace. Then you bring it down to zero, which would mean a day off with rest two days before the marathon. The day before the race, you will need a little increase in work again. Run 10 minutes on the day before the race. Women, of course, need to increase that to 12 to 15 minutes the day before, also at marathon race pace.

According to *Tapering and Peaking for Optimal Performance* by Inigo Mujika, Ph.D. (see Appendix B), studies of different athletes indicate that you can have an increase of .05 percent energy on race day with this slight increase in workload on the day before the race, after taking it to zero. See the application of this idea at the end of the marathon training schedule in Appendix D. Women will need to add about 10 to 15 minutes to each run during the taper on that schedule.

The work during the last taper serves to keep you running-ready while not stressing the body any more than necessary. In other words, you are maintaining your efficiency. You're maintaining an elevated red blood cell count, an increase in capillary veins and arteries, additional mitochondria, and an increase in hormones. Don't forget, you should also match your diet to your reduced mileage so that you don't add any weight during this important time.

Rehearse Race Day Strategy

At the three-week mark, you finalized your race day strategy. Now is the time to actually rehearse it, taking into consideration any new information you have learned in the last few weeks. With the weather and your general state of wellness in mind, begin tailoring your choice of clothing, equipment, and nutrition and hydration. Each day may bring new information, so be prepared to remain flexible. Imagine what you will need during the race itself. How many carbohydrate gels and how much water will you be comfortable carrying? Pack up your fanny pack if you're using one, and run with it once or twice during this week so you understand how it will feel on race day. Think through your entire race again so you can prepare as completely as possible.

COACH SAYS …

If possible, visit the marathon race course before race day. If you can either walk some of it or drive the entire route, you will learn a tremendous amount that you wouldn't otherwise know. Visualization can only go so far. If you drive the route, you may want to stop on any hills if possible, and walk or jog them so you know what to expect. At this point, the more information you can glean about the route, the better, so put on your detective hat and investigate.

Double-Check Travel Arrangements

If you haven't done it already, reconfirm all of your travel arrangements at least once during the final week. Make sure you understand where and when any shuttles will pick you up and drop you off. Memorize where the start and finish line are in relation to any amenities you may need, such as parking or your hotel. If you are traveling, it is a good idea to research where pharmacies, groceries, and sporting goods stores are in relation to your hotel in case any last-minute needs pop up. If your race is local, you should rehearse your method for getting to the starting line. If a friend is driving you, confirm your plans. If you are driving yourself, double-check the parking arrangements at the race. Don't forget that there will probably be a tremendous amount of traffic that morning, as thousands of people try to do exactly what you're trying to do. Race organizers usually publicize road closure plans, so try to familiarize yourself with those conditions as well. Nearly all roads that the race will use are going to be closed to traffic early on race morning. At this late stage of the game, the last thing you need is for some small problem to turn into a crisis. Again, preparation is the best prevention.

Organize Your Gear

Whether your marathon is in a distant city or in your hometown, you need to start organizing all of your equipment and supplies. A little military training might come in handy at this point. As you get closer to race day, you can start winnowing down the possibilities. The idea is to keep all your viable choices handy so you don't have to think when it comes time to pick the best options. Some runners like to lay everything out on a bed or couch during the last few days before the race. It's a good idea to give your running shoes a once-over as well. Make sure your laces and soles are in good shape. If you are traveling, you should pack any critical items in your carry-on luggage such as your bib, chip, running shoes, at least one complete outfit, and your preferred foods. You should also be sure to bring any second-choice options as well as extra items that you can use to adjust to unexpected differences in weather or temperature. And, if you forget anything, the research you've already done to locate local suppliers will come in handy.

Carbo Loading

The concept of carbo loading has gone through many unfortunate misinterpretations. The theory behind it has sadly morphed into something unrecognizable. Many runners think that carbo loading is a free ticket to gorge on carbohydrates for the last few days before a race. Not only can this wreak havoc on your blood sugar, but it can lead to feeling bloated and gassy on the morning of the race, which translates into a difficult and uncomfortable marathon experience.

Carbo loading is much more complicated than that. In fact, it begins with a complete reduction of carbohydrate intake. This usually takes place approximately one week before the big race. The athlete's diet may only include some vegetables as carbohydrates, if even that. The rest of the diet would be proteins and some fat intake. When your body is starving for something, it usually responds by storing that nutrient as much as possible in a kind of "famine" response. This is true even when finally fed that thing in abundance. So following a period of two or three days of completely depleting your body of carbohydrates, you set your body up to be ready to absorb more carbohydrates than normal.

For the next two or three days, you go in the opposite direction. You begin to load a lot of carbohydrates into your body. But be careful—if you eat too many carbohydrates, you could end up storing them as fat. If done correctly, you will end up with a higher amount of carbohydrates than normal to use as fuel on race day. That is the idea of carbo loading. Incidentally, this decrease in carbs would mesh nicely with your very low mileage during the final week of tapering.

YELLOW LIGHT

If you're considering carbo loading, seek the guidance of an experienced nutritionist. This extreme diet concept must take the individual into consideration, and everyone has different needs. What may work for one person could be disastrous for another. We merely report this concept so you will understand the idea, but please use discretion in implementing it.

The Day Before the Race

It's finally here! If you have followed your training program and have disciplined your mind as well as your body, you are ready. Don't let any doubts or anxiety diminish your confidence at this point. It may be a good time to draw upon the bonds you created in your training group or with any running buddies you may have recruited. You're all in this together, and solidarity feels good when facing a new challenge.

The best thing you can do as race day approaches is to not set any expectations. After all, this is your first time, so it's very easy to get caught up in unrealistic predictions. And you don't need to place any unnecessary pressure on yourself at this point. Today, envision yourself doing your best and not trying to live up to some preconceived notion. In this way, you will remain present, you will listen to your body, and you will be able to react to any issues that pop up appropriately and without prejudice. Today you can take a very short, 10-minute run at marathon race pace just to keep yourself limber, or 12 to 15 minutes for women. But don't exert yourself any more than is necessary. Try to stay off your feet, even if you are in a new city and want to see the sights. Swollen, tired feet tomorrow morning would be a disaster. Try to eat light and stay away from items that are difficult to digest, such as dairy or fried foods. In general, take it easy today, focus on how far you have come, take comfort from the preparations you have put in place, and visualize a smooth and safe marathon for tomorrow.

Expo—Pick Up Your Bib

Most race organizers set up an expo on the day or two before the race in order to hand out bibs and chips. The expo usually entails a gathering of sports supply vendors and race sponsors who tempt you with their wares while you pick up your bib, chip, and T-shirt. Always try to check that your timing chip works. When you pick up your chip at the expo, you can check it on a pad connected to a computer, usually at the end of the pickup area. It should register your name, bib number, and personal information. If not, make sure to mention it to a volunteer. They'll need to get you a new timing chip and program it. A certain percentage will always be defective, so beware. This is true of the new throwaway chips being used by more and more races as well.

You can often leave the expo with a bagful of food and equipment samples to use during the race or in future training. Of course, don't try anything unfamiliar during the race. Race organizers will be present and will be available to help you find your bib number if you've lost it, and other such administrative issues. You can ask questions, pick up any handouts you might not have received, and schmooze with your fellow runners. Expo organizers also often reach out to the community, setting up sign-making stations and the like. Make sure you understand the where and when of your expo, as it's usually your only chance to pick up your bib and chip. Smaller races may allow you to pick up your bib on the morning of the race.

A typical expo is very crowded and includes bib pickup stations as well as vendors and sample products.

Mental, Physical, and Spiritual Preparation

While your body may be doing all the hard work during the marathon, it's your spirit which has pulled you through this far. It's the mind, not the body, that initiates training and sets goals. Therefore, you must prepare mind, body, and spirit for the challenge that lies ahead. An overactive mind can work against you when you need to stay focused for long periods such as a marathon, so try to calm yours. Use your own rituals, or other simple practices to relieve stress. Deep breathing, stretching, and creative visualization all can help keep negative thoughts away, as can favorite hobbies. To keep your spirit—another of your vital engines—running smoothly, pay attention to your morale and your outlook. Positive thinking and an emphasis on your recent accomplishments keeps your spirits up. And, as discussed in earlier sections, your body now simply needs appropriate nutrition, hydration, and rest in order to be as primed as possible for your first marathon challenge tomorrow.

Traditional Pasta Dinner

The pasta dinner that most marathon organizers provide on the night before the race really doesn't provide the best or most strategic nutrition. Pasta is more of a refined, simple carbohydrate that does not carry many other nutrients. And, the sauces that are offered at such gatherings are generally of poor quality, such as cream-based or heavy meat-based choices. While the camaraderie of such events is important and invigorating, the food leaves much to be desired. You would do better to eat a balanced meal of complex carbohydrates along with a little protein and fat. If you are carbo loading, your meal would emphasize carbohydrates, but you still need to exercise portion control. Eating too much tonight of any kind of food could make you sluggish and uncomfortable in the morning. Don't forget to drink water and avoid dehydrating beverages such as alcohol. If you are sensitive to caffeine, make sure to avoid it tonight as well.

> **YELLOW LIGHT**
>
> Pasta is usually made from durum wheat flour which has a relatively high protein content. However, only the heart of the grain is used, and not the germ or bran which carry more fiber and nutrition. Therefore, whole-wheat pasta would be a better choice if you simply must have pasta.

Fine-Tune Your Clothing and Equipment

This is your last and best chance to prepare your clothing and equipment for the race tomorrow morning. You've winnowed down your choices, and now you have a pretty good picture of what tomorrow's weather will be. You should do your final preparatory run-through in your head, and finish packing up your fanny pack or any other items you will be bringing with you to the race, such as your after-race bag. Make sure to keep a few options available and in easy reach in case of any surprises or last-minute changes in the morning. If your race starts very early, don't forget to pack for a cold morning start and a warmer finish line. And above all, don't forget to take your running shoes with you on the morning of the race. Believe it or not, people do sometimes forget to pack them or wear them!

Prepare Strategic Nutrition and Hydration

By now, you know what works for you in terms of nutrition and hydration. You also should know how many water stops are provided on the race course, and whether sports drinks are offered or not. In the last couple of weeks, you've already estimated how much reinforcement you will need in terms of carbohydrates and hydration.

Now is the time to think it all out again, one last time, and make any adjustments that seem necessary. Again, keep a few options out in case you change your mind in the morning or need some additional fortifications. You may feel differently than you expected when you wake up, and you want to be able to adjust to that possibility as quickly as possible.

Sleeping the Night Before

Don't be overly concerned if you cannot sleep the night before the marathon. This is a common occurrence, most often caused by anxiety and adrenaline. While rest on the night before a race is important, you can still perform well if you managed some decent sleep on the nights leading up to today. Getting a good amount of sleep (eight hours a night) two or three nights before the race will help even out any sleep debt you might develop on the night just prior to the race. However, on that final night, be strategic and do what it takes to push yourself naturally into sleep. You may have your own rituals, but you can also try these tips:

- Don't eat too late at night.
- Don't do anything too strenuous before bed.
- Keep your room cool, quiet, and dimly lit near bedtime.
- Take a warm bath or shower before bed to help relax.
- Don't watch television as it can irritate you or keep you up too late.
- Start getting ready for bed early so you don't feel rushed.

 COACH SAYS ...

It is easiest to sleep in a cool room. Your body must slow down and cool down in order to start the descent into slumber. To help with this process, try turning your thermostat down to 64 or 65 degrees.

The use of sleep aids is not recommended as they can have lingering effects the next day, which would negatively impact your performance. Often marathoners wake every hour, and when the alarm finally goes off, it is almost a relief. If you keep waking up, get out of bed and briefly do something else that is low-key and usually makes you feel sleepy, like reading. Often that can relax you and help you fall asleep. But rest assured, less than optimal sleep on the night before the race won't affect your performance in any quantifiable way.

The Least You Need to Know

- Your longest run in your training plan will take place approximately three weeks before the marathon. It is your last chance for experimentation and a full "dress rehearsal."

- Tapering is a proven strategy to improve performance, even if it seems counter-intuitive.

- With one week to go, your training is as much mental as physical. Don't forget to rehearse your race day strategy, recheck those travel plans once more, and carefully plan your carbo loading strategy to maximize your energy.

- The day before the race, you need to pick up your bib, chip, and T-shirt, but don't be tempted by goody bags with nutritional supplements you have never tried.

- Proper rest is key, but insomnia on the night before a race is common. Therefore, strive to get enough rest on the last few nights leading up to the race.

Race Day

In This Chapter

- Waking up early with enough time for prerace preparations
- What to expect when you get to the marathon
- Preparing physically and psychologically for the race ahead
- How to avoid hitting the wall on race day

So it's finally here! The day for which you have prepared like no other. Your training has done its job and you are ready for your first marathon. If you're like most people, you've been feeling more and more nervous as this day grew nearer. That's normal. And today your stomach may feel queasy. You may feel like you have a weight on your chest. And your eyes may be half-closed from not enough sleep. That's all normal, too, believe it or not. In fact, you'll probably feel nervous, and a little bit of all of the above, until the race begins. Again, completely normal.

Once you take your first step onto the race course, you should be on auto-pilot and your training will guide your every step. But before that gun goes off, you need a structured plan to get you through your marathon morning. Just as preparation and strategy have been the hallmarks of your training for the last several months, so too must they dictate the hours before and during your race.

The Morning of the Race

Last night probably wasn't the best night's sleep you've ever had, but that's okay. Even if you didn't get as much sleep as you'd like, you still need to make sure that you'll wake up on time on race morning. And "on time" should really mean two to three hours before the race, depending on how much traveling you must do to get there.

Hopefully you've only left a few last-minute things to do on marathon morning. To help ease your nerves, try setting up a couple of alarms, or one alarm with some backup systems. For example, if you're staying at a hotel, you could use your cell phone alarm as well as the hotel's wake-up call service. Or use two alarm clocks. Or you and a fellow marathon participant or running buddy could agree to call each other at a set time. The last thing you need right now is to stress out about whether you'll wake up on time.

MILE MARKER

Most but not all marathons start early in the morning, so make sure you know exactly what time your division is expected to start. The 2010 San Francisco Marathon started at 5:30 A.M. because of time restrictions on the Golden Gate Bridge, which is part of the course. In contrast, the 2011 Boston Marathon is expected to start at 9:00 A.M. Obviously, getting up at 3:00 A.M. is a lot different than getting up at 6:00 A.M. A little rehearsal in either case makes for good insurance on race day, so try a few practice runs at the same time as your chosen marathon in the weeks leading up to the race.

Finalize Nutrition and Hydration Choices

If you have been following your training and the advice in this book, specifically in Chapter 6, you have already thought out your food and hydration needs during the marathon. Hopefully you have mentally run the course and you have done your research to find out how many water stops there will be, and where they'll be located on the race route. Therefore, you have already packed the majority of what you expect to use. However, now on marathon morning you have a better idea of the weather forecast. If it's going to be warmer than expected, you'll need to allow for additional hydration and electrolytes. If it's going to be colder, you may need some extra calories to help keep you warm.

Additionally, what you eat for breakfast is very important. Now isn't the time to try anything new. Whatever you have found to be the easiest on your stomach, and a good source of energy, is the way to go. It's the same with caffeine—if you don't normally have it for breakfast, or before your long runs, don't change now. If you're staying in a hotel and won't have time for room service, make sure you stock your room ahead of time with familiar foods that you can eat for breakfast. You should also listen to your body, and if you are especially hungry or not hungry, adjust your intake accordingly. But don't start out on an empty stomach, unless you're one of those who suffer greatly from eating before a run. Even a gel or bar will help to get your blood sugar going. It is best to eat the bulk of your prerace food about two hours before the start of the race, to allow your body enough time to start digesting it. Running with a full stomach is uncomfortable at best, and can lead to nausea or even worse.

COACH SAYS ...

Popular premarathon breakfast foods include oatmeal, bagels, apples, or bananas. They are all relatively easy to digest and deliver a good amount of energy. Dairy products can be a bit heavy for some, as they take longer to digest and don't offer as much energy in the form of carbohydrates.

It's also important to think out what you'll eat just before the race. Depending on what you decided to eat for breakfast, you'll need to choose wisely. By the time you get to the race, breakfast should've already started to leave your stomach and your blood sugar may be starting to wane. Something light and full of carbohydrates is a good choice. For this prerace snack we have found bagels, oatmeal bars, or gels can do the trick pretty effectively. However, avoid the brands of these foods that are filled with processed sugars. You don't want to spike your insulin levels right before a race. This will cause your energy levels to drop during the race. Don't forget you're looking into the immediate future when you eat. You might not be starving now, but you must plan diligently to prevent any low energy problems from developing after you have started the race. Don't fill up but don't wait too long between snacks either.

Make sure you also drink adequately before the race. Many runners cut back on hydration within the hour or two before the race to reduce the need for pit-stops, but you should always drink when you are thirsty. Some water with breakfast, and up to a cup or two again within the last couple of hours before the race will usually set you up well. Some runners prefer to use sports drinks instead of water, or sports drinks slightly diluted with water. Again, you should do whatever has worked best for you in the past on your long runs. And this is all predicated on the expectation that you have hydrated well in the days leading up to today, as well as before bed yesterday evening.

Finalize Your Clothing and Equipment

Last night, you likely fine-tuned your clothing and equipment for today. Now that race day is here, you have a little more information to work with. Naturally, the latest weather forecast will dictate many of your choices in apparel and equipment. It may also affect what you choose to pack in the bag you will bring to the race. If you think you'll be too cold at the starting line, you can layer up, though this can leave you with the dilemma of what to do with the extra clothing once you start running and warm up. Some runners simply tie extra clothing around their waists, though others find this too clumsy and troublesome. It can also hold in heat and moisture. Many marathons have contracted with local charities to pick up discarded clothing along the marathon route. Therefore, if you're so inclined, you can don some outerwear that you don't mind parting with for good during the race.

You will probably not need to make any changes to the equipment you've laid out unless there is some extreme condition to deal with. For instance, if it's expected to be an especially hot or humid day, you may want to use a backpack water system instead of just a water belt. Most water belts can't hold any more than about 40 ounces, which is a little over a quart. Backpack water systems, on the other hand, can hold up to 100 ounces. And, if you're drinking at least 4 ounces per mile as you should, the smaller water bottle will only last you 10 miles at most. Of course, there will be water stops as well, and some races offer sports drinks as well as water. But it's best to have too much water available than not enough. (See Chapter 4 for more on hydration systems.) Don't forget to slather on some sunscreen before leaving your home or hotel.

YELLOW LIGHT

You must hydrate in the morning. However, beware of developing hyponatremia, a dangerous imbalance of sodium in your body caused by overhydration. Too much water can dilute electrolytes, upsetting your fluid balance and disturbing electrical signals like nerve and cardiac muscle impulses. Add some mineral pills or electrolytes to your morning hydration (see Chapter 6 for more information).

Here are some items you may want to carry with you during the race:

- Identification
- Emergency contact information
- Key to your car or hotel room
- Water and/or sports drinks
- Electrolyte pills
- Carbohydrate gels, blocks, or beans
- Energy bars
- A travel-sized bottle of sunscreen
- Hard candy or any other carb sources you like
- Small bandages for blisters

This is by no means a comprehensive list, and many runners prefer to carry much less.

Pack Your Postrace Bag

Most point-to-point races (they start and end in different places) will allow you to bring a bag of supplies that they will store for you during the race and that you can pick up at the finish line. Common items that runners wish to have at the end of the race are:

- A change of shoes and socks
- Clean, dry, loose-fitting clothing, including underwear
- A jacket, sweatshirt, and/or hat for warmth
- Cell phone
- Favorite recovery food or drink

Usually, you can use the goody bag you received during the expo for this, and it will have a place on which you can write in your bib number. Some races insist upon clear plastic bags, which you can also label with your bib number.

Get There Early

Not enough can be said about arriving early on marathon day. Do yourself a favor and do not schedule yourself too tightly in the morning. You'll appreciate the stress-busting effects of taking your time to get ready and to get to the race. Once you're certain you have all of your early morning preparations completed and you're ready to head off to the race, there is still a lot to do before leaping across that starting line. After you're dressed and you've packed—or are wearing—all of the equipment and supplies you will need for the race, you still need to get to the race. Don't forget to bring your prerace snack and postrace bag, too. If you're lucky and you planned well, you'll be able to walk to the starting line. If not, you must allow for traffic whether driving or taking a shuttle. Parking may also take time just because of the volume of drivers trying to park at the same time, but also because the lot may not be near the starting line.

Once you have negotiated the logistics of actually getting to the race, you need to figure out where all the most important services are located. Some races are organized better than others, so you may need patience to find your way around. But that's not too stressful because you have plenty of time, right? Once you've found the starting line, there are a few other important things you may want to think about. For example, it would be a good idea to locate the postrace bag drop-off, the bathrooms, and the medical personnel, all of which are described in the next sections. Take some time to refamiliarize yourself with the layout of the course, as well as the locations of the water stops. You wouldn't want to finish up your water, expecting an upcoming water stop 2 miles before you actually get to it. It's also a good time to chat with your fellow runners. You can learn a lot that way, about the race in particular, about running, and about who knows what else.

YELLOW LIGHT

Many races do not provide bathrooms at the first mile stop. Boston recently started their bathroom facilities at mile 2, and New York currently starts at mile 3. Make sure to do your homework so you can plan your bathroom stop accordingly.

Postrace Bag Drop-Off

In most races, you can check your bag near the starting line, and if the finish line isn't nearby, the bags will be transported to the finish line. They'll be arranged in order by bib number. Using the bag drop-off is a lot more convenient than leaving something in your car for after the race, or trying to find a relative at the finish line after you're already exhausted from your first race. However, most races that start and end at the same place will not have a bag drop-off or transport.

Bags are lined up by bib number for easy pickup after the race.

Bathrooms

Most likely, one of the first things you'll need when you arrive at the starting line is a bathroom. Facilities at the starting line will, of course, be very crowded, and the lines can be quite long. This is where you will probably use up most of the extra time you've allotted yourself for the start of the race. Our empirical evidence suggests that with most large races, at an hour before the race, bathroom lines can take 20 to 30 minutes on average. You wouldn't want to skimp on time to take care of absolute necessities, and just about everybody has a nervous stomach at this point. And, being stressed out about the time would certainly not help the situation. You don't want to find yourself standing in line for a bathroom when the starting gun goes off.

Usually, the bathrooms will be portable toilets with only the minimum amenities, so you may want to carry hand sanitizer. Marathon runners aren't known for spending a lot of time in the bathroom, so don't expect any kind of luxuries (such as soap in some instances). While standing in line for a bathroom, try this relaxation technique. Inhale deeply and hold it for a few seconds, then exhale. Do this three times, and stretch your arms over your head. It can also be a good time to get in some standing progressive and active stretches. This movement will also keep your blood circulating better in your legs. This is much better than standing still for the 20- or 30-minute wait time.

COACH SAYS …

The average runner will lose at least 5 to 10 minutes to bathroom breaks on the marathon course. You should loosely figure this delay into your targeted finish time.

Once you are on the marathon course, bathrooms will usually be spaced at definite intervals, which are hopefully described in the race's literature and on its website. If you haven't familiarized yourself with your race's particular arrangements already, ask questions now. You should note that some smaller marathons have very few if any amenities. Be sure to do your research ahead of time and plan accordingly. Sometimes, a restaurant or gas station along the course will come in handy, and it pays to know where they are located ahead of time. The bathrooms early in the course will generally be the most crowded, so if you can wait you may save some time. Don't wait too long, however, and add unnecessary discomfort to what is going to be an already challenging time. You'll also probably find that you have to urinate less toward the end of the race, as your kidneys begin to work more slowly due to your level of exertion.

Medical Personnel

One of the most crucial aspects in any marathon race is its medical support. Ideally, medical personnel will be staked out along the course as well as at the start and finish lines. Should a runner have any medical difficulties during the race, medical support can be radioed and the runner can be picked up and transported to the nearest medical tent. Several such tents are likely to be positioned along the course, most often near certain water stops. In an emergency, of course, an ambulance will be called. Medical tents are usually equipped with basic medical supplies, equipment and medications, as well as stretchers or cots. Paramedics, doctors, and/or nurses are typically available to attend to any injured or ill runners. The most medical personnel will usually be assembled at the finish line, when runners are most likely to need some support. Larger races can be quite sophisticated in their medical support arrangements.

> **MILE MARKER**
>
> Some of the most common injuries suffered by marathon runners are sprained ankles, shin splints, stress fractures, and various maladies of the tendons and connective tissues of the knees, ankles, and feet. See Chapter 12 for more about common running injuries.

Getting in the Zone

Getting in the zone means different things to different people. You may find it helpful to chat and joke with your fellow runners. Or some people find it more sustaining to focus inward and think quietly. Whatever works best for you, now is the time to do it with intention. This is the point at which you need to transition from preparation to implementation.

Your mind has been the driving force behind your training, and now it's your biggest asset as you prepare to start your first marathon run. All of your focus and determination have brought you to this point. It's a good time to reflect upon all the lessons you've learned in your training, as well as to do some forward thinking about the course that's laid out in front of you. You may find it relaxing to close your eyes for a few moments and focus on your breathing. Or you may have other rituals that help you center and prepare. As you look around at the other runners who are also striving to organize their thinking and get control of their nerves, you will see a wide variety of tricks and techniques. You're in good company as you prepare to take that first step of your first and most meaningful marathon.

Warming Up

Your efforts to get to the starting line have already gotten your muscles moving and have warmed you up a bit. However, it is a good idea to start some specific prerun work to get your body primed. Gentle stretches, a little jogging in place or a few very short, slow runs can get you ready for running. Just like a boxer who shadowboxes in preparation for his big fight, it will help you to go through the same motions you will be using in your run. You can, for example, lightly step from foot to foot while swinging your bent arms back and forth as you would when running. Some people use yoga or meditation before the starting line. Whatever has worked for you before your long runs should work for you today as well. As with all of your other activities today, don't try anything new or different.

Managing Negative Thoughts

If you can get your mind under control, you have won the battle. Although the power of your mind is the strongest tool in your running toolbox, it can also trip you up if you let it run wild. Nervousness stems from worry, which is an entirely useless endeavor. You have trained diligently for today's race. Your body is as ready as it can be. But if you find yourself descending into negative thoughts, worry, or dread, you can pull your body right down with you. You can get your stomach in a tizzy and cause your heart to race. Your muscles may tighten up and your perception could become skewed. But if you can recognize that your body itself is not worrying, perhaps you can see the futility of negative thoughts. Imagine a pilot with an airplane. The pilot can worry himself sick, and if he hasn't prepared himself and his plane, he has a right to. But if the plane is in top shape and is ready to go, it's only the pilot's mind that is causing the problem. The plane, objectively, is prepared. It can only do what the pilot instructs it to do. And if the pilot is telling it to over-rev its engine or run on low fuel, it will do that for as long as it can, and then it will fail. Hence, be careful how you use your mind because its power is immeasurable.

Therefore, it's important to learn how to manage negative thoughts. Your body has already run close to the marathon distance before, possibly more than once. You have thought out everything you'll need to keep your body as happy as it can be. Amenities along the race course are designed to do the same thing. Everything is in place to support you as much as possible. So you need to let go of negative imaginings and focus on the positives. That may sound easier said than done, but with a few realistic and effective tools, it's entirely within your reach. You can use many of the same strategies you used during training (described in Chapter 11) to stay focused and positive.

COACH SAYS ...

When confronting fear, the best thing to do is to imagine the worst possible scenario coming true. If you can survive that, then you have nothing to worry about. And the worst thing that can happen on a marathon is that you don't finish. So you will do a different one!

Imagine Your Entire Race

By now you have a mental map of the course itself, as well as the approximate locations of water stops and bathrooms. You can also recall what your longest runs so far have been like. Put those two thoughts together and you should be able to imagine yourself running this particular marathon course. You should know, approximately, when you'll be getting hungry and thirsty, and when you might need a bathroom break. You can now mentally prepare to deal with each of those needs as they arise because you have brought whatever supplies you will need. You also know that you must start out slowly and conserve your energy for as long as possible.

What will you do if you have to take a bathroom break but none of your running buddies need to stop? Will you tire yourself out by trying to catch up with them? Or will you stick to your plan and run at your marathon pace, trusting that you may catch them later on? The bottom line is, you should not increase your heart rate above your marathon pace in order to catch up. Or what if your musical device fails to work (assuming they are allowed in your race)? It may be a big disappointment, but if you have already thought about the possibility, you can decide how you will handle it ahead of time. Distractions and annoyances can be fatiguing; it's best to think everything out ahead of time to minimize time or energy lost on unimportant things.

Mantras and Rituals

Many runners use mantras or rituals to help them stay focused and positive throughout the race. Repeating a simple mantra such as "I can do this" or "one step at a time" can help distract you from any negative thoughts you might be fighting. Some people pray, some repeat favorite inspirational quotes, or even visualize scenes from movies. You can break up the race into smaller bits, imagining something like five 5-mile runs, and count them down as you progress. You could focus on how good, and how proud, you will feel at the finish line. If you developed any rituals before your long runs that gave you comfort, you should also use them now.

During the race, many runners play mind games to help keep them going. They try to guess runners' ages, or count the number of people wearing red, for example. Jeff Galloway, a renowned running coach and author, describes imagining a giant rubber band that he attaches to faster runners as they pass him, or ball bearings that he can shake from his hair to make his feet glide more easily. He says he collects extra oxygen molecules and keeps them handy for when he needs an extra boost. Your mind may be very creative at convincing you of negative things, but you can harness that power and use it ingeniously for positive thinking. Be creative in imagining your success, and you'll get there sooner than you expected.

Another great psychological tool to get you through the last few miles of a marathon is to count your steps. That's right. Simply start counting every time, or every other time, your left or right foot hits the ground. The point is that you create a kind of mantra that causes you to focus on the rhythm of your body. That focus helps you to maintain the same pace. In addition, any negative thoughts are stopped by your concentration on counting. You can't have a negative thought while counting. It's virtually impossible. Actually, you cannot really have many thoughts at all while counting. This is a good lesson in how to begin meditation as a runner. After using this ritual of counting your steps several times, you'll eventually learn to channel out negative thoughts and meditate while running, even without the counting. This type of focused distraction can also help you recover in case you went out too fast and find yourself struggling to get to the finish. Start counting your steps, and before you know it, you will be crossing the finish line and accepting the medal you deserve.

Plan to Avoid the Wall

Another important situation you must plan to avoid is "hitting the wall." This is the point at which you have used up all your glycogen stores and you simply cannot go on, except perhaps to walk slowly. It's a torturous feeling, and can ruin your race experience completely. Many experienced marathoners believe that everyone always hits the wall at mile 21. This simply is not true, and there is absolutely no reason for this, except ignorance and poor strategy. It's quite simple to avoid the problem altogether. One important strategy is to plan your nutrition and hydration carefully, so you can keep your energy up and stay as strong as possible. It is also imperative that you take in enough electrolytes as you run. You should plan to consume a good amount of easily digestible carbohydrates throughout the race, such as gels, blocks, and beans, some of which also contain electrolytes. Sports drinks can also supply carbs as well as electrolytes.

In addition to proper nutrition and hydration, an important factor in avoiding the wall is to keep to your training plan in terms of pace. It's critical to keep your level of energy output as level as possible. When there are hills, for example, you need to slow down on the uphill and speed up only slightly on the way down. If the hill is steep, quite often even moderately paced runners won't be able to slow down enough to continue running, and will need to walk. This is especially true if the hill is in the first three quarters of the race. Also, make sure you do that *negative split*, to ensure that you do not hit the wall. Early on, and always in the first half, keep it a few seconds slower per mile than the second half of the race. And, if it turns out to be a significantly hot day, you'll need to lower your average pace as well.

DEFINITION

A **negative split** is when you spend less time (negative) in the second half of the race than the first. This means you run more slowly in the first half of the race. This allows you to utilize that abundant fuel source of fat, which you do at a lower heart rate.

It's most common to hit the wall around mile 20, as that is the point at which the human body reaches the limit of its glycogen stores. If you haven't been replenishing that glycogen at an adequate rate, or you have not kept control of your heart rate and energy output, you may find it impossible to complete that last 6.2 miles. Keep in mind, if you lower your heart rate, which you can do by walking, your body will begin to use more fat again as a fuel source. Obviously, walking slowly isn't the optimal way to finish your race, but it can help keep you going. During your long runs, you should have learned how to pace your eating, and which foods work best for you to keep your energy up for the longest amount of time. You should do the same thing for the marathon, and be sure to bring a little extra for the final miles that you might not have covered in training runs. Also keep in mind the fact that your digestive system will progressively slow down as your mileage increases, so simple, easy-to-digest foods will work best. And, if in the last few miles you find you have a good amount of energy, speed up and use it.

The Least You Need to Know

- Plan to wake up two to three hours before the start of the race to allow for preparation time.
- Allow extra time for traffic on the roads near the marathon course and lines for bathrooms at the starting line.
- Plan to arrive one to two hours early. Once you are there, locate the bag drop-off site, bathrooms, and medical personnel stations.
- You can avoid hitting the wall by controlling your level of energy output and consuming carbohydrates throughout the race to keep your energy up.
- Gentle stretches get you ready physically, but also prepare mentally by visualizing the entire race and confronting your fears.

The Race

In This Chapter

- What to expect at the starting line
- Run through your strategy again
- Staying on pace
- What to do when you need to stop
- What your fellow competitors are really like
- Don't forget to enjoy the experience!

There is nothing quite like a marathon starting line. The anticipation, the excitement, and the anxiety all add up to a unique and unforgettable energy and atmosphere. You'll want to get there extra early in order to take it all in. Before you get into position behind the starting line, enjoy this moment. Not many people earn the right to stand at a marathon starting line. Look at the tents, the banners, and the sea of people. Give a grateful and appreciative nod to the organizers and volunteers who have already worked so hard to make this event possible. Note the medical personnel who are ready to help at a moment's notice.

After you have breathed it all in and taken care of last-minute concerns, go over to the starting line. Instead of being nervous and overwhelmed by the people all around you, stop and really take note of them. These are your fellow competitors—or running buddies, depending on how you look at it. They have just gone through months of training like you have, and most of them have probably not slept in a night or two just like you. You're in good company.

At the Starting Line

As you head to the starting line, clear your head and focus on your race. Mentally walk yourself through the course and what will happen during the race. Make sure you're imagining a happy outcome. Picture the finish line and the cheering crowds. Imagine how it'll feel to cross that finish line. What will you do as you cross the finish line? Will you punch the air? Jump off the ground? Do a cartwheel?

Now that you're in a positive state of mind, relax with some deep breathing. Inhale deeply, hold it, and exhale slowly. Do that three times. Stretch your arms over your head. Continue with some additional gentle stretches. If you haven't done it already, this may be a good time to apply some sunblock if you're using it. Don't forget to perform the ritual you created that has some personal meaning to it. And know deep down in your heart, we will see you at the finish line.

COACH SAYS ...

Psychological preperformance routines all suggest similar things. First, take it all in, see it, feel it, imagine it, relax, stretch. Then dial it in and focus, and finally let go of the stress and perform. Focusing on fear will defeat you. Instead, focus on positive thoughts and reinforce your self-confidence.

Corrals

At the starting line, especially in larger marathons, runners will be grouped into "corrals" based on their estimated finish times. Corrals are usually marked with ropes, barricades, or small signs that indicate the various estimated finish times or average pace times. The signs will have average per mile pace, from fastest in the front, to slowest in the back.

Even when there are no signs designating corrals, you still need to line up with the idea that the fastest runners will be in front with the slowest in the back. How do you figure that out, without corral signs? Take a good guess. It's easier if you honestly calculate whether you are a fast or slow marathoner. If you get into the starting area too far up, mobs of runners will pass you and you will be motivated to go too fast. Too slow, and you may have to hold back too much. Try to err on the side of being too far back rather than too far forward. Keep in mind, it can take more than 10 minutes for all the runners in a large marathon to cross the start line, so this is an important issue. No one wants faster runners stuck behind walkers or slow runners, so pay close attention to the time slot for each corral. Competition for position at the front of the pack can be fierce, as every second counts for faster, competitive runners.

A sea of runners at the Los Angeles Marathon 2010 starting line.

Staggered Start

Some races use staggered starts or waves. Instead of using corrals only, they group or corral their runners by estimated finish time and start them off in batches separated by a few minutes. This can help keep larger races more organized and safer for the runners, as there is less of a crowd starting at any one time. This method requires slightly more sophisticated timing so that the later start times will be correlated with the later finish times of each subsequent group of runners.

Start Time

Your start time won't necessarily be 9:00 A.M. or whatever time the race officially starts. Because of the corral system and/or staggered starts, it may take you quite a few minutes to get from your starting position to the actual starting line, when your chip will register your official start time. If there are thousands of runners in your race, start times will naturally be staggered because of the time difference between when the first runners cross the starting line and when the slowest walkers cross. If there are wheelchair participants, they will usually start first because they are the fastest.

When the gun goes off and the crowd moves forward, you will need to stay very alert in order to remain safe and on your feet. Competitive runners will dart in front of you and around you, so you will need to watch your step to ensure you don't trip.

Also watch the ground for water bottles, clothing, or debris that runners may toss as they start off. If you're using a stopwatch, turn it on as you cross the starting line. The chip timing company will record the time at which you cross the start line as well as the time you cross the finish line, and the difference will be your total finish time. It's a good idea to use your own timer, too, however, as mistakes can happen. This won't give you an official time, but at least you will know your own time with relative certainty.

COACH SAYS ...

Especially when it comes to hills and heat, remember that pace is meaningless. You want even levels of energy output. Do a negative split, with the first half of the race slower than the second. That will help ensure that you don't run out of glycogen and hit the wall.

Mentally Run Through Your Strategy

It may feel repetitive to keep mentally running through your strategy, but remember that you are training your mind as well as your body. The captain of the ship has to know her ship and the sea, and even so, she recognizes that both will be different every time. You need to develop visionary powers in order to run your best race. The ability to see potential and literal stumbling blocks can determine the difference between a successful finish and a difficult and painful run.

We emphasize this mental preparation and awareness because it's a necessary tool in any endurance athlete's toolbox. You'll be out there for several hours, and many unexpected things can happen during that time. Remind yourself of the lessons you learned in your "dress rehearsals" on your longest runs. Use these few moments before the starting gun goes off to collect your thoughts and organize your running plan. Even after you cross the starting line, you'll need to continue this mindfulness during the race and adjust your thinking as the race progresses. Terrain, weather, and your own well-being will all take up real estate in your mind and you need to be focused in order to handle any new challenges appropriately. The fewer resources you need to dedicate to minor problems, the more you'll have to handle the really important ones, if they come up.

Stay on Pace

The single most important thing you can do to ensure a good race is to start out slowly. We cannot emphasize this enough. More races have been ruined by an excited marathoner going out too fast and exhausting herself than by any other mistake. In training you learned how to run slowly or aerobically to build up your aerobic base. Then you learned how to run the same distances a little faster, at race pace. You should know how you feel at both speeds, and you must take great pains to stay at or below your marathon race pace depending on conditions. Your conduct during the early miles of the race is an investment in your later miles. A good general rule is to start easy (slow) and finish strong (fast).

If you're running in a group with a pace leader, staying on pace will be much easier. But you should also fall back if you feel you need to. Listening to your body and your instincts are of primary importance during the race, not sticking to someone else's plan. If you're running on your own, it could be a plus to invest in a pace/distance wristwatch so you can watch your average pace at any given time. Don't forget, GPS watches may not work between tall buildings, so do not base your entire race on a GPS watch. Runner/walkers would benefit from a wristwatch with multiple alarm functions to signal the start and end of each run/walk cycle.

 MILE MARKER

Twice in recent history at the Boston Marathon—one of the most competitive marathons in the country—the first and second place finishers were separated by only one second. And in 1982, Alberto Salazar won by just two seconds.

There are many benefits to maintaining an even level of energy output:

- You will stay below your anaerobic threshold level.

- You will preserve your limited store of glycogen for as long as possible.

- Your race will most likely go as you have so meticulously planned.

- Your supplies will last as long as you expect.

- Most important, you will have great insurance against hitting the wall or bottoming out on energy.

Finding that consistent feeling of energy output is accomplished by focusing on breathing and replicating the same feeling of intensity you had during training runs. Being attuned to your body and "feeling it" will help you go up and down hills with even levels of energy output, so you don't spike your heart rate. This way, you will not lose too much glycogen too early from going up a hill too fast. Basically, there is no reason to go too fast unless a rabid Doberman gives chase, or if you still have extra energy in the last few miles of the marathon. And if you do have energy left in the last few miles of a race, by all means, speed up and use it. If you don't have that energy left, be thankful you held back, or you would have hit the wall. Better to run conservatively and be safe than sorry.

One sure way to keep yourself on pace with your goal finish time and maintain the proper intensity is to carry a pace chart with you. As we discussed in Chapter 9, this is a chart that shows you, based on your pace, what your time should be at each mile as well as what your finish time will be if you stay on pace. The handiest pace charts are printed on paper wristbands for easy reference. You could just do the math in your head and figure out elapsed time versus distance, but with everything else you're thinking about, a preprinted chart is the easiest solution.

You also need to wear a watch in order to keep track of your timing and pace. Most marathons have clocks posted along the course, often at every mile. You can check your watch against your pace chart at every mile marker to ensure you're keeping to your plan. But don't forget, when you hit hills or the weather gets hot, you need to slow down. Each mile will not be at an identical pace unless it is a perfectly flat course.

Eating and Drinking While Running

You know it's important, but how do you do it during a marathon? Undoubtedly, during your training you practiced eating and drinking while running. Ideally, the marathon should be no different other than perhaps a little more volume in what you eat and drink. It's important that you replenish carbohydrates, minerals, and fluids before you start to feel hungry, thirsty, or sick. After the start of the race, gels should be consumed every 30 to 60 minutes. Other preferred carb and mineral sources should be consumed within the first few miles, depending on what they are and how they fit into your overall plan.

Some runners like to use two types of carbs to ensure an even delivery of energy: those that are quickly assimilated and those that take a little longer to digest. For example, gels, blocks, and beans contain simple carbs that your body can burn relatively quickly. Bagels or pretzels, on the other hand, would take a little longer to break down. You probably wouldn't want anything more complex than that although some runners do well with things like nuts or peanut butter. Heavier foods, and especially processed foods such as bagels, can cause some people stomach distress. Again, don't do anything new, unless desperate, but focus on what has worked in the past. The key is to keep the supply of carbs, minerals, and water flowing so you don't come even remotely close to scraping the bottom of your energy and hydration barrel.

COACH SAYS ...

Don't forget to drink water after consuming carbohydrate gels. They may be too concentrated otherwise. The raw gel can make you nauseated, and it would also be best to dilute the sudden carb rush they may give you. Most gels will not dissolve completely in your mouth, so water is necessary to wash them down.

Just like eating, you must be careful and strategic with your drinking and electrolyte/mineral replacement. Some runners experience nausea with sports drinks, though they are handy for electrolyte replacement. They can be diluted to help combat nausea, or mineral tablets may be consumed. Keep drinking throughout the race and don't wait until you feel thirsty—it's already too late at that point. A 3 percent loss in hydration (water in your body) can result in a loss of up to 10 percent in energy output. You also don't want to drink too much, as this can rob your body of electrolytes. If you can hear liquid sloshing around in your stomach, you are sodium depleted, and in the initial stages of hyponatremia. The same is true if you find you dislike the taste of water, and there is nothing wrong with it. Go for something salty or a mineral pill quick. Nausea during a race can also signal sodium depletion and/or overheating. There are other possible reasons for nausea, as with sickness, but in a race those are the two big ones.

Be Strategic

It's not only what you eat and drink during the marathon that matters, it's also when. Whatever you choose to bring with you, keep a plan in mind regarding when and how you'll eat or drink it. After your first food intake during the race, you will need to take in carbs at a rate determined in your training (and based on what you're capable of taking in). You should also be drinking at least 4 ounces of water or sports drink every 10 minutes. Of course, you will need to adjust these guidelines based on weather and how you feel. Hot or humid weather makes you sweat more, requiring you to replace water and electrolytes at a higher rate. If you are part of a run/walk group you may find it easiest to do the majority of your eating and drinking during your walk breaks.

Bathroom and Water Stops

You should have a good idea by now of where the bathroom and water stops are located on your race course. Usually they are placed every mile or every 2 miles. Many beginning runners carry some water and hydration equipment with them during the race. It's purely a personal decision as to how much to carry with you. Often sports drinks will be available at certain mile markers in addition to water. It's a bit of a toss-up, as carrying a lot of water keeps you from having to stop often, but the added weight and bulk could slow you down. It's possible that you didn't have this decision to make during your long training runs, because there probably weren't water stops at every mile and you had to carry water with you. But you can use that experience to extrapolate how you will want to proceed during the marathon. Your first marathon may be a bit of a learning experience in this regard.

To go or not to go, that is the question you will face at some point during your race. If you're proactive about it, you can pick and choose when you will stop based on the shortest waiting lines. Don't wait so long that you become uncomfortable, however, as a full bladder bouncing up and down is no one's idea of a good time. Keep in mind, some smaller races don't offer bathrooms along the course, so again your advance planning will come in handy here.

COACH SAYS ...

Once you get into the meat of the race, you will probably need to urinate at least once. Take care of business as it arises and you will enjoy a less stressful race. Then, as you near the last several miles of the race, your kidneys may stop working as efficiently and the need to urinate may not come up again.

Yes, You Can Stop Running

The point of a marathon, of course, is to keep moving until you cross the finish line. Beginners may not realize that you can stop running or walking any time you need to. There is no rule that says you must keep moving forward at all times. If you do intend to stop or walk, make your way to the edge of the road and ensure that you don't block any runners behind you. Or, if you need to walk for a while, stay to the far right side of the road if possible. It is very easy to get injured in collisions with other runners so stay alert and out of the way. If you are injured or in pain, seek out a volunteer or other race personnel to summon help. When you're ready to run again, make sure that you find an opening with few or no runners before you jump back in.

Keep in mind, it can be difficult to start running again if you stand or walk for too long. Once you stop, waste products, predominantly lactic acid and hydrogen, may pool in your legs. This could make them feel heavy and uncomfortable. Your joints may also start to swell and stiffen if you stop suddenly. If you feel you need to stop completely, try to walk for a while first before stopping. Even run/walk programs only allow a short walk break between run cycles, in part to prevent too much discomfort from developing. Depending on how you feel, you may want to walk a little while before resuming your running. When high volumes of waste product build up in the muscles, it may signify that you needed more low heart rate aerobic work in training. A solid aerobic base, among other benefits, could keep you from facing this uncomfortable situation on race day.

What to Expect from Fellow Competitors

Spend any time at a marathon starting line, way up front, just before the gun goes off and you will learn the true meaning of competition. But the meaning of sportsmanship? Maybe not so much. American track and field athlete Jesse Owens once said, "Sportsmanship itself is the ultimate victory." But for runners who are serious about their finish times, positioning behind the starting line is critical and competition can get ugly. Tempers can flare as runners jockey for position, refusing to let each other through. Simple courtesies may not survive. For us middle- and back-of-the-packers, though, this should be less of an issue. You should not assume, however, that any runner you come across isn't concerned with his or her time and is happy to slow down to chat with you. Respect your fellow runners' space and goals and be polite.

Just like there are all kinds of people, there are also all kinds of runners. Needless to say, if you are in a pace group you will probably find people who are very much like yourself. Some will like to talk while they run; others will prefer solitude. Some will be on their cell phones or listening to music. Usually there is a spirit of camaraderie, a feeling of "we're all in this together," and the mood is upbeat. Toward the end of the race, everyone will be feeling a little stressed and tired, so be careful to not step on any toes—literally and figuratively. And watch your own as well!

Have Fun Out There!

Don't forget why you got into this race in the first place. Maybe you were looking for a challenge or an incentive to get back into exercising. But the ultimate reason probably had something to do with having a good time or enjoying a new adventure. The only way to do this is to keep a light attitude about your training and your running.

This isn't the Olympics, and any pressure you put on yourself is self-generated. Try to stay away from preconceived ideas regarding how your race should go and you will immediately cut out a huge source of stress. Attitude plays a big part in perception, and if you decide ahead of time that this will be a positive experience no matter what, in all likelihood you will be right.

Sticking to your training plan also goes a long way toward ensuring a happy race. Your nutrition, rest, and training are all structured to make the marathon a positive experience. If at any point in training you stopped having fun, it probably meant that you were overtraining, were not ready for what you were doing, or got injured. It's the same with the marathon. Do whatever has worked in training and you'll know what to expect during the marathon. No surprises equals a lot more fun.

It's been said before, but try to see the journey as the destination. Running a marathon is kind of like going to Vegas in a way—you should be focused on having a good time whether you win or lose at the casino. With marathons, the experience itself should be your reward, whether you make it to the finish line or not, or whether you make it at your expected time or not. You've done everything you could possibly do to be prepared for this challenge. Now it's time to enjoy the ride!

The Least You Need to Know

- At the starting line, runners line up by estimated finish time, with the fastest runners in front and slower runners and walkers in back.
- Starting out slowly is the single most important thing you can do to ensure a successful finish. Focus on holding back and maintaining an even level of energy output.
- It's okay to stop if you need to; just make sure you move to the side of the road without cutting off other runners. Be equally careful of this when starting up your run again.
- Your fellow competitors will include serious athletes for whom finish time is everything. You'll do best to stay out of their way.
- If you're not having fun, you're doing it wrong!

At the Finish

In This Chapter

- What to expect in the finish area
- The best methods of cooling down and starting your recovery
- When to seek medical support
- How to do a self-assessment immediately after the race
- What's your exit strategy?

Regardless of whether the runner has reached his or her timed goal or not, the finish line is always a place of accomplishment. It is generally a rather quiet place, with the muffled cheering from the crowds behind it now fading off in the distance. At the finish line, triumphant runners experience an enormous swell of pride over their tremendous achievements. This is followed by the need to relax, recover, and for some, the need to eat and/or go to the bathroom. Restroom facilities are usually abundant following the finish line.

The Finish Line

Each marathon's finish area is different, depending on the race. However, they all have similar things:

- If you have a removable timing chip, there will be volunteers available to remove the timing chip from your shoe. If it's one of the new throwaway chips, obviously that service is not needed. Throwaway chips are not reusable, so take it home as a keepsake.

- There will be a first aid tent with medical personnel available to help anyone who doesn't feel well or is injured.

- There will be several enthusiastic people ready to place a marathon ribbon with a finisher's medal on it around your neck. Enjoy it, as you've earned this moment!

- There will be tables where you can get something to eat and drink. For some reason, smaller races seem to have the best postrace free food selection. Go figure. Larger marathons seem to get whatever they can from sponsors, and that's it for the food they put out.

- There will be a place to pick up your postrace bag of personal belongings. This would only be on a point-to-point course, where you start at one point and finish at another. This service is not provided at races that start and end at the same, or similar, points.

YELLOW LIGHT

Putting a cell phone in your bag before the race can help you find friends and family at the finish line. However, these bags tend to be thrown into a truck and piled high, so don't put something in there that you absolutely cannot stand to lose or that may break.

The marathon finish line is a place of exhilaration.

Although the order can change, those are generally the things found in a finish area. Next, you exit and meet the crowds. A sea of people, especially in larger races, may be milling about looking for friends and family. There may even be a bit of a crowd keeping you from exiting the finish area. Be patient, with a little time, you will get beyond the crowd, and on to your postrace plans.

Medical Support

Most marathoners will never need any kind of medical aid during the marathon. The greatest need for medical attention is usually at the finish line, when runners have exhausted themselves or pushed themselves through the pain of an injury. Whether it's something as minor as a chafing problem or something more serious, there is always a great deal of medical support available at the finish line. Most injuries are remedied with icing to reduce inflammation, mineral pills, water or carb- and mineral-based fluids for hydration, or massage. In an extreme case, such as when someone can't hold down fluids, the runner may receive an IV of saline solution.

MILE MARKER

Five hours into the 2004 Los Angeles Marathon, there had already been over 1,000 phone calls for emergency medical help. The temperature had risen to 93°F. Many runners were not prepared with additional mineral pills or fluids, and hadn't compensated for the heat by lowering their intensity (heart rate). Emergency medical units could not respond to all of the 911 calls for help. Marathoners were found lying on some strangers' front lawns. Residents took many of those runners into their homes to get them out of the heat and aid recovery. A massive outpouring of humanity emerged that day, when strangers helped hundreds of marathoners in the City of Angels.

Getting Your Time

With the advent of the timing chip, most marathons quickly post times online. Many will now have immediate postings, which include your split times. A split time is when you complete a quarter or half the course, as well as finish. That way, friends and family can often track you by looking for your statistics on line. This would include the pace at which you completed each section. That way, if you're slowing down and struggling, friends and family will be able to see that with your slower statistics. The breakdown of distances recorded online for each marathon will change slightly. Some show the first or last 5K or 10K of the marathon, others do not.

Larger marathons usually don't have the ability to post results on a board somewhere. There are simply too many people to create print outs and post them. Some smaller marathons do have that ability to post a long print out with each athletes' results and finish time placement. However, this is more of an older method, and rarely used anymore. Nowadays, it's all about computers. On rare occasions, your chip may not register properly on the *timing mats*, which they connect with out on the course.

> **DEFINITION**
>
> **Timing mats** are long rubber mats which usually stretch across the entire width of the street. As marathoners cross over each mat, there will be an audible beep heard for each athlete registered by the mat. When you have hundreds going over a mat, you will hear endless beeps.

If you find a timing discrepancy, you can fix the record online. If you were wearing a stop watch, or noticed the finish clock as you crossed the finish line, simply send an e-mail with that time to the race director, or call them. Often a race will have a video camera at the finish line. If they can look up a time range, they can probably spot your bib number and easily see the exact time you finished. If you aren't going to upset a win in your age group, they may simply trust you and change your time. That is entirely dependent on the race and race director.

Finishers' Medals

Following a few steps across the finish line, you will receive your finisher's medal. This is a treasured keepsake for most runners, given out at nearly all marathons. The Nike Women's Marathon actually gives away a Tiffany necklace instead. It is a popular, always sold-out race. Though the marathon day may have come and gone, your medal can be with you for the rest of your life. Quite often runners will pick a marathon solely because of the cool medal. Disney medals usually have big Mickey Mouse ears around a circle face, with the name and date of the marathon or half marathon. Rock 'n' Roll marathons often have a rocker on the thick, cool-looking, heavier medal. Often they get creative, based on the location. Silicon Valley had a computer chip as part of the medal. You get the picture. At the finish, a volunteer will place your medal around your neck. Following the simple but powerful moment of accepting the medal, you enter a new, small but proud group called marathoners. Every finisher receives a medal, regardless of finish time. (Winning a trophy, however, is another story.)

Photos

As you cross the finish line, remember to smile, because undoubtedly a photographer is taking your picture. This is common especially at all larger marathons. In fact, often at the big events, there is scaffolding behind the "finish" banner. Photographers are standing on that platform, looking down and shooting pictures.

Throughout the course, there are usually photographers shooting all the marathoners. Most races set up websites, usually in cooperation with the photography company, to sell digital copies and printed copies in any size imaginable, including a giant rock star–sized poster, from many races. They will frame a picture, put it in a case with your medal, mount it on a plaque, you name it. In fact, some marathons will sell you a DVD of highlights of the marathon, with a clip of your finish. So don't forget to smile!

Recovery

At this point, you have crossed that finish line, and the dream is a reality. It's now time to take care of you. As best as you can, it's beneficial to keep walking. There may be a mob in the way, but try to keep moving. You want to rid your body of as much hydrogen, lactic acid, and other waste products as you can, as soon as possible, and keeping your blood moving is the best way to do this right after you stop running.

Cool Down

Everyone responds to training differently. Likewise, everyone recovers from long, intense exercise differently. That said, it is also true that every marathon runner will benefit from cooling down gradually, and not stopping abruptly and sitting down. Although you may not want to, it is best to keep your legs moving for as long as possible after you cross the finish line. Even a mile-long walk will help, though it may be the last thing you want to do. The only reason to stop entirely after crossing the finish line is if you are in pain.

Postrace Stretching

We're going to recommend something that no one ever seems to do right after a marathon, but it is so beneficial. Stretch. After you walk around a bit and eat something, head over to an open area and gently stretch. Perform the gentle progressive stretches found in Appendix E. The five second gentle stretch and release will help squeeze some of the hydrogen, lactic acid, CO_2, and other waste products out of your legs. This will ease the growing tightness in your legs, which increased the moment you stopped running. That is what happens with waste product. You stop and it will build up. Work your legs a little with walking and progressive stretching, and it will start to go away. After two hours, most waste products such as lactic acid and hydrogen will be gone. The more of those aerobic runs you did during training, the more efficient your capillary veins and arteries, and the faster you will rid your legs of that waste product.

Postrace Icing

As soon as possible after the race, and after some gentle stretching, you can also benefit from icing any areas of soreness or inflammation. The more areas you can ice, the better. If you skip icing entirely, you will likely be sore for about three days and walk around rather rigidly, especially for the first day or two. Refer to Chapter 12 for the best way to apply ice.

An even better method to treat soreness and inflammation is to take an ice bath, if you can stand it. The sudden cold shock will force the waste products from your legs. This method is a bit more dramatic, as you need to submerge your entire legs in ice water. If you must wait until you get home, do this as soon as possible upon arrival. Fill a clean garbage can or your bathtub with ice and water. Get in, submerging only your legs up to your hips if possible. Pray that 10 minutes goes by quickly. (It won't.) But this method really works, and the normal three days or so of soreness can virtually be eliminated in the 10 minutes of an ice bath. Many feel as if they never ran a marathon after taking an ice bath.

> **YELLOW LIGHT**
>
> If the finish line is near a lake or ocean where the water temperature is below 60°F, try going into that water for 10 minutes instead of using an ice bath. But be careful not to go in above your waist or you could develop hypothermia, which is a dangerous reduction in body temperature.

Replenish Nutrients and Water

After completing a marathon, or really any exercise, you have an approximately 30- to 45-minute window in which your body absorbs carbohydrates at an alarming volume. This is true of any of your training runs, and a good thing to plan for, following a marathon. Your body absorbs carbs and turns them right into glycogen, storing it in the muscle. This window of time diminishes gradually, starting at the moment you stop running after crossing the finish line. If you miss this window of opportunity to replace an important energy resource (carbohydrates), it can take up to one full day (24 hours) to accomplish the same thing. This might mean that you have less energy for that entire day than you otherwise might have had. So go for those carbs.

If you hydrated appropriately throughout the race, you should not be terribly thirsty at the finish line. However, you should still drink enough water to satisfy your thirst and continue to hydrate throughout the day. Drinking during the first two hours especially can help flush waste products from your muscles. Taking a mineral pill with some water, or drinking a sports drinks that contains electrolytes, may also help to prevent cramping after you stop running.

MILE MARKER

Science does not completely understand the causes of muscle cramping. It often occurs when the body is depleted of minerals or nutrients, or under the stress of extreme fatigue. Replacing electrolytes before and after the race may help you avoid this painful phenomenon.

Self-Assessment After the Race

It's important to take an honest assessment of yourself, both mentally and physically, immediately following a marathon. Most people will have some soreness upon reaching the finish line, but they are not usually injured. You will need to determine which category you fall into as soon as possible, as it's important to take action quickly to address any injuries. Similarly, you will probably be focused on how you did and whether you met your goals. It's a good idea to do a mental check now, right after you finish the race, and compare it to how you feel in a few days. Your outlook will likely improve as you feel physically better a little further into your recovery.

Check for Injuries

If you're indeed injured during the marathon, it may not be obvious, and it may not reveal itself right away. You probably won't have a bone sticking out, or blood spurting, or even minor cuts or bruises. In order to determine whether you need professional medical care following a race, consider this. You will undoubtedly have some sore muscles, but that is different from an injury, and can be dealt with by icing and stretching, as we have discussed. If you feel a strong pinching or stabbing feeling, you probably have something worse, like an injured tendon, ligament, or muscle. If you cannot walk normally without pain, or if you have to significantly change your stride to compensate for any new pains, seek medical attention. When in doubt it's best to check it out, and the sooner you get to a medical professional the better. You don't want an injury to become worse, or heal improperly, by ignoring it. Take advantage of the medical personnel at the finish line if you have any doubts or any new or substantial pains.

Did You Meet Your Goals?

Now that you're on the other side of the finish line, you can assess whether you've met your goals. Did you finish in the time you predicted? Or did you simply finish? Was the experience of training for and running a marathon fulfilling to you? If not, perhaps your expectations were unrealistic. Or perhaps you didn't finish the marathon due to injury or another mitigating factor. But can you still find satisfaction in the fact that you did your best? No matter the specifics of your intended goal, isn't that the bottom line? Perhaps the most important result in running a marathon isn't your timing or your placement but the fact that you set a goal for yourself and you reached it. It's another paving stone in your path to growth and self-realization.

With one step across the finish line, you create an accomplishment and you lose a goal. Often achieving a goal isn't where the greatest pleasure lies. In most cases, it's the pursuit, not the completion of the goal, that is most enjoyable. And when we cross a finish line, that acknowledgment creates change. You begin to think, "If I could do this seemingly insurmountable challenge, maybe there are other challenges I have ignored. Maybe those other seemingly insurmountable challenges I ignored, I could actually do." Fear destroys goal setting, and quite often athletes lose that fear after crossing the finish line. That is when doors can open. So consider having a new goal in mind before you cross that finish line, and go for it!

Postrace Transportation

When you are ready to leave the finish area, you will want to find your friends or relatives, or you will need to find your car or shuttle. Most races have a "Family Reunion Area" that may be arranged alphabetically by last name. Generally, parking is near the finish line, and on a point-to-point course, runners are usually bused for free from the parking area to the starting line. That way, you finish the race near your car. But above all, when you leave your car, remember where you left it.

If you are lucky enough to be staying at a hotel near the marathon course, a postrace shuttle may be provided by the hotel. Or, if your hotel is near the finish line, you might consider walking there to help aid in your recovery. Even a mile or two walk to a hotel is not a bad thing after a marathon, as the walk will help you get some waste product out of your legs and the additional blood flow will help get more oxygen into those damaged muscles to aid repair.

The Least You Need to Know

- Finish areas in most marathons are similar, with your finisher's medal, some food, a medical area, possible chip removal, and trucks with your postrace bag (on a point-to-point course).
- Following a marathon you benefit from continuing to walk, gently stretching, and using some ice or an ice bath for 10 minutes.
- Soreness is common following a marathon, but if you feel a pinching or stabbing feeling, you may want to seek medical attention.
- Planning your exit strategy is important, with friends or family, a hotel within walking distance, or remembering where your car is.

Beyond the Finish Line

In This Chapter

- Recovery in the days following the marathon
- Dealing with postrace depression
- Cultivate a new lifestyle
- When and how do you start training again?
- Your next marathon

Well, the finish line is now behind you. In crossing it, you now know what the victory feels like, and in all likelihood it was a great feeling of accomplishment. If you had specific goals, hopefully you achieved them, but regardless, two things were probably true: it was tough and you finished. If for some reason, you did not finish, no worries, there are probably tons of other marathons in your area, within the next few months. Whatever the case, at this point you need to recover from your marathon experience before looking too far into the future.

After a marathon, your muscles and joints are probably sore and you feel fatigued. Your hormone levels are also depleted at this point, including human growth hormone (HGH) that aids in healing muscles. You have micro-tears in your muscles that need to heal before you exert yourself again. You may also feel a little out of sorts. Many runners get sick right before or after their first marathon, or something goes wrong. Hopefully this marathon was a positive learning experience and next time you will avoid the overtraining or other mistakes that may have made you sick or vulnerable to injury.

In the weeks following the marathon, you may wonder what to do next. There is a huge gap in your once busy calendar. But before you can fill that schedule again, you need to hold yourself back a bit and listen to your body. Allow yourself a little recovery time before you start thinking about running again. You may also experience changes in mood during this postrace period, and you need to stay active to help keep mind and body on the road to recovery.

Recovery Timeline

Within about two hours of completing a marathon, most waste products have been eliminated from the muscles. Though everyone recovers at a different pace, many take about three days to completely eliminate all soreness. (That is, unless they use icing techniques, walking, or gentle stretching to accelerate the process, as described in Chapter 16.) Pain from micro-tears in the muscles may take longer to abate, and healing can take up to four weeks. An icing, warm bath, and stretching regimen over the next few days can help speed recovery.

Being sedentary and doing nothing lengthens the healing process. During periods of recovery, light exercise with little or no impact is preferred. The day after the marathon, instead of sitting on the couch and pounding down a box of well-deserved donuts, drink plenty of water all day and get out for some easy, low-impact exercise. You will recover more quickly from the greater blood flow and increased delivery of oxygen to your muscles. While rest is of critical importance, it's also necessary to keep moving a bit during this period of recovery. Running in water, walking, and even some light strength training over the next few weeks will help your body to heal and will help you to maintain some conditioning at the same time.

YELLOW LIGHT

Be sure to consult a doctor or physical therapist regarding exercising during this time if you are injured. In some cases, sitting and waiting for an injury to heal is the wrong way to go. It can take longer and never heal properly. With medical advice, you may find that some movement or light exercise of the injured area will speed healing when done correctly.

Relieving Pain and Speeding Recovery

Hopefully you were able to use stretching and an ice bath immediately after the marathon to help force waste products out of your leg muscles. Now, a continued regimen of ice, heat, and stretching can be useful tools in the days following a marathon to help combat soreness and promote healing. Fill an ice bag with ice and water and squeeze out as much air as possible. Close it and place it right on the sore area for no more than 10 minutes. If this is too cold, you can put an old T-shirt or a thin piece of cloth between your skin and the bag of ice. After 10 minutes, move the bag to another sore area for the same amount of time.

When you have hit every sore spot on both legs once, make an assessment. If you are still sore, fill the bathtub up with warm water and jump in. Water is a very good conductor of temperature—a heating blanket wouldn't be as effective. Remain in the warm water for another 10 minutes. The warm water is used to get your circulation going and ensures that you do not freeze the areas you iced. Following this, get out and ice again with the same bag of water and ice again for another 10 minutes only. Following all this, do a gentle stretch, especially hitting those muscles affected by soreness. After all that, you should feel like mush and should take it easy for a short time. You could repeat the process every few hours for three days, during which time you will dramatically reduce inflammation and soreness or discomfort. Beyond three days, there is little benefit.

Running in Water

Running in water can help you in your postrace recovery and also helps maintain your endurance base while eliminating the pounding effects of running. This would be a good thing to do right after a marathon. The best way to run in water is to go to a pool that has aqua-joggers (described in Chapter 12), or to use some workable type of floatation device that enables your arms and legs to move freely as you run with normal running form in the water. Pick a deeper area of the pool where your feet cannot touch the bottom and run normally. Don't lift your arms or knees up too high. You can also look down and make sure you maintain proper form. As with jogging or walking, running in water increases the circulation of blood and oxygen, which promotes quicker healing of injured muscles.

COACH SAYS …

It can take approximately four weeks to eliminate all micro-tears in the muscles even though you may not feel them. Light exercise is beneficial during this time. Additional movement from exercise causes greater blood flow throughout the body, which brings more oxygen to injured muscles, enabling them to heal faster.

Walking

Walking is an exceptional exercise in the days following a marathon, as it keeps the blood and muscles moving without any great effort. Gentle hikes can also be very beneficial. Just don't overdo the time spent exercising. The benefits you are seeking come from gentle movements and short periods of exertion. Obviously, there is no need to worry about getting faster or stronger during this period. You are on an extended taper and want to give your body every opportunity to recover and heal while still remaining active.

Light Strength Training

Any movement, even some light strength training, will help increase circulation, and get more oxygen to help heal muscles. Use low weights and not quite as many repetitions as usual, and as always, never take a movement to "failure" at which point you cannot do one more repetition.

Nurture Yourself

Allow yourself abundant rest during this time and follow a healthy diet. Listen to your body and don't push yourself in any way. Strive for at least eight hours of sleep per night. Combined with light exercise every day, these habits help you reach your former level of activity in the least possible amount of time and with the least discomfort. A full recovery after every running event will enable your body to go on racing nearly indefinitely, should you so desire. After a few weeks of light activity and abundant rest, you may already be thinking about starting training again.

Injuries and Healing

If you find you have an injury following the race, you will first need to go to a doctor or sports orthopedist to get checked out thoroughly. Find someone who specializes in running-related injuries. Orthopedists usually treat serious issues that only surgery can cure. However, a sports orthopedist is probably the best doctor to assess you and write you a prescription for physical therapy if it's warranted. Such a prescription could enable your health insurance to kick in and pay for the physical therapy, which may call for several weeks or months of treatment.

Beware of the surgery-happy orthopedist. There are a high percentage of surgeries performed in this country that are unwarranted. Orthopedists are generally not trained to heal you without surgery and medication. It may be a good idea to try physical therapy first, as quite often it can accomplish more than surgery can, and with better results for the future. In 80 percent of cases, strength training, stretching, and/or different shoes will solve the problem. Rarely is an injury simply attributable to one problem.

It's a rare orthopedist who is trained in any form of injury prevention. This can sometimes lead the orthopedist to mistakenly tell an injured runner to never run again. Before leaving an orthopedist's office, make sure to ask what caused your injury. If you don't uncover what caused it, you are destined to experience that injury again. Often runners with repeat injuries begin to see themselves as not being able to run. Generally speaking, most injuries stem from a lack of strength and/or flexibility, which prevents the athlete from running with proper and efficient form. Those are two of the key ingredients in avoiding repeat injuries. So in your quest to heal and not get injured again, you will do well to focus on developing these two disciplines. Then, once you're healed, stronger, and more flexible, you will probably find that you are going faster than before you were injured.

YELLOW LIGHT

Common injuries following a marathon range from mild, such as sprains and strains, to severe, such as torn muscles and broken bones. While RICE (rest, ice, compression, elevation; see Chapter 12) can help treat most minor injuries, visit a sports medicine doctor immediately for anything more serious. Don't wait—any delay in treatment can compound the issue.

Whether you suffered an injury during the marathon or not, you should only begin running again when there is no pain or achiness. Only then should you try the following progression. First, go for a 10-minute aerobic (low heart rate) run. You may also call this a jog. Take the next day off. Two days later, if the first run went well, with no pain, start with another 10-minute jog or aerobic run, followed by a 10-minute walk. If all is still okay, keep going with another 10-minute aerobic run. Two days later, with another day off in between, you may want to repeat this 10-minute jog, 10-minute walk, and 10-minute jog again. Or if feeling strong, and strength training is also going well, go for one 20-minute aerobic run, with a few minutes walking following that. Building up slowly this way can get you back in the game with less risk of injury. If you feel any pain or achiness at any time, during any of these runs, stop immediately.

Postrace Depression

For many, a sense of depression may set in following a marathon. You have accomplished your goal and may feel you have nothing left to aim for. A lot of time went into achieving your marathon goal, and now there is a big hole in both your daily schedule and in your long-term objectives. The time spent recovering after a marathon is an abrupt change from the highly scheduled, goal-oriented behavior that you cultivated over the last several months. Often people feel as if that marathon training portion of their schedule gave them a purpose, which they also enjoyed. Plus, your hormone levels are shifting; you may be physically uncomfortable or in pain; and you're not sure if or when you should start running again. All of these factors can contribute to some frustration, impatience, and sadness. While your body adjusts to "life after a marathon," your mind has to do the same thing. Just understand that this is all a normal part of the postrun recovery period and it won't last forever.

Let's face it, running can be fun. That is, as long as you're not overdoing it. And you can do it again soon enough if you take the time to recover properly. You can use this down time to set a new goal and concentrate on the future. Finding a new goal is of critical importance just after a race, as a way to focus your energy and concentration. Once you feel physically better, your mind and spirit will pick up again, too. Then you can really focus on what you enjoyed in your training and in the marathon experience, and find ways to work that sense of accomplishment into the rest of your life. But first, be patient with yourself and let yourself heal. You can't skip this period any more than you could have skipped your training.

A Lifestyle for a Lifetime

Now that you have completed a marathon, what are you going to do next? Will it be a short distance triathlon, another marathon at higher intensity and greater efficiency, an ultra-marathon, or possibly an Ironman Triathlon?

Many feel as if they did not quite achieve the goals that they set out to do on their first marathon. Maybe you didn't do as well as you hoped because you went out too fast and burned out before the end, and you would like the opportunity to try again. Although there is no such thing as getting a marathon right, there is nothing wrong with wanting to do another marathon, for any reason. Obviously, competition and doing better at an endurance event is the reason many become wrapped up in the endurance lifestyle. For many, it's years later, after they have done it all and achieved it all, when they realize that they really benefitted from all the endurance work in many other ways which go well beyond athletic achievement.

Lessons Learned

Crossing a marathon finish line is the culmination of many lessons learned, and is perhaps the start of a good many more. Your training brought you many physical and emotional lessons, and the marathon itself brought its own unique lessons. Then, in your postrace recovery you likely thought about your experiences and found patterns and associations you had never seen before. You undoubtedly learned about your own abilities and limitations, and how to improve both. You probably realized you can achieve a great deal more than you had previously thought. And you figured out what great things you can accomplish by setting goals, breaking those goals into manageable parts, and then sticking with the plan to achieve them. Of course, these lessons are applicable to much more in life than just marathons. How you apply these new tools to your life in general is limited only by your imagination.

> **MILE MARKER**
>
> Statistically speaking, men between the ages of 40 and 44 consistently score the fastest marathon finish times. This seems to underscore the fact that the focus, determination, strategic thinking, and adaptability required to finish a marathon come with experience and maturity. The average age of all finishers has hovered around 38 for the last decade.

Hopefully, throughout this process, you have learned that exercise is fun, when you build up to it slowly and do not kill yourself by pushing too hard too early. Bill Bowerman, the Olympic and University of Oregon coach who invented the prototype that became the Nike shoe, has said, "If you have a body, you are an athlete." Upon finishing your marathon, maybe now you believe that.

Your New and Different Body

You may have lost a lot or a little body fat, especially during all the aerobic work you did in preparation for the marathon. Outwardly, from the weight loss, you could look dramatically different. But even if you still look the same, internally you are dramatically different, and often in ways you don't feel. Endurance-wise you're able to do more. This is due to the increase of capillary veins and arteries, and mitochondria from aerobic work. There is more oxygen now going to the cells which make up your muscles, due to the increase in red blood cells and hemoglobin, which carry that oxygen. The greater volume of additional capillaries also enables more lactic acid to get to your liver for recycling into glycogen, which gives you more fuel at higher intensities. You are engaging more muscles and nerves (motor nerves), which make you stronger with regard to running, walking, or both, depending on how you trained.

An increase in *buffering agents* will also help you by reducing any burning sensation from acids caused by hydrogen waste products binding with other chemicals. Your heart's left ventricle may be larger and stronger, pumping a greater volume of blood throughout your body. Blood return from the muscles is also increased for several reasons. And many other benefits occur from endurance training.

> **DEFINITION**
>
> **Buffering agents** are compounds that occur naturally in your body and regulate the amount of hydrogen ions in the blood.

In general, physiologically, you're able to go faster and farther, and you are more efficient in many ways. Your assimilation of nutrients in food is more efficient, and your metabolism may be at a higher rate. Sleep may even be more efficient, and you may be capable of doing well with less sleep for short periods of time. Some endurance athletes get to a point where they can run all night long, before shutting down and sleeping. But the biggest question of all is what are you now going to do with all of these benefits? You now have a wealth of knowledge from all of this science stuff you just learned. And psychologically, you may now feel stronger and better equipped to take on the challenges of the world. So go get 'em!

Keep the Momentum Going

It does take a few years to fully reach your potential as a marathoner, even with the most efficient training programs. Instead of putting the brakes on all training for several months after you complete a marathon, it's a good idea to maintain your hard-earned endurance base. However, this is a long shot from immediately jumping back into speed work, hill training, and longer runs. Immediately following a marathon it is good to allow your body to rest for a short period, and build back slowly. You don't need to become flabby and put on weight, but you cannot maintain that high level of performance for long. This does not mean you stop all exercise immediately upon completion of a marathon, or at any time. Do not forget, you still want to heal. Some light exercise helps with that. But you do benefit from a dramatic reduction in the volume, frequency, and intensity of exercise, for a few weeks. Your central nervous system needs to rest as well, following the season of building for a marathon. Maintenance, and maintenance only, is the key to the period following the marathon. As with any period of taper, you need to let your body recover and adapt to the marathon stress you just placed on yourself.

When to Start Training Again

In most cases, you have the capacity to start running with low intensity, low volume, and low frequency shortly after a marathon. The actual start date for greater volume in training following a marathon is quite an individual thing. It can take up to four weeks, for example, for the micro-tears in your muscles to heal, so be careful to not start back too soon. When you start up again has to do with the timing of your next big race. We don't recommend setting another race any sooner than four months after the marathon, for a beginner. If you do not have another race lined up, it's still a good idea to maintain your aerobic base by starting to run again. In general, if you feel well-rested, energetic, and recovered by your third or fourth week, it's probably safe to start running. Start slowly and pay close attention to your body. The one rule that is critical following a marathon, or at any time during training, is if it hurts to do it, stop doing it immediately.

How Much, How Soon?

The best plan for starting a new season can be exemplified by the same training strategy that is used at the start of a race: start slow and finish fast. Far too many nonpro (age grouper) athletes keep training at the same frequency and intensity all year, regardless of what they are training for, or when that event is. They may cut back a little on volume (distance and time), but they continue to do threshold runs and possibly track work. This is destructive, and only implements the later part of the training season, leaving out aerobic runs. Unlike a taper, where you need to continue with the same intensity and frequency, but drop volume, this is a new season. You need to cut back on everything and start all over again from the beginning. Your efficiency will continue to grow even more than it did your first time around. Therefore your capacity to go faster will increase. But your levels of energy will stay high.

On the other hand, if you just want to maintain your fitness level and don't have another race in mind, you still need to cut way back in volume in the early season. Training could be more random in this case, but that depends greatly on listening to your body and what it needs.

Light Training Runs

When you are sure you're ready to start running again, you need to start with the same level of low intensity and low heart rate work as you started with in the last season. It is all about low heart rate. This includes the period right after a marathon as well as the beginning of any training season. When it's the appropriate time to truly begin training with greater volume for the next marathon, start at the beginning of your schedule with low heart rate work and volume. Schedule some short aerobic training runs to get you back in the saddle again. After several weeks or months of increasing distance, you can start to increase your intensity. If the next training program is scheduled rather close to the end of the last marathon, you may not need as much aerobic work early in the season. That may also depend on how much of a training season you have left for the next race, and when you need to peak and taper in preparation for it.

> **MILE MARKER**
>
> Quite often your experiences, and watching you do what you do, changes the habits of people around you. If you eat a healthy meal, chances are those around you begin to do the same. The same can be said of exercising. Those around you may not set out to do a marathon, but they may begin to walk more or do some strength training, thanks to your example. It happens all the time.

Your Second Marathon

Some people manage to do several marathons in a year. They are generally very experienced runners who can get by with shorter training schedules in between races. If you are determined to start preparing for your second marathon right away, we suggest allowing at least three months of training, which would begin after the recovery period we described earlier (possibly one month). In addition, you will need to design your training regimen around one very important concept: pick your "A" race—the most important race you have within a season. You may have two or three training seasons a year, but only one "A" race in any one of them. Your build and taper are absolutely tied to this race, in which it is essential to do your best.

Keep in mind, you cannot be at your best with every race unless you give yourself time to recover and then build, peak, and taper. Needless to say, there is a lot more to it than just that. But you can only build then peak and taper most efficiently once a season. Therefore, any other race that year becomes a "B" or a "C" race, or slightly less important.

Imagine the drama of being a high school, college, or pro coach with an athlete who has several races in one season. When designing the athlete's build and taper schedule, does the coach choose the Olympic qualifying race as the "A" race, or does he make the Olympics the "A" race, if they're only a few weeks later? You can't peak effectively for both in such a short time. If the coach screws up, and his training schedule causes the athlete to peak at the wrong time, he may not be able to qualify for the final race. Or he may do well in the qualifying run but not be at his best for the actual race, depending on the placement of the peak training in his schedule. This shows you how critical it is to schedule your training accurately for your "A" race.

On a lesser scale, you face the same dilemma. If you want to have a P.R. (personal record) or go faster, or even be at your best, you need to focus on that "A" race. For instance, if your "A" race is a marathon, and you have a big 5K coming up, you may be doing all aerobic runs to train. The 5K would require doing some threshold work (higher heart rate), but that would go against your marathon training for efficiency. This does not mean that you should not do the 5K. No, go for it. However, understand you will not be at your best for that particular 5K. In this scenario, with the marathon as the "A" race, if it's early in that season, keep doing the aerobic work only. So choose that "B" race wisely, and give yourself enough time to reasonably recover, then build and peak and taper, with all the training elements which go along with any training season: aerobic work, threshold work, hill training, building in volume, and then in intensity, tapers, etc.

With all of this new knowledge, both researched and experienced, can you ever simply screw around and have fun? Absolutely. Don't forget rule number one of endurance athletics: you need to have fun. On the other hand, it's also pretty easy to screw up. You may wonder, do pro athletes whose income depends on performing at a high level, ever screw up and go too fast? Absolutely. In fact, Lance Armstrong's coach, Chris Carmichael, suggests that "Most athletes do their slow workouts too fast due to ego, and their fast workouts too slow due to exhaustion." There is some great truth to that statement. On the other hand, if you do screw up, now you at least know you're screwing up and what the ramifications will be. So please do not screw up too often, or it'll negatively affect your season and race day. But sometimes, will even the best of all of us go too fast or too far, because we get excited, just as pro athletes do? Sure. And we enjoy it.

The question is, why do a marathon at all? Why should major cities with normally heavy traffic close the roads for hundreds or thousands to run in the streets? What is the value to a community for doing all of this? Also, why is it that complete strangers come out in the heat, or cold, or rain, and for hours watch runners and walkers going by? They don't simply watch the front runners go by, but they stay and watch thousands of us seemingly normal people run or walk past them. We believe one answer is that the endurance athlete shows the world that the boundaries and limitations of what we once thought existed, do not exist beyond the realm where we can dream. And for that reason, when we do an endurance event we do it not just for ourselves, but we do it for those around us, in hopes that they too may have a dream.

In other words, when you finish an endurance event, you show yourself and others that the endurance limits you once thought you had, never really existed. This can have a profound effect in many different ways. In smashing one limit you thought was out of reach, you find that your confidence grows stronger, and you realize that setting difficult goals doesn't have to be scary. Removing fear from the equation of success is often how the world is changed. And on some occasions, for some people, it might be at the finish line, where that change begins for yourself and those around you. May your life be filled with many finish lines, and may they all be fulfilling.

Have an inspired run or walk!

The Least You Need to Know

- Recovery following the marathon can take up to a month and can be improved with gentle stretching, ice, and heat.
- Do not sit and do nothing following a marathon, as healing will take longer. On the other hand, do not start off with too much too soon. If you have any pain, stop immediately.
- Some depression or lethargy following a marathon is normal and won't last long. The best medicine is to get back on your feet again and keep moving.
- A lifestyle of endurance athletics can lead to personal growth and healthy change.
- Begin training the next day, with a walk or run in water, but build each season from the beginning, and do not peak too early. Build your seasons as you do a well-run race, start slow and finish fast.

Glossary

5K A distance equal to 3 miles, 564 feet, 2.4 inches.

10K A distance of about 6 miles, or 6.21371192 miles to be exact.

"A" race The most important race within a season.

actin One of the protein filaments that makes up muscle tissue.

active stretches A specialized type of movement that might loosen up the muscles. These are effective before a hard workout or race.

adaptation phase A period of about six weeks before formal marathon training begins during which the runner prepares all the muscles, ligaments, and tendons for the stresses to come, bringing all body parts into balance with strength training and easy aerobic runs.

aerobic Describes any chemical reaction that requires oxygen to progress. It is only at this lower level of exercise intensity where more capillary veins and arteries are created and mitochondria are increased in number.

aerobic base The range of activity intensity over which your body transitions from using primarily fat as fuel to primarily glycogen use. A longer aerobic base is most desirable.

age grouper Any nonprofessional runner; usually runs in races organized by age group.

allergen Anything that triggers an allergic reaction.

anaerobic Without or lacking oxygen. An anaerobic process can progress in the absence of oxygen. At this higher level of exercise intensity, glycogen becomes the only source to create fuel.

anaerobic threshold (AT) The exercise intensity point at which the runner no longer uses fat or oxygen in the muscles that are used for running. The body transitions to glycogen as its main fuel.

anemia A lack of healthy red blood cells and a corresponding low level of hemoglobin, which carries oxygen in the blood.

antihistamine Any natural or medicinal compound that mediates the effects of histamine, which is released in the body during an allergic reaction.

antioxidant   A molecule that prevents certain damaging chemical reactions in the body. Antioxidants protect the cells against free radicals, which are rogue atoms and molecules that can cause mutations to normally healthy cells.

aqua-jogger   A flotation device that holds the runner upright in the water, allowing running movements with the arms and legs.

ATP   Adenosine triphosphate, a molecule that stores energy and is continually being produced and broken down by your body.

base   *See* aerobic base.

bonk   This is a slang runners' term for running out of energy, specifically glycogen.

buffering agents   Compounds which occur naturally in the body and regulate the amount of hydrogen ions in the blood.

cadence   The speed or rhythm with which your feet hit the ground.

capillaries   The tiniest blood vessels in the body which connect veins and arteries. Walls of capillaries are only one cell thick, allowing oxygen and nutrients to pass through.

carbohydrate   A compound that contains carbon, hydrogen, and oxygen. Your body uses carbohydrates in your diet, such as sugar, for energy.

centrifugal force   The outward force experienced by an object in rotation around a central point.

chronic condition   A condition that can be managed but not cured. It generally lasts longer than three months but does not necessarily progress.

complex carbohydrate   A larger molecule than a simple carbohydrate; it takes the body longer to process. Found in beans, nonstarchy vegetables, and whole grains.

corrals   Holding areas for runners of different per-mile paces or finish times. They are usually arranged from fastest in the front to slowest in the back.

cortisol   The stress hormone that affects the metabolism in various ways. It can aid in energy production and even dampen the immune system depending on the type of stress experienced by the runner.

creatine phosphate   A biochemical energy source for the body that is available in less than 10-second bursts.

cross-training   Athletic training in sports that is different but supportive of the main sport.

detraining   A loss of conditioning due to lack of training or overly aggressive tapering.

electrolytes   Minerals such as sodium and potassium that allow electrical impulses to flow inside the body.

elevation map   A cross-section of the entire race course, illustrating the altitude gained and lost along the route.

endorphins   A type of hormone found in the brain and nervous system which acts as an opiate by suppressing pain and soothing the emotions. They are responsible for the legendary "runner's high."

ergonomics   The science of designing products to fit the human body and its movements.

essential fatty acids   Certain fats that your body cannot produce; they must be obtained from the diet. They can aid with the regulation of such things as blood pressure, blood clots, immune response, and inflammation.

expo   An event sponsored by race organizers at which runners can pick up their bibs, timing chips, and T-shirts. Sports supply vendors, community services, and race sponsors usually participate as well.

fartlek   Swedish for "speed play." A form of loose interval training using ever-changing random speeds and distances.

fascia   Flexible connective tissue in the body that bind muscles and nerves as well as other structures.

fast oxidative glycolytic, type 2a muscle fibers   Trainable muscle fibers that control your speed, and can help you go faster. They can utilize fat and glycogen.

fast-twitch muscle fibers   Nontrainable muscle fibers which allow higher speeds in running. These fibers are generally thicker in size than other muscle fibers, and the amount one has is attributed to genetics.

fat   An essential, energy-storing nutrient that is available in many foods such as dairy products, meat, and nuts. It is also stored in the body as a fuel source.

frequency   How often one runs.

glycogen   An altered form of glucose, a sugar, capable of residing in the liver and muscles.

GPS   Short for global positioning system, which tracks location and altitude based on satellite information. GPS watches made for runners can also calculate pace and distance in real time.

hamstring   The set of muscles that comprise the back of the thigh.

hand crank wheelchairs   Wheelchairs that are operated differently from push-rim wheelchairs. The rider uses an upright crank system to generate movement.

hemoglobin   A protein in the red blood cells that carries oxygen.

hip flexor   The muscle group that begins about halfway between the hip and knee, in the front of the leg. It wraps around the side of the hip and connects in the lower back.

hit the wall   *See* bonk.

HR Max   Maximum heart rate. A point of highest exercise intensity, at which the body will begin to shut down rather than race the heart any faster.

human growth hormone (HGH)   A naturally occurring hormone which dictates the rate of growth of many tissues in the body. It also controls the rate of healing after injury.

hypertrophy   Cellular growth within the muscles which occurs when stress is applied to the muscle, and proper rest and recovery follow.

hyperventilation   Out of control, rapid breathing. It is a reversible condition that can result from physical or emotional stress. If not treated, it can cause dizziness, numbness, and even fainting.

hypoglycemia   Low blood sugar; a condition in which there is not enough energy-storing glucose in the blood. This can lead to fatigue, confusion, headache, and hunger.

hyponatremia   A dangerous imbalance of sodium in the body which can interfere with the flow of electrical signals in the nervous and cardiac systems. It can also disturb the body's fluid balance.

insulin   A hormone that helps glucose get into the muscles for energy and into the liver for storage as glycogen. Diabetics do not create enough insulin, or their cells are resistant to the insulin they do have.

intensity   The level of energy output or heart rate. It is not necessarily connected to terms such as "fast" or "slow" running.

lactate shuttle   A metabolic system that carries lactate to the liver to be recycled into glycogen for use as fuel.

lactate threshold (LT)   The level of high heart rate activity at which lactate starts to build up in the tissues.

lactic acid   A by-product or waste product created by the muscles at all times. Its formation increases exponentially at higher levels of exercise intensity, when the runner is burning mostly glycogen.

lateral build   A training schedule that simply builds without any taper, which usually leads to fatigue and a depletion in hormonal output.

ligament   Connective tissue that binds bone to bone or which supports organs within the body.

lottery   A blind system of chance employed by some marathons with a tremendous pool of applicants.

low blood sugar   *See* hypoglycemia.

mantra   A word or sound used for concentration and spiritual centering.

marathon   A run of 26.2 miles. In Greek, it means "fennel" and has no relation to running.

micro-tears   Tiny rips in the muscle tissue caused by intense exercise. As they heal, the muscle becomes stronger.

mitochondria   Specialized, microscopic structures within each cell of the body that provide energy by creating fuel in the form of ATP.

myosin   With actin, one of the filaments that make up muscle tissue.

negative split   This is when less time (negative) is spent in the second half of the race than the first, meaning the first half of the race is run more slowly.

net finish time   The elapsed time between your actual start and finish times.

orthotics   A support device used in the shoes to correct pronation issues.

osteopenia   A precursor to osteoporosis. Osteopenia indicates reduced bone density, but not enough to be classified as osteoporosis.

osteoporosis   A severe thinning of the bones that can increase the chance of fracture.

P.R.   Personal record (or P.B., personal best), which describes the fastest race finish ever by an individual athlete at a specific distance.

patella   Another name for the kneecap.

peak   The point in training where you reach your longest and most intense runs in time or distance.

Pilates   A form of exercise that strengthens the core muscles of the torso by using one's body weight for resistance.

progressive stretches   Stretches that are designed to elongate the muscle and are held for 5 to 10 seconds.

pronation   The rotation that the foot makes as it strikes the ground.

proprioception   The perception of one's own body and its actions. It is an instinctive understanding of how the body moves and how it is oriented in space.

protein   Commonly called the building blocks of muscle. Protein is a nutrient found in animal products as well as some grains, nuts, and vegetables.

quadriceps   The set of four muscles comprising the front of the thigh.

qualifying time   A certified finish time for an approved marathon race.

race pace   The pace or speed at which a race will be run.

RICE   An acronym for rest, ice, compression, elevation. This is the best treatment for many minor running injuries.

singlet   A loose-fitting tank top worn by many types of athletes.

slow-twitch muscle fibers   Trainable muscle fibers that contribute to endurance, but are slower than fast-twitch muscles.

SPF   Short for sun protection factor, a measure of the strength of sunscreen expressed in terms of time.

static stretches   Traditional stretches, often the same as progressive stretches, but usually held for a period of 30 seconds.

stress hormone   *See* cortisol.

stride   The distance your foot reaches forward and backward with each strike of the ground. One stride can also mean one step.

taper   A structured reduction in volume of training runs while frequency and intensity remain the same.

tendon   Connective tissue that binds bone to muscle.

timing mats   Long rubber mats used by marathon chip timing companies which usually stretch across the entire width of the street or race course so that runners must step over them as they pass.

titin   A springlike structure within muscle tissue that helps muscle fibers and filaments to contract.

ultra-marathon   A race that is longer than a marathon. Popular distances are 50 and 100 miles.

VO$_2$ Max   The volume of oxygen an individual is capable of using. VO$_2$ Max is one factor in calculating athletic efficiency. It defines aerobic and anaerobic levels. VO$_2$ Max also indicates the maximum heart rate at which the athlete still uses oxygen and fat as a source to form ATP.

volume   The amount of time or distance covered during a single exercise. It can also refer to how much training is performed over a certain amount of time, such as volume per week.

Books

Bompa, Tudor O., and G. Gregory Haff. *Periodization: Theory and Methodology of Training, 5th edition.* Human Kinetics, 2009.

Bompa, Tudor O., and Lorenzo J. Cornacchia. *Serious Strength Training.* Human Kinetics, 1998.

Daniels, Jack. *Daniels' Running Formula, 2nd edition.* Human Kinetics, 2005.

Dreyer, Danny, and Katherine Dreyer. *ChiRunning, 2nd edition.* Fireside, 2009.

Fitzgerald, Matt. *RUN: The Mind-Body Methods of Running by Feel.* VeloPress, 2010.

Friel, Joe. *The Triathlete's Training Bible, 2nd edition.* VeloPress, 2004.

Galloway, Jeff. *Galloway's Book on Running, 2nd edition.* Shelter Publications, 2002.

Hagerman, Patrick. *Strength Training for Triathletes.* VeloPress, 2008.

Ley, Alan, ed. *USA Triathlon Level One, Coaching Certification Manual.* USA Triathlon, 2003.

Lovett, Charlie. *Olympic Marathon.* Praeger Publishers, 1997.

Mujika, Inigo. *Tapering and Peaking for Optimal Performance.* Human Kinetics, 2009.

Noakes, Tim. *Lore of Running, 4th edition.* Human Kinetics, 2001.

Powers, Scott K., and Edward T. Howley. *Exercise Physiology: Theory and Application to Fitness and Performance, 5th edition.* McGraw-Hill, 2004.

Sedava, David, et al. *Life: The Science of Biology, 8th edition.* Sinauer Associates, Inc., W.H. Freeman and Company, 2008.

Seebohar, Bob. *Nutrition Periodization for Endurance Athletes.* Bull Publishing Company, 2004.

USA Track & Field Coaching Education. *Level Two Endurance.* Sport Court, 2010.

Websites

Online marathon and other event registration and information: www.active.com

Altitude information: www.altitude.org

American Association of Orthopaedic Medicine: www.aaomed.org

American Diabetes Association: www.diabetes.org

American Heart Association: www.heart.org

American Lung Association: www.lungusa.org

Arthritis Foundation: www.arthritis.org; www.arthritistoday.org

Centers for Disease Control and Prevention: www.cdc.gov

Jeff Galloway (author of *Galloway's Book on Running*): www.jeffgalloway.com

Marathon Guide: www.marathonguide.com

Mayo Clinic: www.mayoclinic.com

Olympics: www.olympic.org

The Pose Method (Nicholas Romanov): www.posetech.com/pose_method

Runner's World magazine: www.runnersworld.com

Running in the USA: www.runningintheusa.com

Running Planet: www.runningplanet.com

Trail and ultra running: www.backcountryrunner.com

Trail Runners Club: http://trailrunnersclub.com

USA Track & Field: www.usatf.org

To rank these races, we took every list we could find online from a running organization who reported on well-known races or marathons. Most of them were numbered by favorites. The numbers were added up and divided by the number of lists they were on. If a marathon was on three lists or more, one number was subtracted. That is how we came up with our list of most popular marathon races in the United States. They also happen to include the largest marathons in the United States.

15 Most Popular U.S. Marathons

1. **Boston Marathon:** Billed as the most legendary and oldest marathon in the United States. It is held on Boston's holiday, Patriot's Day, when the city is closed and it seems as if the entire town comes out to watch and cheer. You need to qualify in most cases. In April. www.bostonmarathon.org.

2. **New York Marathon:** A huge, amazing race, with great crowd support like Boston, this race runs through five boroughs of New York, with a spectacular Central Park finish. There is a lottery to enter. In November. www.ingnycmarathon.org.

3. **Los Angeles Marathon:** This was the only race not at the top of a few lists. We bumped it up due to the exciting new "Stadium to the Sea" course, from Dodger's Stadium to Santa Monica's famous Pier. This is a huge change in course for this enormous race, which is one of the largest in the United States, and it will continue to grow in popularity. In March. www.lamarathon.com.

4. **Chicago Marathon:** The joke about this rather flat course is: Do you know what the biggest hill is on the Chicago Marathon? Answer: The curb. Not completely true, but always among the largest, exciting, faster races in the United States. In November. www.chicagomarathon.com.

5. **Houston Marathon:** Southern hospitality for contestants is at a premium here, at this large (22,000), sell out race. They also give out a T-shirt, a finisher's shirt, medal, and mug. In January. www.chevronhoustonmarathon.com.

6. **Marine Corps Marathon:** Hosted by the U.S. Marine Corps, this marathon is fairly flat and goes past numerous monuments in Washington, D.C. Given the time of year, it could be cold, but a great race with lots of spectators. Be forewarned, this race sells out in a few days in early April at 30,000 participants. In late October. www.marinemarathon.com.

7. **Honolulu Marathon:** Beginning before dawn to avoid the heat, there are fireworks, torch-lit roadways, and stunning views on this big, spectacular race. The humidity is a factor and this is not a fast course, especially with a big hill at the end. Plenty of elegant vacationlike amenities abound, at affordable prices. In December. www.honolulumarathon.org.

8. **St. George Marathon:** Many run this Utah course to achieve a personal record, or to qualify for Boston. Though there is a good uphill at mile eight, there is also plenty of comfortable downhill (nearly 2,600 feet of descent) to take you down this breathtaking country road and mountainous area. Begin with a long drive out to the point-to-point start on a cold dark morning, complete with fires in trash cans to stay warm and a glorious sunrise while running. They have a competitive lottery to get in. On the first Saturday of October. www.stgeorgemarathon.com.

9. **Grandma's Marathon:** Held in Duluth, Minnesota, next to Lake Superior and the north woods, this fast and rather flat country course, with an elevation of 610 feet to 740 feet, boasts a great postrace party and dance. The small town is packed for this event, so book a room early. In late June. http://grandmasmarathon.com.

10. **Big Sur International Marathon:** The breathtaking and scenic California coast via Highway 1 is the site of this spectacle. It is a slow, hilly course, occasionally with head winds, along amazing cliffs overlooking the ocean. Not a lot of spectators, but popular on marathon lists, with nice touches such as a grand piano played at the halfway point, next to a scenic expansive bridge. In late April or early May. www.bsim.org.

11. **Philadelphia Marathon:** This growing race sells out with over 20,000 participants, which includes entrants in other shorter races on the same weekend, including a half marathon. It runs past some nice scenery and historic landmarks, beginning and ending near the Philadelphia Museum of Art. Held the weekend before Thanksgiving in November. www.philadelphiamarathon.com.

12. **San Francisco Marathon:** This is not a fast course, but a bit hilly and certainly scenic, which boasts fun and wacky participants. It crosses over the Golden Gate Bridge, through Fisherman's Warf, down famous Haight Street, ending in Golden Gate Park. Besides the high-tech (polyester dryweave)

running T-shirt you are given, the medal is also a coaster. Temperatures usually start in the 60s and end in the 70s. In early July. www.thesfmarathon.com.

13. **Twin Cities Marathon:** This scenic urban Minnesota marathon is run with a background of fall colors, starting in downtown Minneapolis near the Metrodome, which offers warmth and bathrooms. It runs past lakes and streams and elegant neighborhoods, and finishes on the State Capitol grounds in Saint Paul. There is a six-hour time limit on this course, so it is not for everyone. In early October. www.twincitiesmarathon.org.

14. **Rock 'n' Roll Las Vegas Marathon:** Formerly the Las Vegas International Marathon, this race is filled with Elvises, or Elvi, as they are called. After running part of your race on the Vegas strip, with some miles run outside of town in a desolate area, you are treated to an evening party for all participants, in a posh casino bar. It is a fairly flat course, but often windy. In early December. http://las-vegas.competitor.com.

15. **Portland Marathon:** This race in Portland, Oregon, begins and ends in the interesting downtown area, surrounded by charming old and new architecture. It follows the Willamette River, and continues on into beautiful park areas, and boasts that it's a friendly marathon with 4,500 volunteers and over 70 bands playing music. The course is fairly fast, but hilly in areas, and mostly scenic, with temperatures usually around 50°F at the start, rising to 60°F or so at the end. There is also a half marathon as well as other shorter races, providing a distance for everyone. In early October. www.portlandmarathon.org.

There were several popular marathons from one or two lists, which did not quite add up enough points to land on our list of 15. San Diego's Rock 'n' Roll Marathon and the Cincinnati Flying Pig Marathon are only two.

15 Most Popular U.S. Short Races

1. **Peachtree Road Race:** This 10K, Atlanta, Georgia, July 4th race remarkably seems to be at the top of a few lists. It began in 1970 with 110 participants, and has grown to its current size of 55,000. www.peachtreeroadrace.org.

2. **Bolder Boulder 10K:** Boulder, Colorado, is the site for this Independence Day race, which is so large, it has 92 waves of people starting at different times, with the first at 7:00 A.M. and the last at 9:24 A.M. Each year, runners sign up to get one of the 55,000 slots. The race is televised locally and features some Independence Day festivities. On July 4th. www.bolderboulder.com.

3. **Walt Disney World Half Marathon:** The event weekend takes place at the theme park in Orlando, Florida. There are some nice unique touches. For instance, the race will be run at night, and feature a "Wine and Dine" finish area, with a lot of food. The Mickey Mouse finish medal is unique to Disney races. In October. http://espnwwos.disney.go.com/events/rundisney/wine-and-dine-half-marathon/.

4. **Cooper River Bridge Run 10K:** Charleston, South Carolina, hosts this large scenic race, which also features a wave start and a green innovative idea called the "Racelet," which you can wear. It holds all the information needed for the race on a chip, viewable with nearly all electronic media devices, rather than printing it out on paper. In April. www.bridgerun.com.

5. **Bay to Breakers:** The San Francisco 12K (7.46 miles) race has become a standard since it began in 1912. It is the seventh longest, consecutively run road race in the world, and the largest in California. The event recently had to ban alcohol, as it was a bit of an unruly circus. Many were finishing the race naked or in their underwear. Many still finish in costumes, behind the impressive world class running talent. Mid-May. http://baytobreakers.com.

6. **San Francisco Half Marathon and 5K:** *Runner's World* ranked this course as one of the most scenic in the country. This is a flat, fast course which goes by Golden Gate Park and the Pacific Ocean. Participants take a free shuttle to the start from the finish. All contestants receive a free long sleeve shirt and goody bag, which they get after crossing the finish line. In February. http://xnet.kp.org/sanfrancisco/index.html.

7. **Freihofer's Run for Women:** This 5K in Albany, New York, attracts top women in running, from Olympians, to local talent, to women from across the country. Approximately 4,000 women compete in this race, now in its third decade. Held on a Saturday in early June. www.freihofersrun.com/womens_5k.htm.

8. **Austin Half Marathon:** Austin, Texas, is the home for this event. The race is capped at 5,750 participants, and hails as the second-largest foot race in this capital city. You can run this race as an individual or as a two-person relay team. In late January. http://solutions.3m.com/wps/portal/3M/en_US/HalfMarathon/Home.

9. **Colonial Half Marathon:** Historic Williamsburg, Virginia, is the site for this event, which begins on the college campus of William and Mary. The course is a bit hilly, with fewer flat areas than most. Held in late February, the climate

can still be quite cold, with temperatures in the 30s to 50s. Proceeds from the race go to the Track and Field program at William and Mary. www.tribeclub. com/past_events.html.

10. **Crescent City Classic 10K:** New Orleans, Louisiana, hosts this fast, popular point-to-point 10K course, with a field of almost 20,000 participating athletes. The 2002 event saw a world record broken. Organizers of this event boast of a great expo and a large postrace party. It's held the Saturday before Easter, usually in April. www.ccc10k.com/site.php?pageID=3.

11. **Austin American-Statesman Capitol 10K:** Held in Austin, this is the largest 10K race in Texas and the fifth largest in the country. Now in its third decade, this race attracts the "silly to the serious," according to the website. There is a costume contest for the silly. And money from the event benefits two youth-based charities, a children's shelter, and a learn-to-swim program for children. Held in late March. www.statesman.com/cap10k.

12. **Carlsbad 5000:** Held in Carlsbad, California, just north of San Diego, this race bills itself as the World's Fastest 5K. This flat, fast course runs for 2 miles along the Pacific Ocean. There are separate starts dividing different groups into separate races, all racing the same 5000m. These separate group starts begin with masters' men and women, 40 and over, who go in the morning; wheelchair invitational is next followed by men and women in their 30s. There's a fair amount of time before the men and women 29 and under race. Finally the elite men and women's invitational completes the day. In early April. www.carlsbad5000.com/Home.html.

13. **Canyonlands Half Marathon:** The red rock formations around Moab, Utah, are a highlight for this race setting, now well into its third decade. This is a rolling, and often challenging race, set at a reasonable 4,000 feet of elevation. Average temperature for this region in March is 35°F to 64°F. The course is limited to 4,000 for the Half and accompanying 5-mile race. The lottery is conducted in December for the March race. www.moabhalfmarathon.org.

14. **Caesar Rodney Half Marathon:** Located in Wilmington, Delaware, organizers bill this race as the "Granddad of all Delaware road races," with the race entering its fifth decade in 2013. More than 1,000 runners from 20 states and several other countries participate in this scenic, interesting course. Average temperatures in March, when the race is held, range from 32°F to 50°F, with a fair chance of rain. www.halfmarathons.net/usa_half_marathons_delaware_caesar_rodney_half_marathon.html.

15. **New Bedford Half Marathon:** This scenic New Bedford, Massachusetts, race is a New England championship race, in a series from USA Track & Field. The entire town seems to come out to embrace the race and make all feel welcome, at this Half. Now in its third decade, the Half saw record participants in 2010, at 2,665. In March. www.newbedfordhalfmarathon.com.

Although the next three races do not completely fit into this category, we threw them in as a bonus, due to their popularity, intrigue, and uniqueness:

16. **Hood to Coast Relay:** 12,000 runners take turns on teams to go 197 miles, from Mt. Hood to the Pacific Ocean at Seaside Oregon, and raise money for the American Cancer Society. In August. www.hoodtocoast.com.

17. **Pikes Peak Ascent:** Simply stated, you run up 13.32 miles, and climb 7,815 feet of elevation while you do it. In August. www.pikespeakmarathon.org.

18. **Rock 'n' Roll Los Angeles Half Marathon:** With 14,000 for their inaugural race in October 2010, the terrain is a bit hilly, but you can't beat the scenic and interesting view of Los Angeles—but it does not include Hollywood or Beverly Hills. http://los-angeles.competitor.com/.

15 Most Popular International Marathons

The top five international marathons seemed to clearly rank above the others, in this order:

1. **London Marathon:** This is one of the largest and faster (flatter) marathons in the world. Similar to the New York Marathon, this race has three different starts, on three different streets. Each start is named by a color (red, green, or blue), rather than a number, which might indicate that number one is more important than number three. All three courses begin near each other, and all go the same distance, merging together after a few miles. One interesting statistic holds that in 2010, four out of five of the fastest marathon times run in the world by women, on any marathon course, were run at the London Marathon. This race crosses the famous Tower of London Bridge, and ends in front of Buckingham Palace, after going past the Houses of Parliament and other famous sites. In April. www.virginlondonmarathon.com.

2. **Berlin Marathon:** This is another of the largest marathons in the world, with more than 40,000 runners and power walkers, and over 7,000 skaters, with additional wheelchair and hand-crank contestants. This faster course also goes past old historic sites, ending just after going under the famous Roman-built

Brandenburg Gate. In September. www.real-berlin-marathon.com/events/berlin_marathon/2010/index.en.php.

3. **Stockholm Marathon:** Features enthusiastic spectators and a course that is usually near the water. Only 20,000 are allowed into this race, which runs two identical laps around the Swedish capitol. A big highlight for this race is the thousands of fans who greet the runners at the finish in the classical 1912 Olympic Stadium. In June. www.stockholmmarathon.se/Start/index.cfm?Lan_ID=3.

4. **Rotterdam Marathon:** This is another fast marathon, boasting four out of five top male finish times in any marathon in the world, in 2010. Only 22,000 are entered into this event each year, with 900,000 spectators. There is a five-and-a-half-hour time limit. In April. www.abnamromarathonrotterdam.com.

5. **Marathon de Paris:** This is a historic marathon, started in the late 1800s, with a rather flat, fast course. It begins in front of the Triumphal Arch and continues down the Champs-Elysees, past the Seine River and other scenic and famous historic sites, such as the Eiffel Tower and Notre Dame Cathedral. The race features wine and cheese at the 35th kilometer of the course (approximately the 22nd mile). There are 250,000 onlookers and 70 areas with music. In April. www.parismarathon.com/index.html.

The following international marathons are listed by calendar date, and not by a specific numbered ranking:

6. **Mumbai Marathon, India:** This race has the richest purse of winnings in Asia, at $310,000, and claims 36,000 runners in all of its different distance events. Though the purse brings a fair amount of international talent to the marathon, only about 3,000 will participate in the marathon. In January. http://mumbaimarathon.indiatimes.com/index1.html.

7. **Tokyo Marathon:** This newer marathon, only a few years old, is enormously popular, selling out many months in advance (in August for the February race). Only 32,000 will be allowed to participate, so a lottery will be held to determine the exact entrants in the race. The course runs past several tourist attractions. There is a seven-hour time limit, and you must be 19 years of age to participate. In February. www.tokyo42195.org/2011/index_en.html.

8. **Seoul International Marathon, Seoul, Korea (South):** This is a well-organized, flat, fast course, with 23,000 runners, mostly Korean, and a rather large but subdued crowd. The finish is exciting, with one lap of the Olympic Stadium. In March. http://marathon.donga.com/seoul/international_e1.html.

9. **Maratona Di Roma, in Rome, Italy:** The 15,000 marathon participants begin in front of the 2,000-year-old Colosseum, making up only a small portion of the 100,000 overall athletes who are doing the 4K and Marathon. They continue past old picturesque sites, including Saint Peter's Basilica, the Trevi Fountain, Piazza Navona, and the Spanish Steps. The course is rather flat, but there are a lot of cobblestones, which can be difficult to run on. In March. www.maratonadiroma.it/default.aspx.

10. **Hamburg Marathon:** This quarter-of-a-century-old marathon sees a little more than 15,000 participants. It is a fairly flat course with some downhill at the beginning and less of an uphill at the end. There is a 5-hour-and-20-minute time limit for this event. In April or May. www.marathon-hamburg.de/index_e.php.

11. **Comrades Marathon (89 Kilometers/56 miles), Durban, South Africa:** Entries are only open from September to November, with a cutoff of 18,000 athletes. This is a long, grueling, and historic distance race, which requires that you qualify to get in. It was first run in 1921, as a tribute to those comrades who had died in World War I. Though it clearly is an ultra-marathon, it is still called a marathon. In May. www.comrades.com.

12. **Beijing International Marathon:** This marathon was first run in 1981. It begins in historic Tiananmen Square and finishes at the National Olympic Sports Centre stadium. It is a rather flat course except for one hill around the 25K (about 15.5 miles) point. Along with the full marathon, a half marathon, a 9K, and a 4.2K "mini-marathon" are also run. All four races fill up with a combined total of 30,000 participants, which is maximum capacity for Tiananmen Square. Reports indicate this is a well-organized race, and not too crowded on the course. In October. www.beijing-marathon.com/en/index.html.

13. **Amsterdam Marathon:** The organizers of this marathon are expecting 30,000 participants in all of their distance races, but only 11,000 for the marathon. This is reported to be a flat, fast, scenic course, in a great city to visit. Not a lot of crowds, but an exciting finish in the Olympic Stadium. In October. www.amsterdammarathon.nl.

14. **Athens Classic Marathon:** This race features poor air quality, few crowds, and an occasional cobblestone street, which is difficult for running. However, it is a great tour of an ancient Greek city, as well as the historic location of the battle of Marathon which occurred 2,500 years ago. The people and volunteers are helpful and always nice. In October. www.athensclassicmarathon.gr/MARATHON/fMain.aspx.

15. **Frankfurt Marathon:** The flat, fast course has a lot of twists and turns in it. The scenery is not as spectacular as in some other European marathons, though there is a lot of music on the course, as well as organized, helpful volunteers throughout. The finish is incredibly exciting with a big crowd at an indoor arena, a red carpet, confetti, and four large video screens. In October. www.frankfurt-marathon.com/en/home.html.

Another challenging and historic marathon that may not be as popular as some but is worth mentioning is The Great Wall Marathon, staged in China's Tianjin province. This is a slow marathon with steps and a lot of uneven stone, which make running difficult. It is an impossible marathon to race through, but it is a cool 26.2-mile running tour of the area.

Sample Training Programs

Welcome to marathon training! This is a 27-week marathon program, and an 18-week half marathon schedule, as an example. Rule #1 of endurance athletics: have fun!

Marathon Training Schedule

The one-size-fits-all schedule does *not* fit all. And when you find a schedule that fits, something will happen, and it won't fit for long. If you are tired the day after an exercise, you are overtraining and need to do less, until you recover and regain your energy levels. If you are in pain, stop immediately. Heal first and train second. Of course, things such as family life or work issues can come up, and you may not be able to run one day. So once you find the perfect schedule for you, be prepared to change it. Just don't miss too many days, or you will lose some of your hard-earned endurance ability. Also, remember that if you are doing too much or too many hard workouts in a row, you are overtraining. A good mantra to live by: proper exercise and rest create optimal performance, which equals your best race.

For both the marathon and half marathon training schedules: women need to add 10 minutes to every workout for the final exponential taper, except the 20-miler and the Saturday before race day. The reason for this has to do with the fact that women do not benefit from as much of a taper as men do. Testosterone, a hormone that motivates, is limited in women, and they benefit from holding on to as much as they can by not tapering too much.

Please refer to the terms in the table when looking at the marathon or half marathon training schedules.

Have an inspired workout!

Term	What It Means
Aero or aerobic	Aerobic; zone two; an intensity level where you feel as if you could go forever; you can talk without noticeable pauses for breathing; slower than marathon pace; easy.
LT	Lactate threshold; zone three; marathon "race pace" intensity; higher than aerobic.
AT	Anaerobic threshold; zone four; higher heart rate; heavier breathing; 5K or 10K level of intensity, 85 percent of HR Max.
XT or X-train	Strength training, swimming, biking—anything but running.
4 x 6:30 @ AT off 3:30	Four sets of 6½ minutes at AT intensity, with an off period in between each set of 3½ minutes. Try and run LT (marathon race pace) during off periods, or do what you can to recover quickly.
Taper week	Occurs every fourth week, when the athlete works out with the same intensity and on the same days of the week, but with much less volume as the previous week.
Exponential taper	Following the peak of training comes a taper where volume (distance) drops immediately, while intensity and frequency (days working out each week) stay the same.
Fartlek	Swedish term meaning "speed play," in which one simply chooses a distance and a pace. Once achieved, the athlete chooses a different pace and distance and does that. This is used as higher-intensity work, especially by beginners in these schedules.

Week 1 / 27	Mon	Tues	Wed	Thurs	Fri	Sat	Sun
Beginner	DAY OFF	30 mins. aerobic	DAY OFF	30 mins. aerobic	DAY OFF	4 miles aerobic	Strength train
Intermediate	30 mins. aerobic	DAY OFF	45 mins. aerobic	30 mins. aerobic	DAY OFF	5 miles aerobic	X-train
Advanced	DAY OFF	30 mins. aerobic	50 mins. aerobic	30 mins. aerobic	DAY OFF	8 miles aerobic	40 mins. & XT
Week 2 / 26	**Mon**	**Tues**	**Wed**	**Thurs**	**Fri**	**Sat**	**Sun**
Beginner	DAY OFF	30 mins. aerobic	DAY OFF	30 mins. aerobic	DAY OFF	5 miles aerobic	Strength train
Intermediate	30 mins. aerobic	DAY OFF	45 mins. aerobic	30 mins. aerobic	DAY OFF	6 miles aerobic	X-train
Advanced	DAY OFF	30 mins. aerobic	55 mins. aerobic	30 mins. aerobic	DAY OFF	10 miles aerobic	40 mins. & XT
Week 3 / 25	**Mon**	**Tues**	**Wed**	**Thurs**	**Fri**	**Sat**	**Sun**
Beginner	DAY OFF	30 mins. aerobic	DAY OFF	30 mins. aerobic	DAY OFF	6 miles aerobic	Strength train
Intermediate	30 mins. aerobic	DAY OFF	45 mins. aerobic	30 mins. aerobic	DAY OFF	7 miles aerobic	X-train
Advanced	DAY OFF	40 mins. aerobic	1:00 aerobic	40 mins. aerobic	DAY OFF	11 miles aerobic	40 mins. & XT
Week 4 / 24	**Mon**	**Tues**	**Wed**	**Thurs**	**Fri**	**Sat**	**Sun**
Taper Week Beginner	DAY OFF	30 mins. aerobic	DAY OFF	30 mins. aerobic	DAY OFF	3 miles aerobic	Strength train
Taper Week Intermediate	30 mins. aerobic	DAY OFF	30 mins. aerobic	30 mins. aerobic	DAY OFF	3 miles aerobic	X-train
Taper Week Advanced	DAY OFF	30 mins. aerobic	30 mins. aerobic	30 mins. aerobic	DAY OFF	5 miles aerobic	40 mins. & XT

Base phase one. Focus: build volume (low heart rate), form, and strength.

Week 5 / 23	Mon	Tues	Wed	Thurs	Fri	Sat	Sun
Beginner	DAY OFF	30 mins. aerobic	DAY OFF	30 mins. aerobic	DAY OFF	8 miles aerobic	Strength train
Intermediate	30 mins. aerobic	DAY OFF	45 mins. aerobic	30 mins. aerobic	DAY OFF	9 miles aerobic	X-train
Advanced	DAY OFF	40 mins. aerobic	1:00 aerobic	40 mins. aerobic	DAY OFF	12 miles aerobic	40 mins. & XT
Week 6 / 22	**Mon**	**Tues**	**Wed**	**Thurs**	**Fri**	**Sat**	**Sun**
Beginner	DAY OFF	30 mins. aerobic	DAY OFF	30 mins. aerobic	DAY OFF	9 miles aerobic	Strength train
Intermediate	30 mins. aerobic	DAY OFF	45 mins. aerobic	40 mins. aerobic	DAY OFF	10 miles aerobic	X-train
Advanced	DAY OFF	40 mins. aerobic	1:05 aerobic	45 mins. aerobic	DAY OFF	13 miles aerobic	40 mins. & XT
Week 7 / 21	**Mon**	**Tues**	**Wed**	**Thurs**	**Fri**	**Sat**	**Sun**
Beginner	DAY OFF	30 mins. aerobic	DAY OFF	30 mins. aerobic	DAY OFF	10 miles aerobic	Strength train
Intermediate	30 mins. aerobic	DAY OFF	45 mins. aerobic	40 mins. aerobic	DAY OFF	10 miles aerobic	X-train
Advanced	DAY OFF	40 mins. aerobic	1:10 aerobic	50 mins. aerobic	DAY OFF	13 miles aerobic	40 mins. & XT
Week 8 / 20	**Mon**	**Tues**	**Wed**	**Thurs**	**Fri**	**Sat**	**Sun**
Taper Week Beginner	DAY OFF	30 mins. aerobic	DAY OFF	30 mins. aerobic	DAY OFF	5 miles aerobic	Strength train
Taper Week Intermediate	30 mins. aerobic	DAY OFF	30 mins. aerobic	30 mins. aerobic	DAY OFF	5 miles aerobic	X-train
Taper Week Advanced	DAY OFF	30 mins. aerobic	30 mins. aerobic	30 mins. aerobic	DAY OFF	6 miles aerobic	30 mins. & XT

Base phase two. Focus: more volume (low heart rate), form, and strength.

Week 9 / 19	Mon	Tues	Wed	Thurs	Fri	Sat	Sun
Beginner	DAY OFF	30 mins. aerobic	DAY OFF	30 mins. aerobic	DAY OFF	12 miles aerobic	Strength train
Intermediate	30 mins. aerobic	DAY OFF	45 mins. aerobic	40 mins. aerobic	DAY OFF	13 miles aerobic	X-train
Advanced	DAY OFF	40 mins. aerobic	1:15 aerobic	50 mins. aerobic	DAY OFF	15 miles aerobic	40 mins. & XT
Week 10 /18	**Mon**	**Tues**	**Wed**	**Thurs**	**Fri**	**Sat**	**Sun**
Beginner	DAY OFF	30 mins. aerobic	DAY OFF	30 mins. aerobic	DAY OFF	13 miles aerobic	Strength train
Intermediate	40 mins. aerobic	DAY OFF	50 mins. aerobic	40 mins. aerobic	DAY OFF	14 miles aerobic	X-train
Advanced	DAY OFF	50 mins. aerobic	1:20 aerobic	50 mins. aerobic	DAY OFF	16 miles aerobic	40 mins. & XT
Week 11 /17	**Mon**	**Tues**	**Wed**	**Thurs**	**Fri**	**Sat**	**Sun**
Beginner	DAY OFF	30 mins. aerobic	DAY OFF	30 mins. aerobic	DAY OFF	14 miles aerobic	Strength train
Intermediate	40 mins. aerobic	DAY OFF	50 mins. aerobic	40 mins. aerobic	DAY OFF	15 miles aerobic	X-train
Advanced	DAY OFF	50 mins. aerobic	1:30 aerobic	50 mins. aerobic	DAY OFF	16 miles aerobic	40 mins. & XT
Week 12 /16	**Mon**	**Tues**	**Wed**	**Thurs**	**Fri**	**Sat**	**Sun**
Taper Week Beginner	DAY OFF	30 mins. aerobic	DAY OFF	30 mins. aerobic	DAY OFF	7 miles aerobic	Strength train
Taper Week Intermediate	30 mins. aerobic	DAY OFF	30 mins. aerobic	30 mins. aerobic	DAY OFF	7 miles aerobic	X-train
Taper Week Advanced	DAY OFF	30 mins. aerobic	45 mins. aerobic	30 mins. aerobic	DAY OFF	8 miles aerobic	40 mins. & XT

Base phase three. Focus: more volume (low heart rate), form, and strength.

Week 13 /15	Mon	Tues	Wed	Thurs	Fri	Sat	Sun
Beginner	DAY OFF	30 mins. LT	DAY OFF	30 mins. LT	DAY OFF	16 miles aerobic	Strength train
Intermediate	45 mins. LT	DAY OFF	10x300 M @ track	45 mins. LT	DAY OFF	17 miles aerobic	X-train
Advanced	DAY OFF	16x300 M @ track	1:30 LT	50 mins. LT	DAY OFF	19 miles aerobic	40 mins. & XT

Week 14 /14	Mon	Tues	Wed	Thurs	Fri	Sat	Sun
Beginner	DAY OFF	30 mins. Fartlek	DAY OFF	30 mins. LT	DAY OFF	17 miles aerobic	Strength train
Intermediate	45 mins. LT	DAY OFF	8x400 M @ track	45 mins. LT	DAY OFF	18 miles aerobic	X-train
Advanced	DAY OFF	12x400 M @ track	1:30 LT	50 mins. LT w/hills	DAY OFF	20 miles aerobic	45 mins. & XT

Week 15 /13	Mon	Tues	Wed	Thurs	Fri	Sat	Sun
Beginner	DAY OFF	30 mins. Fartlek	DAY OFF	30 mins. LT	DAY OFF	20 miles aerobic Time Trial	Strength train
Intermediate	45 mins. LT	DAY OFF	4x500 M @ track	45 mins. LT	DAY OFF	20 miles aerobic Time Trial	X-train
Advanced	DAY OFF	6x500 M @ track	1:45 LT	50 mins. LT w/hills	DAY OFF	20 miles aerobic Time Trial	45 mins. & XT

Week 16 /12	Mon	Tues	Wed	Thurs	Fri	Sat	Sun
Taper Week Beginner	DAY OFF	30 mins. LT	DAY OFF	30 mins. LT	DAY OFF	8 miles LT	Strength train
Taper Week Intermediate	30 mins.	DAY OFF	30 mins. LT	30 mins. LT	DAY OFF	8 miles LT	X-train
Taper Week Advanced	DAY OFF	30 mins. LT	45 mins. LT	30 mins. LT	DAY OFF	8 miles LT	30 mins. & XT

Building phase four. Focus: building intensity.

Week 17/11	Mon	Tues	Wed	Thurs	Fri	Sat	Sun
Beginner	DAY OFF	40 mins. Fartlek	DAY OFF	40 mins. LT	DAY OFF	12 miles LT	Strength train
Intermediate	45 mins. LT	DAY OFF	4x6:30 @ AT off 3:30	45 mins. LT	DAY OFF	12 miles LT	X-train
Advanced	DAY OFF	1:00 LT	4x6:30 @ AT off 3:30	1:00 LT w/hills	DAY OFF	14 miles LT	45 mins. LT
Week 18/10	**Mon**	**Tues**	**Wed**	**Thurs**	**Fri**	**Sat**	**Sun**
Beginner	DAY OFF	40 mins. Fartlek	DAY OFF	40 mins. LT w/hills	DAY OFF	13 miles LT	Strength train
Intermediate	45 mins. LT	DAY OFF	4x7:00 @ AT off 3:00	45 mins. LT w/hills	DAY OFF	13 miles LT	X-train
Advanced	DAY OFF	1:00 LT	4x7:00 @ AT off 3:00	1:00 LT w/hills	DAY OFF	15 miles LT	45 mins. LT
Week 19/9	**Mon**	**Tues**	**Wed**	**Thurs**	**Fri**	**Sat**	**Sun**
Beginner	DAY OFF	40 mins. Fartlek	DAY OFF	40 mins. LT w/hills	DAY OFF	14 miles LT	Strength train
Intermediate	45 mins. LT	DAY OFF	4x7:30 @ AT off 2:30	45 mins. LT w/hills	DAY OFF	14 miles LT	X-train
Advanced	DAY OFF	1:00 LT	4x7:30 @ AT off 2:30	1:00 LT w/hills	DAY OFF	16 miles LT	45 mins. LT
Week 20/8	**Mon**	**Tues**	**Wed**	**Thurs**	**Fri**	**Sat**	**Sun**
Taper Week Beginner	DAY OFF	30 mins. LT	DAY OFF	30 mins. LT	DAY OFF	7 miles LT	Strength train
Taper Week Intermediate	30 mins. LT	DAY OFF	30 mins. LT	30 mins. LT	DAY OFF	7 miles LT	X-train
Taper Week Advanced	DAY OFF	30 mins. LT	45 mins. LT	30 mins. LT	DAY OFF	10 miles LT	30 mins. LT

Building phase five. Focus: building intensity.

Week 21/7	Mon	Tues	Wed	Thurs	Fri	Sat	Sun
Beginner	DAY OFF	40 mins. Fartlek	DAY OFF	40 mins. LT w/hills	DAY OFF	16 miles LT	X-train 40 mins. easy
Intermediate	1:00 LT	DAY OFF	4x8:00 @ AT off 2:00	1:00 LT w/hills	DAY OFF	16 miles LT	X-train
Advanced	DAY OFF	1:15 LT	4x8:00 @ AT off 2:00	1:15 LT w/hills	DAY OFF	18 miles LT	45 mins. LT
Week 22/6	Mon	Tues	Wed	Thurs	Fri	Sat	Sun
Beginner	DAY OFF	40 mins. Fartlek	DAY OFF	40 mins. LT w/hills	DAY OFF	17 miles LT	X-train 40 mins. easy
Intermediate	1:00 LT	DAY OFF	4x9:00 @ AT off 1:00	1:00 LT w/hills	DAY OFF	17 miles LT	X-train
Advanced	DAY OFF	1:15 LT	4x9:00 @ AT off 1:00	1:15 LT w/hills	DAY OFF	19 miles LT	45 mins. LT
Week 23/5	Mon	Tues	Wed	Thurs	Fri	Sat	Sun
Beginner	DAY OFF	40 mins. LT	DAY OFF	40 mins. LT w/hills	DAY OFF	9 miles LT	X-train 40 mins. easy
Intermediate	1:15 aerobic	DAY OFF	4x10:00 @ AT off 1:00	1:00 LT w/hills	DAY OFF	18 miles LT	X-train
Advanced	DAY OFF	1:30 aerobic	4x10:00 @ AT off 1:00	1:15 LT w/hills	DAY OFF	20 miles LT	60 mins. LT
Week 24/4	Mon	Tues	Wed	Thurs	Fri	Sat	Sun
Taper Week Beginner	DAY OFF	30 mins. LT	DAY OFF	30 mins. LT	DAY OFF	20 miles LT, Time Trial	X-train 30 mins.
Taper Week Intermediate	40 mins. LT	DAY OFF	20:00 @ AT off 5:00	40 mins. LT	DAY OFF	10 miles LT	X-train 30 mins.
Taper Week Advanced	DAY OFF	45 mins. LT	20:00 @ AT off 5:00	45 mins. LT	DAY OFF	10 miles LT	30 mins. aerobic

Peak building phase six. Focus: building intensity.

Week 25 / 3	Mon	Tues	Wed	Thurs	Fri	Sat	Sun
Begin Taper Beginner	DAY OFF	40 mins. Fartlek	DAY OFF	40 mins. LT	DAY OFF	40 mins. LT	Strength train
Last Build Intermediate	1:00 LT	DAY OFF	40 mins. AT Tempo Run	40 mins. LT	DAY OFF	20 miles LT, Time Trial	X-train
Last Build Advanced	DAY OFF	40 mins. AT	1:30 LT	45 mins. hills	DAY OFF	20 miles LT, Time Trial	6 miles LT
Week 26 / 2	**Mon**	**Tues**	**Wed**	**Thurs**	**Fri**	**Sat**	**Sun**
Exponential Taper Beginner	DAY OFF	30 mins. Fartlek	DAY OFF	30 mins. LT	DAY OFF	30 mins. LT	Strength train
Exponential Taper Intermediate	30 mins. LT	DAY OFF	5 mins. LT, 20 mins. AT Tempo Run, 5 mins. LT	30 mins. LT	DAY OFF	30 mins. LT	X-train
Exponential Taper Advanced	DAY OFF	30 mins. LT	5 mins. LT, 20 mins. AT Tempo Run, 5 mins. LT	30 mins. LT	DAY OFF	30 mins. LT	30 mins. LT
Week 27 / 1	**Mon**	**Tues**	**Wed**	**Thurs**	**Fri**	**Sat**	**Sun**
Exponential Taper Beginner	DAY OFF	30 mins. LT	DAY OFF	20 mins. LT	DAY OFF	10 mins. LT	**RACE DAY!** Go out easy and have fun!
Exponential Taper Intermediate	30 mins. LT	DAY OFF	5 mins. LT, 10 mins. AT Tempo Run, 5 mins. LT	10 mins. LT	DAY OFF	10 mins. LT	**RACE DAY!** Go out easy and have fun!
Exponential Taper Advanced	DAY OFF	30 mins. LT	5 mins. LT, 10 mins. AT Tempo Run, 5 mins. LT	10 mins. LT	DAY OFF	10 mins. LT	**RACE DAY!** Go out easy and have fun!

Building phase seven. Focus: exponential taper.

Half Marathon Training Schedule

The four-month training program begins now. Start by building strength, and an aerobic base. This is done by increasing volume (distance or time) at a low heart rate. A good sign of an aerobic-intensity run, run/walk, or walk is the ability to talk comfortably, without pauses to breathe. Relaxed workouts, where you aren't constantly aware of your breathing, are critical now. Later we build with intensity (higher heart rate work). Using multiple intensities helps build efficiency.

The week-long taper every fourth week is critical to rebuild energy and hormone levels. Also critical is the large volume of aerobic work during the first few weeks, which makes up a good percentage of this schedule. You will be increasing capillary veins and arteries; expanding mitochondria, which generate fuel for the muscles; increasing red blood cells and hemoglobin; and improving other important physiological elements. Without true low heart rate work during the aerobic workouts, your higher heart rate work later in the season will not yield as many benefits.

One final note: this training schedule is for a half marathon only. It would not be advisable to use it for a race at a different distance, unless that race is a shorter distance and occurs before the final "exponential taper" in this schedule.

Week 1 / 18	Mon	Tues	Wed	Thurs	Fri	Sat	Sun
Beginner	DAY OFF	Strength 30 mins. aerobic	Cross-train or DAY OFF	30 mins. aerobic	DAY OFF	45 mins. aerobic	DAY OFF or XT
Intermediate	DAY OFF	Strength 30 mins. aerobic	Cross-train or DAY OFF	40 mins. aerobic	DAY OFF	45 mins. aerobic	30 mins. aerobic or XT
Advanced	DAY OFF	Strength 30 mins. aerobic	30 mins. aerobic	45 mins. aerobic	DAY OFF	45 mins. aerobic	30 mins. aerobic or XT
Week 2 / 17	**Mon**	**Tues**	**Wed**	**Thurs**	**Fri**	**Sat**	**Sun**
Beginner	DAY OFF	Strength 30 mins. aerobic	Cross-train or DAY OFF	30 mins. aerobic	DAY OFF	1:00 aerobic	DAY OFF or XT
Intermediate	DAY OFF	Strength 30 mins. aerobic	Cross-train or DAY OFF	40 mins. aerobic	DAY OFF	1:00 aerobic	30 mins. aerobic or XT
Advanced	DAY OFF	Strength 40 mins. aerobic	30 mins. aerobic	45 mins. aerobic	DAY OFF	1:00 aerobic	30 mins. aerobic or XT
Week 3 / 16	**Mon**	**Tues**	**Wed**	**Thurs**	**Fri**	**Sat**	**Sun**
Beginner	DAY OFF	Strength 30 mins. aerobic	Cross-train or DAY OFF	40 mins. aerobic	DAY OFF	1:15 aerobic	DAY OFF or XT
Intermediate	DAY OFF	Strength 30 mins. aerobic	Cross-train or DAY OFF	45 mins. aerobic	DAY OFF	1:15 aerobic	30 mins. aerobic or XT
Advanced	DAY OFF	Strength 40 mins. aerobic	30 mins. aerobic	50 mins. aerobic	DAY OFF	1:15 aerobic	30 mins. aerobic or XT
Week 4 / 15	**Mon**	**Tues**	**Wed**	**Thurs**	**Fri**	**Sat**	**Sun**
Taper Week Beginner	DAY OFF	Strength 30 mins. aerobic	Cross-train or DAY OFF	30 mins. aerobic	DAY OFF	40 mins. aerobic	DAY OFF or XT
Taper Week Intermediate	DAY OFF	Strength 30 mins. aerobic	Cross-train or DAY OFF	30 mins. aerobic	DAY OFF	40 mins. aerobic	30 mins. aerobic or XT
Taper Week Advanced	DAY OFF	Strength 30 mins. aerobic	30 mins. aerobic	30 mins. aerobic	DAY OFF	40 mins. aerobic	30 mins. aerobic or XT

Aero phase one. Focus: building volume (low heart rate) and strength.

Week 5 / 14	Mon	Tues	Wed	Thurs	Fri	Sat	Sun
Beginner	DAY OFF	Strength 30 mins. aerobic	Cross-train or DAY OFF	30 mins. aerobic	DAY OFF	1:30 aerobic	DAY OFF or XT
Intermediate	DAY OFF	Strength 30 mins. aerobic	Cross-train or DAY OFF	40 mins. aerobic	DAY OFF	1:30 aerobic	30 mins. aerobic or XT
Advanced	DAY OFF	Strength 30 mins. aerobic	30 mins. aerobic	50 mins. aerobic	DAY OFF	1:30 aerobic	30 mins. aerobic or XT
Week 6 / 13	**Mon**	**Tues**	**Wed**	**Thurs**	**Fri**	**Sat**	**Sun**
Beginner	DAY OFF	Strength 30 mins. aerobic	DAY OFF	30 mins. aerobic	DAY OFF	1:45 aerobic	DAY OFF or XT
Intermediate	DAY OFF	Strength 30 mins. aerobic	DAY OFF	40 mins. aerobic	DAY OFF	1:45 aerobic	30 mins. aerobic or XT
Advanced	DAY OFF	Strength 40 mins. aerobic	40 mins. aerobic	50 mins. aerobic	DAY OFF	1:45 aerobic	30 mins. aerobic or XT
Week 7 / 12	**Mon**	**Tues**	**Wed**	**Thurs**	**Fri**	**Sat**	**Sun**
Beginner	DAY OFF	Strength 30 mins. aerobic	DAY OFF	40 mins. aerobic	DAY OFF	2:00 aerobic	DAY OFF or XT
Intermediate	DAY OFF	Strength 30 mins. aerobic	30 mins. aerobic	45 mins. aerobic	DAY OFF	2:00 aerobic	30 mins. aerobic or XT
Advanced	30 mins. aerobic	Strength 40 mins. aerobic	40 mins. aerobic	50 mins. aerobic	DAY OFF	2:00 aerobic	30 mins. aerobic or XT
Week 8 / 11	**Mon**	**Tues**	**Wed**	**Thurs**	**Fri**	**Sat**	**Sun**
Taper Week Beginner	DAY OFF	Strength 30 mins. aerobic	DAY OFF	30 mins. aerobic	DAY OFF	1:00 aerobic	DAY OFF or XT
Taper Week Intermediate	DAY OFF	Strength 30 mins. aerobic	30 mins. aerobic	30 mins. aerobic	DAY OFF	1:00 aerobic	30 mins. aerobic or XT
Taper Week Advanced	30 mins. aerobic	Strength 30 mins. aerobic	30 mins. aerobic	30 mins. aerobic	DAY OFF	1:00 aerobic	30 mins. aerobic or XT

Aero phase two. Focus: building volume (low heart rate) and strength.

Week 9 / 10	Mon	Tues	Wed	Thurs	Fri	Sat	Sun
Beginner	DAY OFF	Strength 30 mins. aerobic	DAY OFF	30 mins. aerobic	DAY OFF	2:30 aerobic	DAY OFF or X-train
Intermediate	DAY OFF	Strength 30 mins. aerobic	30 mins. aerobic + optional XT	50 mins. aerobic	DAY OFF	2:30 aerobic	30 mins. aerobic + optional XT
Advanced	30 mins. LT	Strength 30 mins. aerobic	30 mins. aerobic + X-train	60 mins. aerobic	DAY OFF	2:30 aerobic	30 mins. aerobic + X-train
Week 10 / 9	**Mon**	**Tues**	**Wed**	**Thurs**	**Fri**	**Sat**	**Sun**
Beginner	DAY OFF	Strength 30 mins. aerobic	DAY OFF	45 mins. aerobic	DAY OFF	2:45 aerobic	DAY OFF or X-train
Intermediate	DAY OFF	Strength 30 mins. aerobic	30 mins. aerobic + optional XT	60 mins. aerobic	DAY OFF	2:45 aerobic	30 mins. aerobic + optional XT
Advanced	30 mins. LT	Strength 30 mins. aerobic	30 mins. aerobic + X-train	70 mins. aerobic	DAY OFF	2:45 aerobic	30 mins. aerobic + X-train
Week 11 / 8	**Mon**	**Tues**	**Wed**	**Thurs**	**Fri**	**Sat**	**Sun**
Beginner	DAY OFF	40 mins. Fartlek	DAY OFF	30 mins. aerobic	DAY OFF	6 miles LT	DAY OFF or X-train
Intermediate	DAY OFF	3x6 mins. @ AT off 4 mins.	30 mins. LT + optional 30 mins. aerobic XT	60 mins. aerobic	DAY OFF	6 miles LT	DAY OFF or X-train
Advanced	30 mins. LT	4x6 mins. @ AT off 4 mins.	30 mins. LT + X-train	70 mins. aerobic	DAY OFF	6 miles LT	30 mins. aerobic or X-train
Week 12 / 7	**Mon**	**Tues**	**Wed**	**Thurs**	**Fri**	**Sat**	**Sun**
Taper Week Beginner	DAY OFF	Strength 30 mins. aerobic	DAY OFF	30 mins. aerobic	DAY OFF	5K LT	DAY OFF or X-train
Taper Week Intermediate	DAY OFF	Strength 30 mins. aerobic	DAY OFF	30 mins. LT	DAY OFF	5K LT	DAY OFF or X-train
Taper Week Advanced	30 mins. LT	Strength 30 mins. aerobic	DAY OFF	30 mins. LT	DAY OFF	5K LT	30 mins. aerobic or X-train

Aero phase three. Focus: building volume (low heart rate).

Week 13 / 6	Mon	Tues	Wed	Thurs	Fri	Sat	Sun
Beginner	DAY OFF	40 mins. Fartlek	DAY OFF	40 mins. aerobic	DAY OFF	8 miles LT	DAY OFF or X-train
Intermediate	DAY OFF	4x6:30 mins. @ AT off 3:30 mins.	30 mins. aerobic + optional XT	1:20 aerobic	DAY OFF	8 miles LT	30 mins. aerobic + optional XT
Advanced	30 mins. LT	4x6:30 mins. @ AT off 3:30 mins.	30 mins. aerobic + X-train	1:30 aerobic	DAY OFF	9 miles LT	40 mins. aerobic + X-train
Week 14 / 5	**Mon**	**Tues**	**Wed**	**Thurs**	**Fri**	**Sat**	**Sun**
Beginner	DAY OFF	40 mins. Fartlek	30 mins. LT	40 mins. aerobic	DAY OFF	9 miles LT	DAY OFF or X-train
Intermediate	DAY OFF	4x7:00 mins. @ AT off 3 mins.	30 mins. LT	40 mins. LT w/hills	DAY OFF	9 miles LT	30 mins. aerobic + optional XT
Advanced	30 mins. LT	4x7:00 mins. @ AT off 3 mins.	40 mins. LT	50 mins. LT w/hills	DAY OFF	11 miles LT	40 mins. aerobic + X-train
Week 15 / 4	**Mon**	**Tues**	**Wed**	**Thurs**	**Fri**	**Sat**	**Sun**
Beginner	DAY OFF	40 mins. Fartlek	30 mins. LT	40 mins. aerobic	DAY OFF	10 miles LT Time Trial	DAY OFF or XT
Intermediate	DAY OFF	4x7:30 mins. @ AT off 2:30 mins.	40 mins. LT w/hills	30 mins. LT	DAY OFF	10 miles LT Time Trial	30 mins. aerobic + optional XT
Advanced	40 mins. LT	4x7:30 mins. @ AT off 2:30 mins.	50 mins. LT w/hills	40 mins. LT	DAY OFF	13 miles LT Time Trial	40 mins. aerobic +XT
Week 16 / 3	**Mon**	**Tues**	**Wed**	**Thurs**	**Fri**	**Sat**	**Sun**
Taper Week Beginner	DAY OFF	30 mins. LT Strength	DAY OFF	30 mins. aerobic	DAY OFF	10K LT not a race	DAY OFF or XT
Taper Week Intermediate	DAY OFF	30 mins. LT Strength	30 mins. LT	30 mins. aerobic	DAY OFF	10K LT not a race	30 mins. LT
Taper Week Advanced	30 mins. LT	30 mins. LT Strength	30 mins. LT	30 mins. aerobic	DAY OFF	10K LT not a race	30 mins. LT

Building phase four. Focus: begin building intensity.

Week 17 / 2	Mon	Tues	Wed	Thurs	Fri	Sat	Sun
Exponential Taper Beginner	DAY OFF	30 mins. LT Strength	DAY OFF	30 mins. LT	DAY OFF	30 mins. LT	DAY OFF or XT
Exponential Taper Intermediate	DAY OFF	30 mins. LT Strength	30 mins. LT	30 mins. LT	DAY OFF	30 mins. LT	30 mins. LT
Exponential Taper Advanced	30 mins. LT	30 mins. LT Strength	30 mins. LT	30 mins. LT	DAY OFF	30 mins. LT	30 mins. LT

Week 18 / 1	Mon	Tues	Wed	Thurs	Fri	Sat	Sun
Exponential Taper Beginner	DAY OFF	Strength 30 mins. LT	DAY OFF	20 mins. LT	DAY OFF	10 mins. LT	**RACE DAY!** Go out easy and have fun!
Exponential Taper Intermediate	DAY OFF	Strength 30 mins. LT	30 mins. LT	20 mins. LT	DAY OFF	10 mins. LT	**RACE DAY!** Go out easy and have fun!
Exponential Taper Advanced	30 mins. LT	Strength 30 mins. LT	30 mins. LT	20 mins. LT	DAY OFF	10 mins. LT	**RACE DAY!** Go out easy and have fun!

Taper phase five. Focus: all about recovery!

Stretches, Strength Training, and Drills

Postworkout Stretches

Though gentle stretching is good anytime, the best time to stretch is just after exercise, when the muscle is warm and pliable. (Gently loosening up before exercise is also advised, and we'll present some prerun stretches later in this appendix.)

Stretching the muscle too hard can lead to a tightened muscle and injury. Breaking up a stretch into 5- or 10-second segments, 30 seconds total, can rid your muscle of lactic acid, hydrogen, and other waste products following a workout. It's more efficient than static stretching, where you simply hold the stretch for 30 seconds. Hold all of the stretches in this section for five seconds, and do six reps of each stretch for each leg or arm, with a second or two in between reps for a break. Keep them all gentle, at about 50 percent of your ability to stretch further. If you experience any pain, release the stretch immediately.

The following section provides a good routine of stretches to do following your workout. A few of the different versions of these stretches are more advanced. If a certain stretch is uncomfortable or feels awkward, please ease the intensity of that stretch, or stop that stretch entirely.

Knee to chest: While lying on your back, gently pull your knee to your chest. Do both legs, one at a time, for six sets of five seconds on each leg.

Knee to chest stretch.

Pretzel: Lying on your back, with both feet on the floor, knees bent at a 90-degree angle, cross one leg over the other. Pick your remaining foot off the floor. Grab the crossed leg with your opposite hand. Pull it toward you and across your stomach. When done properly, you will feel the stretch in your lower hip. Reverse arm and leg position and then stretch the other leg for six sets of five seconds on each leg.

Pretzel stretch.

Pelvic rotation: On your back, cross your leg at the ankle, not the knee. Roll your upper foot, and your entire body with it, over to that one side. Keep your foot and leg on the ground or leaning toward it. Turn your head to the opposite side, keeping both shoulders on the ground at all times. Repeat with the other leg for six sets of five seconds on each side. This is an important movement for anyone with tight hip flexors. It's also helpful if you have an IT band injury.

Pelvic rotation.

Lying quad stretch: Lay on your side. Reach back and grab the heel of your upper leg. Pull it back behind you gently. Keep the upper leg parallel to the ground, not raised. Repeat with the other leg for six sets of five seconds on each leg. (This is a more effective stretch than the standing quad stretch, presented in the section "Preworkout Stretches.") This may be the only stretch that can cause a permissible, minimal amount of achiness in the knee. If you have a knee injury, be particularly careful and gentle with this stretch.

Lying quad stretch.

Adductor stretch: Sit on the floor with the bottoms of your feet together in front of you. With your hands on your ankles or feet, use your elbows to gently push down on your thighs. A more advanced version of this is to lie on your back, with your legs above you, and gently hold your legs up and then allow them to fall gently apart to either side for six sets of five seconds total.

Adductor stretch.

Seated hamstring stretch: Sit up with one leg extended, the other leg bent, with the bent leg's foot near your knee. Lean forward, gently and slowly, from the hip. Don't bend your upper back. Repeat with the other leg for six sets of five seconds on each leg. A more advanced version would be to lie on your back, with one leg extended above you. Place a strap or towel around your foot, and hold with both hands. Gently pull the outstretched leg back. (See the standing version later in this appendix.) Many runners do a standing bent-over hamstring stretch with their upper body bent over forward. This can be an effective lower back stretch, but isn't an effective hamstring stretch, as you are using your hamstrings to keep from falling forward. For that reason, we did not include that stretch in this book.

Seated hamstring stretch.

Hip flexor stretch: Stand with one leg behind you, bent at the knee. Lean forward, until you feel the stretch in the front of your hip, and hold for six sets of five seconds on each leg. Repeat with the other leg.

Hip flexor stretch.

Kneeling hip flexor stretch: Kneel down on a pad or pillow. Again lean forward until you feel the stretch. Raise your arms straight up for an added stretch of your back and hold for six sets of five seconds on each leg. Repeat with the other leg. This is a more advanced version of the standing stretch.

Kneeling hip flexor stretch.

Standing calf stretch: Stand with one leg behind you. Keep your back leg straight, with your heel on the ground. If you don't feel the stretch, move your back leg farther back, with your heel on the ground and hold for six sets of five seconds on each leg. Repeat with the other leg.

Standing calf stretch.

Downward dog calf stretch: In this more advanced version of the standing calf stretch, keep one foot on the ground. Bend over slowly, placing both hands on the ground. Walk your hands back until your heel is on the ground. Keep your back straight, and hold for six sets of five seconds on each leg. Repeat with the other leg.

Downward dog calf stretch.

Cross arm stretch: Pull one arm across your front, parallel to the floor, while standing or sitting up, and hold for six sets of five seconds on each arm. Repeat with the other arm.

Cross arm stretch.

Trapezius stretch: Bring both elbows together in front of you and hold for six sets of five seconds on each arm.

Trapezius stretch.

Preworkout Stretches

In this section is a good routine of active and progressive stretches designed for loosening up before a workout. Notice that we are again working our way from the ground up (ankles to hips), and from one muscle to the next. These stretches aren't as effective as getting on the ground and doing the progressive stretches, but we understand that we runners don't always like to get on the ground before a run. The stretches done lying down in the previous section, performed even once for 10 seconds each as a prerun stretch, are still more effective than these standing stretches. The stretches outlined in this section are included as a nice preworkout option.

Active stretches are movements designed to prepare the muscle for running. Progressive stretches gently expand components of the muscle. At first, running on a recently stretched muscle will slow you down. A few short warm-up runs of about 50 meters or so will change that. Always begin the workout with lower intensity. Give yourself five minutes or more to simply warm up. On a marathon race day, walking to the starting line and starting out slow may be all the warm-up you need.

Active stretches in this section include ankle rolls, knee circles, hip circles, and rounds, all from the book *ChiRunning* (see Appendix B). These are not held stretches; these are done with a constant cylindrical flow for about 10 times around. The rest of the stretches in this pre-exercise stretch section are all held for about five seconds, with six reps for each leg.

Ankle rolls: While standing on one foot, roll your elevated foot around at the ankle. You can do this with your foot slightly in front of you, or behind. Roll your ankle 10 times in one direction and then 10 times in the other. Repeat with the other ankle.

Standing calf stretch: See the standing calf stretch in the "Postworkout Stretches" section.

Knee circles: Standing with your hands on your knees to help gently guide your knees, roll your knees in one direction and then rotate in the opposite direction. Roll your knees around 10 times in each direction.

Standing hamstring stretch: Stand with one foot in front of you, possibly leaning that heel on an elevated platform, such as a curb, step, or bench. Keep your spine straight, and bend forward from the hips. You should feel the stretch in your hamstrings, which are the long muscles in the back of your leg.

Standing hamstring stretch.

Standing quad stretch: This stretch is a wonderful test of balance, but definitely not as effective a stretch as the lying quad stretch shown in the earlier "Postworkout Stretches" section. Standing on one leg, curl your other leg behind you. While holding the foot or ankle, gently pull your leg up. Hold this for 10 seconds, release, and do a second set for 10 seconds. Repeat with the other leg.

Standing quad stretch.

Hip circles: Standing up straight with your hands on your hips, rotate your pelvis around in one direction. This may feel similar to rolling a hula hoop around. Rotate 10 times in one direction and then 10 times in the other.

Rounds: See the last movement in the "Skills and Drills" section, later in this appendix.

Sample Strength Training

There are two major reasons to strength train. Reducing the risk of injury to muscles and joints is one reason. Increasing power, or the ability to go faster, is another.

Strength Training at Home

The following exercises are designed for runners and walkers of all levels. As a runner, you don't want to perform any of these exercises to failure. Failure would be the point during one movement at which you can barely finish lifting that weight or pushing back to start position. The muscle is literally failing from fatigue.

One good reason to strengthen your muscles is to eliminate muscular imbalances. With any imbalance, or in running a great distance, extra stress is placed on the joints. Strengthening fascia muscles, which support the joints, can brace the impact and save the joint from injury. You can do all of the following exercises in one session, or pick and choose just some of them. Try doing a few of them every morning, alternating which ones you do each day.

High knee (hip flexors—group of muscles that start halfway down the thigh and wrap around each hip): Raise one knee to a 90-degree angle. Gently lower your foot to the floor and repeat—build to 3 sets of 30 or more over a few weeks. Exercise one leg at a time for multiple repetitions, then alternate and work the other leg to complete each set.

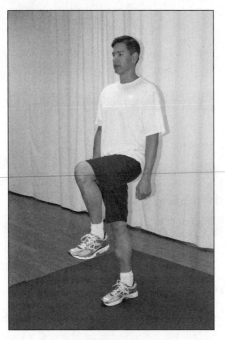

High knee.

Rounds: See the last movement in the "Skills and Drills" section later in this appendix.

Lunges (quads and hamstrings): Step forward on one leg, keeping the other leg behind and bent at the knee. Bend the front leg down, but no farther than a 90-degree angle. Don't lean so far forward that your knee goes in front of your toes.

Repeat with the other leg. Build up slowly over a few weeks to 10 reps per leg. Beyond that, you could hold dumbbell weights in your hands to add resistance.

Lunges.

Sliding wall squats (quads): Put your back and butt against a wall. Slide down the wall as far as is comfortable, but no farther than the point at which your knees are at a 90-degree angle. Hold that sitting/leaning position for 10 to 15 seconds. Then slowly slide back to a standing position. Repeat. The farther your feet are away from the wall, the tougher this is.

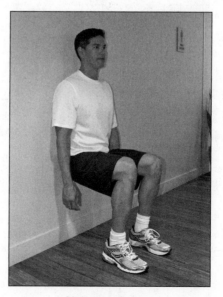

Sliding wall squats.

Hip raises (hamstrings): While lying on your back with your feet apart, raise your butt slightly off the ground. Lower, and then repeat. The farther your feet are away from you, the tougher this is. Don't raise your back up too high as to extend your neck.

Hip raises.

Scissors—abductor raises (outer side of your leg—abductors): Lay on your side with your lower leg bent forward and your upper leg stretched out straight. With your foot parallel to the ground, raise your upper leg up about 2 feet only. Lower and repeat. Build up to 3 sets of 30 or more over a period of a few weeks. Repeat with the other leg.

Scissors—abductor raises.

Adductor raises (inner thigh—adductors): Lay on your side with your upper leg bent forward and your lower leg straight. You may want to put a pillow or ball underneath your upper leg to support it, keeping it parallel to the ground. Raise your lower leg up gently. Repeat. Build up to 3 sets of 30 or more over a period of a few weeks. Repeat with the other leg.

Adductor raises.

Dead bug (core—abdominals): Lying on your back, swing your opposite arm and leg up, then lower and raise your other arm and leg. Repeat numerous times. This is an important movement for runners and walkers, as you are strengthening the same muscles used in running and walking. Some will need to start with 5 or 10 reps, others far more. Do as many as you can do and add reps over time.

Dead bug.

Plank (upper body, core): Hold a push-up position (plank), or start on your elbows (bridge—see next figure). Keep your back and legs straight, as if you could lay a board across your body, at an angle. Hold this position until it becomes uncomfortable. Add more time over a few weeks.

Plank.

Bridge (upper body, core): This is the same as the plank, but on your elbows. Only do one or the other, whichever is more comfortable. Both are equally as difficult and effective.

Bridge.

Flying plank (upper body—one side): The plank on one arm, with the other arm extended in the air above. Do this following the plank or bridge, but only when you are strong enough. This is an advanced movement.

Flying plank.

Kick backs (upper hamstrings, lower gluteus): On all fours, raise one leg behind you to back level. Don't raise your leg above your back. Do a set with one leg and then switch to the other. Repeat and do more, building slowly over a few weeks. Start with a number of reps that is manageable for you, and build up to about 3 sets of 30 reps per leg.

Kick backs.

Advanced Movements

Squat thrusts (not pictured) (quadriceps—front of thigh): From a standing position, squat down, put your hands on the ground, and then thrust out to a push-up position. Do a push-up, then bring the knees in toward the chest and stand up. Repeat this a few times. Perform this on a padded floor or soft grass or you will hurt your hands and wrists.

V-ups (core): Start by lying on your back on the floor. Simultaneously raise your legs off the floor, and raise your upper body off the floor, creating a V with your body. Keep your hands on the floor to help balance yourself if needed, or raise them as pictured. Keep your legs together; bending your knees makes it easier. Repeat until it begins to become uncomfortable, and add a few more reps each week, if you can.

V-ups.

Pistol squats (quads): If you can do this once, you are in good shape indeed. With one leg extended parallel to the ground, or as close to parallel as you can, squat down on the other leg. Then stand up. Only go down to a point where you can still stand back up. Most will do one at best, but do more if possible. An easier version of this would be to simply squat down with two dumbbells in your hands. Do not bend down so far that your knees are below a 90-degree angle. Stand back up and repeat for as many reps as you can and still get back up each time.

Pistol squats.

Skills and Drills

The following skills and drills are designed to improve form. Some runners will never have proper form, due to imbalance issues (such as tight or weak muscles or hip displacement). Improper form and/or imbalance issues can also cause injury. Often, one arm coming up a bit higher than the other, or head tilt to one side, or a shoulder coming forward more than the other, are all signs that there may be an imbalance. Strengthening and stretching can usually solve the problem, though these methods can take a long time. Proper form can often alleviate imbalance issues, especially hip displacement, which leads to a leg length discrepancy. Yet, no one can have proper form without strength and flexibility. It's sort of a vicious circle, which can eventually be overcome.

Front kicks: Standing upright, kick your leg out in front of you with a fair volume of energy. Next, kick the other leg out to the same distance with the same energy. Repeat with both legs alternating at 180 steps a minute.

Front kicks.

Back kicks: Kick one leg back behind you. Only kick it up to a point where it's comfortable. We don't want you to be injured doing this if you have a tight muscle. Kick each leg back in quick repetition, approximately 180 kicks per minute.

Back kicks.

High knee: Thrust your knee up to a 90-degree angle from your torso. Repeat with both legs at about 180 steps per minute.

High knee.

Skipping: Skip as high as you can, getting your knee up as close to a 90-degree angle as you can.

Skipping.

Rounds: Essentially you are nearly creating a circle with your one foot, similar to proper running form, but with one leg. While standing on one leg, bring your other knee up to a 45-degree angle, then kick your leg back. If you could draw a line directly down from your hip to the ground, your foot would strike the ground a few inches in front of your hip. Paw the ground backward and kick your leg back, then bring that bent leg back to the starting position. This puts together all of the preceding skills and drills. Start slow, and when comfortable, speed it up.

Rounds.

Index

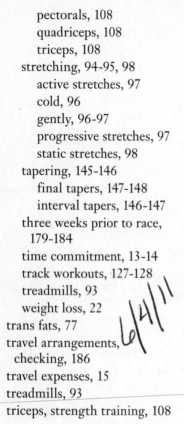